FAMILY INSURANCE HANDBOOK
The complete guide for the 1990s

Les Abromovitz

LIBERTY HALL
PRESS™

This publication is designed to provide accurate and authoritative information in regard to the subject matter covered. It is sold with the understanding that the publisher is not engaged in rendering legal, accounting or other professional service. If legal advice or other expert assistance is required, the services of a competent professional person should be sought.
—from a declaration of principles jointly adopted by a committee of the American Bar Association and a committee of publishers

LIBERTY HALL PRESS books are published by LIBERTY HALL PRESS an imprint of McGraw-Hill, Inc. Its trademark, consisting of the words "LIBERTY HALL PRESS" and the portrayal of Benjamin Franklin, is registered in the United States Patent and Trademark Office.

FIRST EDITION
SECOND PRINTING

© 1990 by LIBERTY HALL PRESS, an imprint of McGraw-Hill, Inc.

Library of Congress Cataloging-in-Publication Data

Abromovitz, Les.
Family insurance handbook : the complete guide for the 1990s / by Les Abromovitz.
p. cm.
ISBN 0-8306-8057-8
1. Insurance—United States—Handbooks, manuals, etc. I. Title.
HG8531.A26 1990
368—dc20   90-30501
CIP

For information about other McGraw-Hill materials, call 1-800-2-MCGRAW in the U.S. In other countries call your nearest McGraw-Hill office.

Questions regarding the content of this book should be addressed to:

Reader Inquiry Branch
LIBERTY HALL PRESS
Blue Ridge Summit, PA 17294-0850

Acquisitions Editor: David J. Conti
Technical Editor: Lori Flaherty
Production: Katherine G. Brown
Books Design: Jaclyn J. Boone

Contents

Acknowledgments

I owe a great deal of thanks to many people who have helped me with this book: I am grateful to Hedy, my wife, who's the most important person in my life and who never wants to hear about insurance again; to my parents, who have always been in my corner and who have promised to buy every copy of the book in South Florida; to Hedy's parents, who raised the best daughter around and who have enough insurance problems for several books; and to David Conti of Liberty House, who guided this project from its inception, and who reminded me that you can't put a joke in every paragraph of an insurance book.

Introduction

IF YOU'RE LIKE MOST PEOPLE, YOU HAVE NO DESIRE TO READ ABOUT insurance. You'd much rather read about how to get a better return on your investments. As a result, you earn a few dollars more on your investments and lose thousands of dollars in wasted insurance premiums.

Chances are, you're on top of your financial situation. On the other hand, you probably know very little about what insurance policies you already have and which ones you really need. Even though you're intelligent and well-read, it's quite likely you know very little about insurance.

If that is the case, insurance companies love you. An uninformed consumer is their best customer. He or she will write checks for protection that is of little value. Of all the products you buy, insurance is the one you spend the most on and know so little about.

Insurance companies have many ways to convince you to spend more money on insurance. They scare you into buying insurance you don't need, offering you peace of mind, while lulling you into a false sense of security. They confuse you with technical jargon that makes little sense to even the most intelligent purchaser.

In this book, you will learn to understand that jargon. You'll be given the tools to analyze any insurance policy. You'll develop a strategy for buying insurance.

A number of books discuss life insurance or one particular policy at great length. In this book, I have provided information about every policy you'll ever need to know about over your lifetime. Throughout this discussion, you'll see how much these policies have in common. When you learn how to analyze one, you will be able to understand most of them.

You won't just find out how to save money on auto insurance. There are enormous savings on homeowners, disability, travel, long-term care, and health and life insurance policies. You'll learn whether medicare supplemental policies are worth the money or if you should buy the collision damage waiver at the rental car counter.

You'll find out how to guard against lawsuits that can destroy the financial well-being of your family. For less money than you are paying now, you can increase the amount of protection you have against the risks that every family faces.

Too many people view insurance as being too complicated to understand. You know you need it, but you aren't sure why. You pay your premium and keep your fingers crossed. It doesn't have to be that way. With a modest amount of intelligence and a willingness to learn, you can make sense of it all. You really only need to know three things about insurance: Do I need it? Am I totally protected? If I have to buy it, how can I save money?

Perhaps there is legislation pending in your state aimed at lowering the price you pay for insurance. Even if you live in California, which has passed Proposition 103, a landmark voter initiative, or your state has taken similar steps to reduce insurance premiums, you still can control how much you pay. No matter what reform measures are passed, the greatest savings on insurance will be brought about by your own actions. Put this book back on the shelf if you're content to let others dictate what you pay for insurance. The ball's in your court.

You don't have to know a lot about insurance to be your family's insurance planner. You must simply be willing to change your attitude toward insurance. A significant portion of your family's budget is going toward insurance premiums. In the 1990s, it's time you stop paying for insurance that you don't need, and start paying less for the insurance you must have.

1

Understanding your insurance policy

IF YOU HAVE TROUBLE UNDERSTANDING INSURANCE, YOU ARE NOT ALONE. My Uncle Phil summed up many people's perception of insurance when he told me: "In the big print, they give you coverage. In the small print, they take it away."

After trying to read your own policy, you might feel the same way. A recent Gallup survey conducted for *Best's Review*, an insurance periodical, found that almost 75 percent of all consumers have trouble reading their homeowners or automobile policies. Not surprisingly, consumers listed technical terms and jargons as the major reason for their difficulty in understanding the policies.

Recently, insurance companies have attempted to write easy-to-read policies. Many insurance companies even advertise that their policies are easy to understand. Despite these claims, however, this same survey found that the newer policies are not any easier to read than they were five years ago. In fact, a sizable percentage didn't believe they were *any* clearer.

This book is concerned with the coverage you are about to buy and the coverage you already own. Hopefully, you will develop an understanding of that policy you keep in your desk drawer, and the additional policies the insurance industry wants to sell you to keep in that drawer. We'll start by making sense of the insurance lingo used in virtually all policies, not just homeowners and automobile insurance. Examples of how the policy actually works should remove any of the mystery created by complex language.

Although many of the technical terms and jargon are found in every policy, the insurance coverage itself can differ from company to company. There are hundreds of different policies, and it is often difficult to make specific statements about how your particular policy will treat a problem. Although many policies are

1

adapted from standard forms used throughout the insurance industry, they differ in the types of coverage offered. While generalizations can be made, there will be occasions when you can't avoid the dreaded reading of your own policy. There are also different state insurance regulations that affect your policy.

If you're reluctant to read the policy, you can take a step in the right direction by examining the promotional literature. It might even make you laugh. One brochure for an accidental death policy boasts that no medical exam is required. Of course there's no medical exam required; the company could care less if you die of an illness or old age. They only have to pay if there's an accident, and only for some accidents at that.

There are some shortcuts that can help you through the literature. If the price you're paying is absurdly low in relation to the amount of insurance you're supposed to get, keep reading. An unusually low price is a tip-off that there are a great many situations where benefits won't be paid. As you plow through the material, be on the lookout for them.

APPOINTING AN INSURANCE PLANNER FOR YOUR FAMILY

The Gallup survey also found that more than a third of the participants read a new policy completely and thoroughly. The rest either skimmed it or filed it away without reading it. Many of those who didn't read the policy indicated that someone else in the family would read it. If the responsibilities in your family are divided, it's time to appoint an insurance planner to handle these duties. Otherwise, you could discover later that everyone was filing away the policy without reading it.

The insurance planner for your family should have an aptitude for reading complex documents. Even if you have one of the so-called easy-reading policies, it takes a special person to pour through the "simple documents" and understand them. If you're the only adult in your family, congratulations! You're the newly-appointed insurance planner for your family. If you haven't already turned this book over to someone else, I'll assume you have taken the job.

The role of insurance planner involves much more than just reading through insurance policies and brochures. It is up to the insurance planner to identify any potential hazards faced by the family. His choice of policies will depend upon an analysis of those dangers. Analyzing risk is not just a question of buying insurance and then ignoring the hazards you face. If you know your child is a reckless driver, you won't just shrug your shoulders and take comfort in the fact that you have insurance. Sometimes, the stakes are much higher than just purchasing insurance and how much that coverage will cost.

The family insurance planner's duties are similar to those of a risk manager for a corporation, who identifies and analyzes the dangers that could jeopardize the assets of the corporation. While the risk manager does focus attention on how to handle problems after they occur, considerable emphasis is placed on loss prevention. Similarly, you should also take such steps. You should be isolating potential trouble spots and taking corrective action before an accident or loss occurs.

To take a simple example of analyzing risk, suppose you have a priceless vase. It's not enough that you have an insurance policy for it. The vase is special to you, and you would like to keep it in one piece.

The question becomes: Where do I keep it? Suppose I keep it at home. What potential hazards are faced? If I leave it on a pedestal at home, one of the kids could knock it over while playing. It could be stolen. Perhaps, I could get a security system at home to reduce the likelihood of theft. Maybe I could keep it under lock and key.

Maybe it would be better kept at work during the week. What if one of the cleaning people knocks it over? Are the chances of theft greater at work or home? Are there greater chances of it being damaged in transport? After you have analyzed the risk, you still owe it to your family as risk manager to practice loss prevention. Protecting personal property is just one small aspect of your job.

Even more than the priceless vase, you want to keep your family in one piece. Risk identification and loss prevention is a full-time endeavor that can help you achieve that goal. Loss prevention can include everything from wearing seat belts to practicing fire-prevention procedures around the house. It involves reading about which cars are safer and are involved in less accidents. The insurance planner can protect the family unit in many ways that are far more important than just insurance.

POTENTIAL HAZARDS FACED BY MOST FAMILIES

Whether you know it or not, your family lives with risk daily. Hopefully you can identify and prevent many of those dangers from striking your family. Certain risks, however, are unavoidable, no matter how careful you are or how many steps you take to guard against those potential problems.

Without digging too deeply into our anxiety closets, we soon realize that there are a host of dangers we can't avoid. We are all at risk of dying before we're ready to die and before the financial needs of our dependents are met, of contracting a health-related problem that generates catastrophic medical expenses or impairs our ability to work, of being sued for our role in an event that causes harm to someone else, or of being a victim of a natural or man-made disaster that can take away our property.

For all of the bad things we might believe about insurance, it does serve a useful public purpose. It spreads risks among a large group, so that individuals do not have to bear the entire burden themselves. Insurance lets individuals with similar risks join together so that one individual does not have to deal with the financial exposure alone. Insurance protects people financially when disaster strikes, so they can deal with the problem itself and not the economic consequences.

SELF-INSURANCE

There is no way to avoid the purchase of insurance. You can, however, limit your expenditures for insurance by taking more risk upon your own shoulders. If you have the financial means to cope with a loss when it occurs, there is no need to spread the risk among a large group. The risk manager for a corporation won't always buy insurance to protect the company against losses. Many companies have gone to self-insurance programs to deal with potential hazards. Within reason, your family can carry more risk on its own shoulders by self-insuring. While you are unlikely to have the same assets to work with that a risk manager does, you can incorporate many of the same ideas into your own life-style.

You might already be administering a self-insurance program. You're undoubtably familiar with the deductible on an insurance policy. When you carry a deductible on a policy, you are agreeing to insure yourself up to a specified dollar amount. The actual coverage provided by the insurance carrier does not start until your deductible has been satisfied.

If you're like most people, you hate deductibles. You're probably thinking that if self-insurance involves deductibles, you want no part of it. If deductibles do offend you, you're most likely unaware of the true purpose of insurance, which is to prevent a catastrophic financial loss from occurring. The idea behind insurance isn't to reimburse you on a dollar-for-dollar basis on every loss. Deductibles are designed to keep every small incident from turning into an insurance claim.

Deductibles aren't the only form of self-insurance that you've unknowingly practiced. Many disability and long-term health care policies contain an elimination period. This is the waiting period until benefits begin. If you become ill in May, your benefits might not begin until June. This waiting period puts some of the risk on your shoulders, which is where it belongs. The idea is totally consistent with the true purpose of insurance.

The question to ask yourself is whether the possibility of loss is a realistic one. You should be able to sleep with your risks. It's the same philosophy you practice with investments. If your investment strategy keeps you up at night, it is too risky. Therefore, if intentionally failing to insure against a risk spoils your night's sleep, you definitely should buy the insurance. More than likely, you are now sleeping like a baby while many areas go uncovered. Nevertheless, if you are specifically aware of an area that you would like protected through insurance and that knowledge bothers you, go forward and buy the policy even though it might not be a good investment.

ANALYZING RISK

Before you choose to go without insurance, you must learn to analyze risk in a setting you understand. When you refine this skill, you can then determine if it is worthwhile to self-insure against losses rather than transferring the risk to an insurance company. It is helpful to examine some different forms of protection that you don't usually think of as insurance. These are quasi-insurance policies that normally are not state-regulated. They do, however, resemble insurance in many ways.

A common policy of this kind is the extended warranty on appliances. When you buy a major appliance, you are likely to receive a call offering to extend the manufacturer's warranty beyond the prescribed duration.

Another policy of this type is the mechanical breakdown coverage for automobiles that is available in many areas. With this vehicle breakdown coverage, you are entitled to reimbursement for the damages that result from a mechanical problem. The company that sold you the policy is obligated to pay the reasonable cost of repairing or replacing the parts. Many experts argue that these policies are insurance transactions and should be regulated. The argument is that vehicle service contracts are insurance, unless it is the seller or the manufacturer of the car who is offering the warranty.

Consequently, you should view these policies as insurance and evaluate them accordingly. Even when it is the dealer who is offering an extended warranty, the transaction must be viewed with the same skepticism. The car dealership might make more money on this coverage than from the sale of the car. Again, you should be examining the issue of risk. You need to ask yourself how much risk you face in a given situation and how much of it you can assume. This question is also applicable to the more familiar insurance policies that are analyzed later in this book.

Because the same principle is applicable to more complex insurance issues, it is useful to analyze a quasi-insurance policy where you are offered an extended warranty on an appliance. Suppose you extend the warranty on a television set for two years for a price of $45 per year. Would you be better off holding on to that $90 rather than protecting yourself against a contingency that might never occur? Before you try to answer that question, you must first analyze the risk you face in this situation.

After some investigation, you find out that if a problem occurs, it will most likely happen within the first few months of use. At that point, the television would still be covered by the manufacturer's warranty. Therefore, by buying the quasi-insurance policy, you are paying money to guard against a remote risk.

Although you know how much the television set costs, you need to estimate how much a new one will be in two years. It would also help to know the terms of the manufacturer's warranty and what parts it covers. You need to know if there is any fine print in the extended warranty that limits the protection it provides. You must determine if the extended warranty duplicates the manufacturer's warranty and if the coverage overlaps in any way.

You also need to investigate the financial integrity of the organization offering the extended warranty. Will they still be in business to honor your contract should that time arrive? There might be additional charges when you take the set to be serviced. The contract might contain conditions that release the company from its obligation to repair the set, such as abuse of the product.

If the company agrees to make the repairs, you might wonder how long this will take. You might find yourself waiting for weeks while the set is being serviced. Were it not for the extended warranty, you could simply go out and buy a new set.

Another factor to consider is whether you will really want the appliance repaired when something goes wrong. Products like VCRs are continually technologically evolving. If you owned a Beta VCR, and bought a service contract, it's doubtful you would have wanted it to be repaired. Rather than having it serviced, you might prefer to replace it with a more popular VHS.

Furthermore, if a problem does occur during the extended warranty, the television would be repaired, but you are left with a television set that is several years old. Perhaps, you would have been better off if you had saved the $90. When the television set goes on the blink, you could then put the money toward a new set. Suppose you had pocketed the $90 and had not purchased the extended warranty. You would now be the proud owner of a new, state-of-the-art television set.

That decision-making process isn't as easy as it sounds, however. The $90 might only be a memory, and the broken television set a reality. When the repair problem occurs, your cash flow could be at a low point and you really can't afford to buy a new television set. Had you paid the $90 for the extended warranty, an amount of money you could afford at the time, your finances would be in much better shape now.

As you can see, there are many issues involved in the seemingly simple decision of whether to buy an extended warranty contract. Because these agreements resemble insurance, analyzing them is good practice for analyzing more difficult exercises in risk. As the insurance planner for your family, you will be scrutinizing the risks and benefits associated with the more complicated policies that will be offered to you.

SELF-INSURANCE AND SERVICE CONTRACTS

When you didn't bother buying those service contracts and extended warranties, you were actually self-insuring against the risk of an appliance needing repair. Corporations do the same thing. They often decide against buying insurance. Many times they'll simply hire an insurance company to process claims for them. The insurance carrier resolves the claims, but it's the corporation's money. The theory behind self-insurance is that they can eliminate the insurance company's profit by paying the claims themselves. You might feel that a corporation can afford to self-insure and you can't. The corporation will often set a limit on how much it can afford to lose. They might self-insure up to $1 million and then buy insurance to deal with the exposure beyond that amount. Likewise, you should establish a dollar amount limit that your family can afford to lose.

Your family's self-insurance program can be understood by looking at these service contracts. In theory, you can buy insurance to cover almost every risk. In reality, you don't. You take on risks rather than spread them among a larger group. When you don't buy an extended warranty, you use the money saved for other purposes. In the self-insurance program that I'm suggesting, you put aside funds to cover inevitable losses.

Looking at our television set example, it's unlikely you earmarked the money saved on this warranty for an insurance fund. When you saved money by not buying the service contract, it went back into your general funds. The problem with segregated funds is that they don't remain segregated. You might end up raiding them when you run short on cash. You never reap the long-term benefits of these funds, which can save you money on insurance.

Buying these service contracts might say something about whether or not you're a smart shopper. When you did research before buying a major appliance, you should have looked at its repair history. Whether you read *Consumer Reports* or asked friends about their experiences with the product, you should have purchased the appliance that your research showed to be the most reliable. Therefore, buying the service contract flies in the face of your initial decision about which product to buy.

Self-insurance works well in an area where you can easily afford to pay the damage yourself. Even if your income is small, the cost of repairing or replacing an appliance is not a catastrophic expense that is worthy of insurance in any form. These are risks that are too small to insure and that you should take responsibility for handling. Your risk of an appliance breaking is small, assuming you've been smart in the selection process. The bulk of the risk is assumed during the manufacturer's warranty period. It is only after that warranty period expires that you take on some of the risk.

SELF-INSURING YOUR AUTO-RELATED RISKS

We've just examined how self-insurance can work in the area of service contracts and extended warranties. Let's look at how it can apply to other lines of insurance. You raise the deductibles on your auto policy from $100 to $500. Let's assume you can save $100 on your car insurance by raising that deductible.

Let's also assume that you have the discipline to put that $100 savings in a special savings account. If you get 8 percent interest on your money, that $100 will double in nine years. On top of that money, you continue to save $100 each year with the higher deductible. You also earn interest on that money.

With this simple example, you can see that you will be better off in the long run by raising your deductible and saving the money. Naturally, if you have an accident in the first few years, self-insurance won't pay off in the short-term. When you have an accident in the first years, you'll lose $500 instead of $100. Your savings on insurance and the interest will negate some of the loss, but your self-insurance fund will have a negative balance. In the long-run, however, this approach will pay off, especially when you don't need to make claims for a number of years.

There are other factors that impact on this approach to insurance planning however, that you must consider. You are paying taxes on the interest you earn on your insurance savings. Thus, you are not really earning 8 percent per year when you consider that part of your interest is lost in taxes. On the other hand, you might end up saving additional money on your insurance. With a higher deductible, you are less likely to report a claim that would adversely affect your premium.

Obviously, implementing a self-insurance program is not something you want to do during your first day as insurance planner for your family. You have a long way to go before you can properly analyze the risk your family faces in a given situation. Once you gain that understanding of the risk you face, your insurance policies will not be so difficult to comprehend. You should be analyzing a risk before you buy a policy. Otherwise, you might not need an insurance company to guard against it.

When you understand the concept of risk, you're on your way to a better understanding of insurance. Reading a policy will no longer be an exercise in futility. You will be able to recognize the risks that you face and how much of it will be protected by the insurance company. While this knowledge won't make these policies any more interesting to read, it will help you understand whether that insurance makes sense for you and your family.

2

How to purchase insurance

IN CHAPTER 1, WE DISCUSSED THE RISKS FACED BY YOU AND YOUR FAMILY during your daily lives. You might think that your awareness of these risks will cause you to buy more insurance, but becoming self-insured means you will be buying less insurance, not more. Nevertheless, there are risks that are too grave to deal with alone, and you need to spread the risk among a large group. Insurance is the most common mechanism to do this.

Before you buy any insurance policy, you must first decide if you legitimately need it. You don't need to insure against every potential loss, just those that will have devastating financial consequences. You should be buying coverage that meets those needs rather than policies that are of no use to you. Your goal should be to develop a comprehensive insurance program, not just pockets of protection.

Once you have established those needs, you should seek out the right policy, not hope the right insurance comes to you. You will receive many inviting proposals in your mailbox each day. You will see wonderful commercials for insurance that scare the living daylights out of you. You will see newspaper and magazine advertisements that speak glowingly about a new insurance policy.

Some insurance companies will try to tell you what your needs are. If you're planning your own insurance affairs properly, however, you already know what your needs are. The decision to buy insurance should be your own and not triggered by junk mail or a commercial.

One mass (insurance) mailing mentions that the decision whether to buy or not is made in 30 seconds. Knowing that 30 seconds isn't necessarily enough to make a decision about insurance, this policy solicitation mentions its 30-day, risk-free look at the policy. If you know human nature at all, you'll realize that few people will change their minds during the 30-day period once the decision is made. Practically speaking, you will end up making a decision in 30 seconds after all.

THE IMPACT OF INSURANCE ON YOUR PURCHASES

The decision to buy insurance takes a great deal longer than 30 seconds as that one solicitation suggested, however. In fact, your insurance needs should be considered at all times, because there are times when purchasing insurance can't be avoided because of the risk involved. In this case, it is imperative that you examine the insurance ramifications before you make the major purchases because you might have second thoughts about whether or not you can really afford it.

The cost of a needed insurance policy should be factored into every discretionary purchase. You should not purchase a new car without considering the insurance you'll need to go with it. If you can't afford the proper coverage for the new Jaguar, you shouldn't be buying it. For example, whenever you buy a status car, you set yourself up as a target defendant for a lawsuit and would need higher liability limits. If you are involved in an accident, you would be viewed as someone with the financial means to pay damages.

People spend exorbitant amounts of money on vacations, yet they shy away from travel insurance. Despite the drawbacks, there are some situations in which a travel policy would be beneficial and should be considered when deciding if you can afford the trip.

The same advice applies to jewelry and artwork. People pay thousands of dollars without flinching, but ignore the necessity of insuring those collectibles. These same people, also won't pay for appraisals to document the value of their purchases, which is necessary to buying the right coverage for those items. It's a lot like buying an expensive home and being unable to afford furniture.

Many people feel they are only getting a piece of paper when they buy insurance. It is, essentially, of no value. You can't put your arms around it. But, you are buying protection, not a vehicle to get you from one place to another or a piece of art to treasure. It might be time to realize that peace of mind and protection are worth paying for, no matter how intangible they are.

The question then becomes: Can you really afford an item if you feel compelled to cut corners on the insurance? Like it or not, it's one of the necessary evils that comes with a higher life-style. Some would argue that they avoid insurance because they are not getting value for their money. They can justify spending $35,000 for a car, because they see what they're getting, but the same can't be said for the purchase of insurance. It has a terrible resale value. People won't swoon over your new insurance policy, but look at the bright side. You don't have to wash it or worry about someone scratching the door in a parking lot.

INSURANCE AND FINANCIAL PLANNING

You should not let convenience influence your insurance-buying decisions. It is not unusual to find invitations to buy life insurance from your credit card company. These offers stress the convenience of buying insurance through the mail. They'll even offer to let you put the premium on your credit card and pay it off in monthly installments—how convenient! No matter, you must still evaluate the underlying policy before you buy.

I know many insurance company employees who receive a discount on the purchase of their personal insurance. Although the discount is significant, most of the policies cost more than those offered by other companies. Nevertheless, a number of employees buy the insurance, not out of loyalty, but because there is a convenient payroll deduction plan. They never price other companies because they like having the insurance taken out in small chunks. It's easier to budget.

These budgeting considerations cause some people to buy insurance they don't even need. In Chapter 1, we discussed how some extended appliance warranties resemble insurance. When evaluating these extended warranties, some people don't care if they're worth the money. Their only concern is whether they can afford to pay for them now and avoid a payment at a later date when they might not have the funds on hand.

These budgeting considerations are just one way in which your insurance decisions are tied to your comprehensive financial plan. They might also explain why the idea of self-insuring is totally unappealing to you. If you're having problems saving money, you probably like paying a fixed amount each month or year and then reaping the benefits as you need them. You might like the idea of being reimbursed in full for prescriptions, x-rays, and diagnostic tests. You'd rather pay the cost up-front, so that you have a good idea what your total outlay will be.

It's a lot like buying a vacation that includes the meal package. You don't want to worry about the cost of those meals once you get to the foreign country you're visiting. Similarly, you'd rather buy your insurance and know it will cover almost all of the contingencies. With health insurance, being sick is bad enough without having to worry about paying for charges that your insurance won't cover. You might even be the type who won't go for medical treatment for fear of the cost. As a result, you find yourself ignoring symptoms. Some people prefer the certainty of regular insurance payments, even exorbitant ones, rather than the uncertainty of expenses that are not covered.

If this sounds like you, you aren't quite ready to operate a self-insurance program. You must also wait until your financial affairs are stable. Most financial planners recommend that you have an emergency fund of at least three to six months salary. This same fund can be used to self-insure against some losses. You can go with a longer elimination period when you have a fund to cover short-term cash flow problems. You can take higher deductibles when your savings are sufficient to cover a higher portion of a loss if it occurs. You can even begin building a separate insurance emergency fund with the money you save in premiums by self-insuring to a limited degree.

INSURANCE AND THE SMART CONSUMER

Purchasing insurance isn't much different than buying any other product. The same Madison Avenue approach is used to sell insurance that you find with laundry detergent or any other product. Just as you are skeptical about the items you buy either at the store or on the Home Shopping Network, you have to view the purchase of insurance in much the same way.

While the difference between insurance and some products is obvious, you can apply many of the lessons you've learned over the years to this purchase. First, take all advertisements with a grain of salt. There will be strong emotional appeals. Recently, an insurance carrier placed a newspaper advertisement for its long-term care policy. The advertisement asked: ''Is this the new bedroom suite you've been saving for?'' In the middle of the page was a drawing of a hospital bed.

The advertisement is an effective one. With insurance, you don't run to the store to pick up the product after an advertisement like this one. You might, however, call for more information. While a long-term care policy is a valuable insurance product as you will see in Chapter 17, you should make a logical decision to buy one, not an emotional reaction to an effective advertisement.

Your experience as a smart consumer has taught you another lesson that can be applied to insurance. It pays to shop around for the best price. Not every store sells an item at the same price. Insurance companies are no different. They offer their products within a wide range of prices. The only difference is there won't be a circular in your Sunday newspaper to help you compare prices, but you can shop around for the best policy.

SHOPPING AROUND

You should periodically shop around for insurance. Usually, a large price increase precipitates your shopping around for another policy that is less expensive. You might not realize that you're being nickled and dimed to death with small increases that don't motivate you to price other policies. Another possibility is that you've been paying too much for too long. A few phone calls at policy renewal time will quickly reveal whether you are getting a fair deal on your present policy.

The one glitch with comparison shopping is when you're trying to compare apples and oranges. This process of comparing prices works superbly with auto or homeowners insurance, where you are buying similar coverages. It won't work as well with long-term care insurance, however, where there are slight but important differences in the policy. Some life insurance policies are easy to compare, while others have many internal features that don't lend themselves to a comparison strictly on price. As you will see in Chapter 11, there are services to help you find the best price for life insurance.

Although price is certainly an important consideration, do not change companies if you're happy with the service you're getting and the company's price is competitive. With auto insurance, in particular, it pays to build up a track record and stay with one company. A carrier is less likely to cancel you if you have an accident. In addition, many companies are fussy about the new customers they take on and might be unwilling to do so if you have had a moving violation within the past three years.

While shopping around is important, it is dangerous to switch certain policies. Certain types of life insurance policies require you to pay a huge, up-front commission. There are also surrender charges when you cash in certain types of life insurance policies. Changing policies on the basis of price alone can cost you money in the long run. Another danger in changing policies is that you risk causing a problem for your beneficiaries. Most life insurance policies have an incontestability clause that protects your beneficiaries. After a period of time, usually two years, the insurance company has very little basis for challenging your beneficiary's right to benefits.

You might also find a less expensive health insurance policy when you shop around. A claim under this policy can be denied if it results from a medical condition that existed prior to your coverage. When you buy any new health-related coverage, you increase your chances of being denied for this reason.

In addition to the money you can save by shopping around for insurance, it helps to remember another rule you learned as a smart consumer. It pays to buy in larger amounts. You'll usually buy the larger size in the store, because it's a better value for the money. Insurance can be like that. When you buy more life insurance, you get a better price. The administrative expenses are fixed. As you buy larger amounts, the price you pay per $1,000 in coverage is smaller. There are some instances where $100,000 in life insurance is less expensive than buying $99,000.

You'll also be able to buy larger amounts of liability coverage for less money. As you increase your liability limits on your homeowners and auto policies, the price goes down. It is not that you are getting a better price because you're buying a larger amount of insurance, however. As your limits increase, the carrier's risk is decreasing, which reduces the price.

Paying your bill in full can also save you money as it does with most consumer purchases. Your premium is lower if you don't pay it on the installment plan.

AVOID THE EXTRAS

When you buy any insurance policy, there is an assortment of bells and whistles you can get along with the basic policy. These frills can add significantly to the price of the policy without adding much in the way of coverage. It's like buying a pizza. The price of the pizza itself is reasonable, but then you must decide if you want to pay several dollars more for mushrooms, pepperoni, or some other condiment. Unfortunately, insurance extras are far more expensive than pizza toppings.

Because each company has its own assortment of bells and whistles, it's important that when you compare prices, you compare the policy itself. These extras are usually added to the policy by way of an endorsement or rider. A rider amends the insurance contract and alters it in some way. It can either expand or restrict the coverage provided by the basic policy. The insurance policy is a contract and the rider changes the terms of the contract. Riders can be a nice way for the carrier to generate revenue. A rider can sometimes add nonessential coverage to a much-needed policy.

An endorsement, or rider, to a policy should customize the policy to meet your particular needs. In too many cases, you end up buying insurance on your insurance. It's a lot like buying an auto club membership that pays for towing when your car breaks down. Many auto clubs then try to sell you a premium membership that pays for towing of greater distances in the event your vehicle breaks down. The additional fee buys you very little in the way of additional protection.

A rider can cost nothing and still be a bad buy. There are riders that automatically increase your coverage each year. The endorsement itself is free. You will pay, however, for the additional coverage you buy. If you need more insurance each year, the rider is worthwhile. If not, you will automatically be buying protection that you don't need.

You shouldn't jump to the conclusion that all riders are a bad deal. A company might offer you a very streamlined policy that doesn't meet your needs, and a rider, or endorsement, might be the only way to add desirable features to the policy. There will even be situations where an endorsement can save you money such as the Social Security rider to the disability insurance policy, which is discussed in Chapter 14.

TIPS FOR PURCHASING INSURANCE

When you're purchasing insurance, there are some general rules you can consider. Policies of limited duration are a bad buy. The flight insurance you buy at the airport begins when the plane takes off and ends when the flight pulls into the gate. Even if it only costs a few dollars, it's a waste of money. You would be better off buying a life insurance policy that lasts all year. No matter how dangerous flying seems to you, the odds of collecting on flight insurance are slim.

Another rule to remember is that you should not buy coverage that is narrowly defined. The worst offenders of this rule are cancer policies and other forms of "dread disease" insurance. Even though they only cost pennies-per-day according to the brochures that promote them, they only guard against one risk. Personal accident insurance is another one-risk type of insurance policy that is too narrow to be of much value.

You need a broad policy that covers a wide variety of risks. You shouldn't be limiting the situations in which you can collect benefits. It's not wise to guard against isolated incidents and to guard against risks that are remote. It's like buying insurance that only pays if you're run over by a General Motors car but not a Chrysler. There is only a narrow band of coverage.

Keep costs down by self-insuring. Raise your deductibles and extend the waiting period until benefits begin. You should have a cash reserve to get you through a short-term financial crunch, while having insurance to guard against long-term problems. You are protecting your family from financial catastrophes, not short-term setbacks. You shouldn't be buying insurance to reimburse you for nominal losses.

Too many people believe there's safety in numbers when they buy insurance. They figure the more policies they buy, the better chance they have of covering every risk on the horizon. As a result, these people spend a lot of money on insurance without getting the comprehensive coverage they need. They'll buy policies that cover one disease instead of a comprehensive medical policy. They'll purchase accidental death policies instead of one life insurance contract that pays for death caused by any reason.

When it comes to insurance, buying more policies is not the best technique to guarantee that you have adequate coverage. You might double your sense of security, but still be woefully underinsured. If there's an exclusion in your policy, it's not going to matter if you have $100,000 worth of coverage or $200,000. You're still not covered for a problem that falls within the exclusion.

You should not be buying insurance to collect a windfall or to make a profit on a tragedy. The idea behind insurance is to make you whole, not to put you in a better position than you would have been had the problem not occurred. When we begin to discuss life insurance in Chapter 11 and discuss the rules-of-thumb for deciding how much to buy, you will see that the idea is not to make the family rich after the breadwinner's death. Rather, the aim of life insurance is to replace the income and earning potential of the deceased.

You should avoid any duplication of coverage. In Chapter 16, we will discuss the supplemental policies you can buy to pay the medical bills that Medicare won't cover. These are commonly called medigap policies. The companies that sell medigap policies are not permitted to duplicate any of the benefits provided by Medicare. Therefore, the medigap policy will not be a wasteful duplication of coverage. Unfortunately, however, many Medicare beneficiaries then make the mistake of buying several medigap policies that duplicate one another.

You should avoid being over-insured. It makes no sense to duplicate coverage that you're already paying for in some other policy. You've probably had this experience at a rental car counter. You buy the $12 per day collision damage waiver because you aren't sure if your own automobile policy covers the use of a rental car. Similarly, you buy baggage protection in a travel insurance policy because you don't know if your homeowners policy covers your belongings. Knowing what coverage you already have can help you avoid buying unnecessary policies that duplicate your current coverage.

You should also avoid policies that encroach upon the territory covered by other insurance. You will see in Chapter 14 that disability insurance is badly needed by most people. Some people take a good disability policy and pay extra for coverage that pays benefits if they're confined to a hospital. This medical coverage should be handled by a health insurance policy, not paid for again when buying disability insurance.

It also helps to know how your policies interact with one another. Your policies should pick up where others leave off, so that you have comprehensive coverage. One policy should pick up the risks where another policy leaves off. Your car is parked at a shopping center. There are gifts in the trunk. The car is stolen and the gifts are gone. The car theft is handled under your auto policy and the gifts are covered by your homeowners insurance.

RISK MANAGEMENT

You *do* have control over how much an insurance company charges you for coverage. You can take steps that will make you a better risk for the carrier to insure. For your own sake and to make your insurance less expensive, drop that excess weight and give up smoking. It will make you a better risk for the company to insure and will keep your premium lower as nonsmokers. In many cases, smokers pay almost double for the same amount of life insurance. It won't just help on policies that take a chance on your staying healthy. At least one company is offering homeowners insurance at a 10 percent discount to nonsmokers.

You can be a better risk in the eyes of an auto insurance carrier if your driving record is clean. You will pay less if the company perceives you as less likely to cause an accident and will insure you at a lower premium.

You can also control the circumstances that might lead to losses. As we discuss each policy, we will look at loss prevention techniques that can help your family reduce its chances of needing insurance. While there are no preventive measures that can help you avoid every peril, you can control your risk to a large extent. Lowering your risk of loss will enable you to buy less insurance and to consider self-insuring against hazards you face.

3

Choosing the right coverage

THERE ARE THOUSANDS OF INSURANCE PRODUCTS ON THE MARKET. IF YOU were to read the many insurance magazines that are published, you would find that pages upon pages are devoted to new policies. Insurance companies monitor the activity of their competitors. When the competition introduces a new product that is well-received by consumers, you can bet that other companies will follow with their own variation. The end result is a hybrid policy that combines the unique features of a competitor's policy with the more common elements you would expect to find in that particular insurance contract.

Over the years, numerous policies have come and gone. You might see them come back again with a new marketing strategy. The idea is to convince consumers that they can't live without this particular policy. Having health insurance is a life-or-death matter, but few policies meet that same criteria. In fact, you have done quite well for many years without the new and improved policies that many insurance companies are promoting.

If you look hard enough, you can find a policy to cover almost any risk. You can buy insurance to reimburse you in case it rains while you're on vacation. You can purchase a policy in case you lose your contact lenses. You can even insure your pet's health, as you will see in Chapter 18. At one time, you could buy mugging insurance, if that possibility frightened you. You can even buy protection in case the wires in your phone go bad.

These specialty policies cover risks that should not be insured under any circumstances. The risks they cover are too insignificant to warrant any kind of protection. While you need to consider insuring against the risk of dying, insuring against the risk of losing your contact lenses is another matter.

These specialty policies do not belong in your insurance portfolio. In their place, you should have the old reliable policies like automobile, homeowners, health, disability, and life insurance. As the population of America ages, you will hear more about long-term health care policies. In the 1990s, these policies might become standard fare. All of these policies cover risks that we really can't avoid, no matter how careful we are. For most people, self-insurance is not an option since the economic consequences are so severe.

NEW WRINKLES ON OLD POLICIES

Even though most people need these old reliable policies, you should be wary of attempts to repackage their contents. When you strip away the wrapping paper, very little has changed. It's the same old familiar policy with new features. The trouble with these revamped policies is that they really aren't giving you any more protection than you previously had.

Often, these changes are simply cosmetic in nature. The substance of the policy remains the same. These improvements are really a marketing ploy to make the consumer believe he is getting more for his money. In its marketing effort, the insurance company will emphasize these new features. The extended coverage contained in the new policy is virtually useless.

One relatively new product is a combination homeowners and auto policy, which is aimed at the over 50 market. The policy is replete with wasted coverage. For example, it replaces lost or stolen Social Security checks. In examining this feature, ask yourself what you are gaining from this coverage. Policyholders younger than 62 certainly won't have much use for it and policyholders over age 62 and on Social Security might not get any benefit either. If their check is lost or stolen, it will eventually be replaced.

This same policy reimburses the insured for expenses incurred in finding a lost pet. Assuming you even have a pet, you might question whether you need insurance to pay the bill if that contingency occurs. This is hardly a risk that insurance should be concerned with in your daily life.

It's not that a policy like this one would necessarily be more expensive because of these additional features. Adding the so-called protection of this kind should not affect the premiums at all. The danger is that consumers will buy a particular policy based on a glitzy marketing pitch that adds very little to the substance of the policy and not look at the policy itself. As you strive to cover the risks your family faces, you should not be sacrificing the basic protection because you are attracted by the packaging of a particular policy.

FIRST-PARTY AND THIRD-PARTY COVERAGE

As you try to determine the right coverage for your family, you'll need to understand the distinction between first-party coverage and third-party coverage. A first-party claim is one brought by the policyholder or beneficiary against the insurance company that issued the contract. If you file a claim against your homeowners insurance policy for items stolen during a burglary, this would be a first-party claim.

A third-party claim is one that is brought against the holder of a policy of liability insurance. The basis for the claim is that a tort has been committed. A tort is simply a wrongful act for which a civil action can be brought. In Chapter 5, you will look at negligence, which is the most common tort. In essence, a third-party claim alleges that you have committed a tort. When that allegation is made, you then look to the liability coverage in your policy for protection. To use our same homeowners insurance example, if someone slipped on your property and was injured, a third-party claim would be brought against you. A lawsuit, or the threat of litigation, represents a third-party claim against the holder of a liability insurance policy.

As the insurance planner for your family, you are responsible for making certain that your policy limits are adequate. There is no simple formula for determining what policy limits you should carry. Your family's financial future is in your hands. You can choose the wrong deductible, and it will cost you a few hundred dollars. If you choose the wrong policy limits, it is a much more serious proposition. Your family could go bankrupt as a result of it.

WORST-CASE SCENARIOS

The difficulty in determining policy limits is anticipating the nature of a possible third-party claim that can arise. All of us hope that we are never involved in an accident. Worse yet, what if the accident is our fault? Even if we can picture that horrible scenario, how do you estimate the potential damages that might result? To choose the correct policy limits, the insurance planner has to assume a worst-case scenario that puts all of the family's assets in jeopardy of a lawsuit. If you have significant assets, a third-party claimant will not stop when your insurance runs out.

As with any decision, there are trade-offs. To protect against this worst-case scenario, you might have to lower your guard on lesser accidents that are more likely to occur. For example, raising liability limits on an auto policy to extremely high levels might mean that you will have to raise your deductibles to offset the increased price of the policy. It is one thing to self-insure by raising a deductible. You should never self-insure against a worst-case scenario.

It is far better to risk that deductible than to bet that you won't be involved in an accident that will place your policy limits in jeopardy. If you hope to have the maximum coverage for the price you pay, you will have to make trade-offs such as this one. As you will see in Chapter 10, a personal liability umbrella policy is an economical way to increase your liability coverage and avoid making difficult decisions about policy limits. Furthermore, an umbrella policy extends the coverage you have in other areas where there might be claims against you.

Analyzing a worst-case scenario is a good way to choose the features you need in other policies. With disability insurance, for example, you can buy a policy that pays benefits to age 65 or one that pays for a shorter amount of time. By lengthening the elimination period, you are able to buy long-term benefits for a reasonable amount. When you approach coverage questions using the worst-case scenario, you recognize that having disability income benefits to age 65 or longer is far more important than putting up with a longer waiting period. As insurance planner for your family, you are saying: I would rather be assured of disability income benefits for many years than to receive payment in 30 days should a disability occur. Trade-offs of this type must be made so that the coverage is affordable.

Looking at these worst-case scenarios can help you buy the right coverage for your family. Surprisingly, it won't cause you to spend more on insurance. Looking at a worst-case scenario encourages you to add a layer of protection. Often, this extra layer of protection is quite inexpensive, because you have already paid the insurance company to guard against most of the risk. When you have already bought $300,000 in liability protection, adding an additional $100,000 adds little to the premium.

Focusing on the worst-case scenario puts the rest of your insurance needs in perspective. It helps you recognize that you can afford to pay for the smaller losses. Having this perspective can make you appreciate the real purpose of insurance, which is to cushion your family from severe financial blows, not to guard against small expenditures that you can deal with yourself.

Throughout this book, we'll be asking how much insurance you need. The answer is more. You'll need more insurance than you get through work. You'll need more insurance than is required by legislation in your state. The good news is that this insurance should cost you less than what you're paying now by using the information in this book to trim your current coverage. At the same time, you'll limit your exposure.

COVERAGE THROUGH YOUR EMPLOYER

You might be surprised to hear that the insurance offered through your employer isn't enough. When it comes to insurance issues, most employees are satisfied with the amount of coverage they get. They might complain about how much they get paid, but they're generally satisfied with the amount of insurance they get. Employers typically offer group health insurance, life insurance, disability insurance, and a variety of other benefits. In most cases, you should exploit your employer's insurance benefits to the fullest extent, but it's still not enough.

Your employee benefits lack the permanence you often need from an insurance policy. Certainly, some insurance policies can be converted when you leave the company. Employer-provided life insurance policies usually provide the option of converting to a private policy up to 30 days after the employment ends. These conversion privileges protect you in the event you are uninsurable when you must resort to a private policy to replace the one your employer provided. This conversion privilege will not help you, however, unless you don't mind buying insurance at any price. There is also a federal law that extends the group health insurance benefit after the employment ends—the Consolidated Omnibus Budget Reconciliation Act or COBRA. In most cases, companies with at least 20 employees must provide medical coverage at group insurance rates for 18 to 36 months after an employee leaves. Although this can buy you time, it is not a permanent solution.

The generous life insurance you have through your employer could evaporate quickly if you lose your job or quit. The lack of a job, and the subsequent financial problems would prevent most people from continuing the life insurance privately. Similarly, the premiums and renewals on group disability policies are infrequently guaranteed. Thus, these insurance contracts lack the portability of individual disability policies that you do not purchase through your employer.

In some cases, you might not be able to meet even your minimum insurance needs through your employer. More employers are now offering flexible-benefit programs, or cafeteria plans, where employees can choose their own coverage from a group of options. Unfortunately, your choice of one insurance policy might force you to pass up another benefit. Therefore, you won't be able to beef-up your insurance coverage through your employer without cutting into another employer-sponsored benefit. Even if you do arrange your benefit package to obtain the maximum insurance coverage available, it is still likely you will need more than is offered.

COVERAGE MANDATED BY LAW

You also need more coverage than is required by law. Often, your choice of insurance coverage is made for you, at least when it comes to the minimum levels. With auto insurance, for example, minimum coverages are usually set by financial responsibility laws or compulsory insurance laws which mandate the minimum amounts of insurance that you should carry. These laws, however, will generally require far less insurance than you actually need. Every state has some type of automobile financial responsibility law that requires drivers to show proof that they are financially able to pay for any accidents they might cause. The usual proof is evidence that you are insured.

Buying the minimum amounts of coverage specified by these laws is sufficient only if you spent your last dollar on this book. These minimum limits are only adequate for people who have no assets worth protecting. Some states only require auto liability limits of $10,000 and property damage coverage of $5,000. You would have to be very naive to believe these limits are adequate for the 1990s.

Despite these minimal limits required in some states, there are still thousands of drivers who do not have insurance. Even though these same laws prescribe penalties for failing to have insurance, high premiums have motivated some drivers to ignore their obligation in this area.

There will be unusual situations where governing bodies will tell you how much insurance you need. The New York City Department of Health established a rule requiring $100,000 of liability insurance coverage for the owners of pit bull dogs. The rule was implemented because pit bulls are involved in an inordinate number of the dog bite cases in New York City. While rules like this one can help in deciding how high your policy limits should be, you should be the one deciding that much higher limits are needed. In that pit bulls have been responsible for many of the nation's documented dog bite deaths, $100,000 would not be sufficient if your pit bull kills someone. Your policy limits should be far in excess of $100,000 if you decide you can't part with your beloved pet.

COVERAGE REQUIRED BY LENDING INSTITUTIONS

People that lend you money will have something to say about your insurance coverage. When you buy a new home and take out a mortgage on it, the bank will insist that you purchase title insurance. This policy protects you and your bank from any defects in the ownership rights you have to a particular piece of property. You also would be required to purchase a fire insurance policy. Often, mortgage life insurance is also required.

When you finance a car, the financial institution will insist that you have collision and comprehensive coverage in your auto policy to protect its interest in the vehicle. The lender might also request that you buy credit life insurance.

Although there are a few instances where a certain amount of coverage is required, you alone must decide what policies to buy and in what amounts by determining your family's insurance needs. To properly assess those needs, you must look at factors such as financial status, occupation, life-style, marital status, dependents, age, and risk.

Keep in mind that your needs will be constantly changing. Major events change your insurance needs—a marriage, the birth of a child, or the purchase of a home. If that new mortgage payment requires the combined income of both spouses, you should look closely at your life and disability insurance needs. As the family's insurance planner, it is your job to pay constant attention to these changing insurance needs.

Don't give up. It's not a daily occurrence. As you enter the various stages of your life, your family will have different needs. Surprisingly, there is a certain symmetry to it all. For example, you might need more life insurance when your children are very young, but your life insurance needs lessens when your children are grown. Then health insurance becomes an increasing concern. Of course, that's not to say that health insurance should be ignored during those years when you are less likely to need it.

It is dangerous to make generalizations about the insurance needs of one particular age group. Although there might be insurance problems that are more common among a particular group, such as the elderly or young newlyweds, their coverage requirements could be very different based on their life-styles.

Typically, young couples are advised to buy term insurance, the least expensive form of life insurance, because they can get more bang for their buck. Presumably young couples have small incomes and the start-up expenses of a new home. This advice won't necessarily apply to couples with a healthy combined income who aren't planning on having children for awhile or buying a home. The insurance needs of a childless couple with two incomes are far different from someone who has a nonworking spouse, children, and a small savings account.

Consequently you need to apply the information in this book to your specific situation. Although there are some policies that are a bad investment for everyone, your family's needs and financial situation will ultimately determine what coverage you should buy. There will be occasions, however, when you will need specific advice and will have to turn to others for help.

USING YOUR STATE INSURANCE DEPARTMENT

The department that regulates insurance matters in your state can help you avoid some of the really bad policies. That department has the power to approve policies offered for sale in your state. If the policy contains unfair or misleading language, the insurance department will not approve its sale in the state. Approval by the insurance commissioner is by no means an endorsement of the policy, however.

The department that handles insurance matters can issue cease-and-desist orders or take other action if the carrier makes false statements about its policy. It can also bring an administrative action against an insurance company that is improperly marketing a particular policy. When a company misrepresents the terms of an insurance policy, your state can withdraw its approval to market it. In some states, the attorney general will be permitted to initiate a lawsuit against an insurance company if it is engaged in a deceptive trade practice.

The insurance department in your state can force a company to rewrite its advertisements in some cases. Failing to do so can result in the company not being able to do business in that state. In many states, the insurance commissioners have the authority to review advertisements to make certain they are not misleading. These regulations can be especially effective against celebrity endorsements for life insurance or medigap policies. But don't let your guard down because of this, you might still see misleading advertisements from another state on a cable station. The state from which the commercial originates might not be as vigorously regulated as your own.

Joining in this effort is the National Association of Insurance Commissioners (NAIC), which is composed of insurance regulatory officials from across the nation and from four U.S. territories. They draft model legislation and regulations that often later become the law in your state. The NAIC recommends new standards for insurance policies. These standards aren't binding, but they frequently lead to changes in your state's insurance regulations.

Nevertheless, you can't expect the insurance regulators in your state to do your job for you. They often have varying degrees of authority to act on your behalf. Some do not have the resources or the power to do an effective job. In some states, the department does not have all of the loss data and financial information it needs to fully evaluate a policy or the rate a carrier is charging for insurance. As the insurance planner for your family, you still have to choose the right coverage from the policies that are approved.

USING INSURANCE AGENTS

An insurance agent can be a tremendous help in choosing the right coverage for your family. First, however, you have to choose the right insurance agent. Your choice of an insurance agent is much like your selection of any professional. You should be asking for recommendations from the people you trust. Your lawyer, banker, friends, business associates, relatives, and others whose opinion you value can supply the names of insurance agents who they respect.

Look for an experienced insurance representative who sells insurance on a full-time basis. You need someone who will be around to provide service. It's a tough business, and you want someone who has made a commitment to his occupation. It should be someone who's in business for the long haul.

A good insurance agent should have the training and skill to evaluate the coverage you need. All agents must usually pass a state examination. The C.L.U. (Chartered Life Underwriter) and C.P.C.U. (Chartered Property/Casualty Underwriter) designations attest to an agent's knowledge. Interview the agent to see if you can work together. Watch out for an agent who sells everything from health insurance to property and casualty insurance, which is homeowners and auto. It's tough to know a lot about each of these lines of insurance. After you interview them, make certain you have faith in the agent's honesty, integrity, and knowledge of insurance.

When choosing an agent, you want someone who will give you impartial advice. The agent should admit to you that a company's price is higher than you can get elsewhere. Don't bank on that, however. You should not be taking every statement as the gospel. You should be checking prices and confirming the information given to you. In this way, you should be able to find out if the agent is acting in your best interest.

A good agent will make recommendations about your insurance coverage. He or she should also be working with you to save money. The recommendations should be unbiased, or as unbiased as you can expect from someone who is selling a product. The agent should also be knowledgeable. Too many agents won't recognize a coverage problem until one of their customers has been burned by it.

You might question whether you need an independent agent or one who works for a particular company. One radio advertisement discusses the benefits of using an independent insurance agent. The announcer promises that the agent won't try to fit your size 12 feet into size 11 shoes. The point of the commercial is a good one. The independent agent has more products to choose from and can find one to meet your needs. The agent tied to one company must choose from the limited products offered by that insurance carrier.

Unfortunately, the question of whether to choose an independent agent or a particular insurance company's agent is not so easily answered. Ideally, the independent agent will select the product that addresses all of your needs. There is a danger, however, that the agent will choose the product that pays the best commission.

The agent tied to one company, might be able to provide better service when you have a claim because he is more familiar with the inner workings of the company and is more familiar with the particular policy you purchased. The independent agent, who sells a variety of policies, might not possess the same degree of familiarity with each product. On the other hand, the agent tied to one company might be afraid to challenge the company's decision.

It can be dangerous to ask someone who sells insurance for advice. You can compare it to looking at time-share properties. You might have no intention of buying a time-share and simply want to pick up your free gift, but a strong sales pitch convinces you to purchase it.

A good insurance salesperson realizes that giving you advice will encourage future business. Few will pass up the opportunity to sell you a policy. If you know how to say "no" to a sales pitch, a reputable insurance agent can offer good advice on how much insurance you need. Try to find a knowledgeable agent who recognizes that meeting your needs will benefit both of you in the long run.

If you are seeking information about life insurance, you are less likely to get impartial advice from a salesperson. On certain life insurance policies, the commission can be as much as 100 percent during the first year with lower commissions during later years. Therefore, you cannot expect insurance agents to give unbiased advice when a commission of that size is at stake. On other policies, their commission is much less, so they would be more inclined to serve rather than sell.

OTHERS WHO CAN HELP YOU FIND THE RIGHT COVERAGE

If you can't trust your insurance agent, who does that leave? Financial planners might be a logical alternative. The financial planner does an analysis of the client's financial exposure as it relates to mortality, morbidity, liability, and property. In theory, then, the financial planner is a good source for the advice you need. In reality, however, some planners make money on the insurance products they recommend just as they do on the sale of mutual funds they endorse. As a way to augment business, planners are advised to work with a property-casualty insurance broker. Even though their purported purpose is to create a program of proper coverage, the arrangement makes you wonder if truly impartial advice is given. The broker and the planner both benefit from the sale of insurance to you.

Many insurance salespeople call themselves financial planners. Although they might have significant training and experience in the financial planning area, they are still people who sell insurance for a living. You might have better luck with a fee-only financial planner. These planners offer advice for a set fee. Unfortunately, many planners who operate on a fee-for-services basis still hope to earn a commission on products they recommend. You can expect a fee-only planner to have a very high hourly rate.

Your family attorney would be a more impartial source of advice on whether you have covered all of the bases with your family's insurance plan. Most attorneys in general practice, however, do not have expertise in all aspects of insurance. Although an attorney can research specific insurance questions you might have, few attorneys in private practice are equipped to work with you on a specific program. Despite that fact, there are undoubtedly a few who will give it a try at their high hourly rate.

Although you can turn to professionals for help in choosing the right coverage, you are the person who has the ultimate responsibility for protecting your family. As we analyze the policies that are on the market, you can determine if your situation warrants coverage of that kind. When you become familiar with the policies, it should be clear if your family will benefit from that insurance.

4

How to evaluate an insurance company

AS THE INSURANCE PLANNER FOR YOUR FAMILY, BUYING THE RIGHT coverage is only the beginning. You must evaluate the company offering the policy. Price is not the only factor you should consider in your evaluation. You must pay particular attention to a company's financial stability and its willingness to provide good service.

FINANCIAL STABILITY

There is a danger that your carrier will become financially insolvent. This is an especially dangerous situation when you have bought life insurance as an investment. When you buy an annuity, you invest a large amount of money now in the hope that the insurance company will make payments to you and your family for many years. Financial insolvency can cut off that stream of income to you.

Don't become complacent if you live where there is a state-supervised guaranty fund which pays claims on behalf of insolvent insurance companies. There could be a considerable delay in getting your money.

It is not enough to know that your insurance department is looking at the financial records and audits the books of companies doing business in your state. In some states, the insurance department does not have access to all of the financial data necessary to make a thorough evaluation of the carrier. The department might also lack the manpower and resources to handle the job properly.

The financial insolvency issue is your responsibility, even though your agent must make an evaluation of his own. The agent should monitor the financial status of insurance companies for whom he sells policies. In some jurisdictions, the agent has a continuing duty to alert you to financial problems.

To evaluate an insurance company, you should be aware of its ability to meet financial obligations. To make this evaluation, you won't have to rely upon reputation or the opinions of your friends and relatives. You won't have to hire an accountant to analyze the company's books or to pour through years of annual reports. There is a reference book that can handle this evaluation for you.

Best's Insurance Reports, which is available in many public libraries, rates insurance companies and translates those ratings into a grading system that is easily understood. The A.M. Best Company is the largest analyst of insurance companies. These reports provide authoritative opinions on the strength of a particular insurance company and its ability to meet contractual obligations.

When preparing its rating system, the company looks at three critical areas and compares them with the industry norms. The three areas looked at are profitability, leverage, and liquidity. Best's classification system also takes note of an insurance company's policy reserves, the expertise of its management, and the caliber of its investments. The ratings also include whether the insurance company has reinsurance, an important criterion of the financial strength of the carrier.

Although this analysis is not an exact science, you are getting an expert's opinion as to whether the company you are looking at is financially sound. In some respects, the evaluation from A.M. Best is similar to a credit report. The difference being that you are getting a credit report on the company rather than the company investigating your own credit-worthiness, which is more often the case.

After going through all of the complex data, A.M. Best rates the carriers much like you were rated during your school days. The top rating is an A+. The A+ rating means a company has exhibited the strongest ability to meet policyholder and other contractual obligations.

The A and A- is reserved for those companies that have demonstrated a strong ability to meet contractual duties. The A and A- rating is considered to be an excellent one.

A B+ is a very good rating and means the insurance company has achieved a very good performance in the industry. The B rating is for those companies that have shown good results in overall performance. The C+ rating reflects a fairly good ability to meet contractual obligations, while a C rating from Best indicates a fair ability to meet the duties pursuant to its contracts.

If you see a small letter next to the rating, you should be asking further questions. With so many well-rated companies to choose from, you should only be considering companies that have the A+ and A rating. Check periodically to make sure the company maintains its rating. Companies should make no secret of their A.M. Best rating. It's often the most convincing proof that they have of their financial strength.

SERVICE

An attractive premium should not cause you to ignore a company's rating from the A.M. Best Company. Good rates will also not make up for bad service. Unfortunately, evaluating the quality of a company's service is not an easy task.

If you had good experiences with a company, and they have always treated you fairly, you have a leg up on those readers who have not been as fortunate in their dealings with insurance carriers. A first-hand look at a company's customer service is the most accurate assessment of their service. It is not just an issue of how they treat you when the time comes to file a claim. Ask yourself some questions: Do they handle routine affairs in a professional manner? Are the bills that you receive completely accurate or are there errors? Do they provide you with regular statements? Are customer service personnel available or do you always get a busy signal? Do they have an 800-number or do you have to make long distance phone calls to resolve problems? Are you constantly switched from one employee to the next? Do they do things right the first time or must you always go back to correct mistakes?

Make certain you are judging the insurance company itself and not the agent who sold you the policy. Although agents do have a great deal of power and can help you resolve a variety of insurance problems, the ultimate decision-maker is the insurance company. In some instances, however, the insurance company relinquishes that authority to the agent. Some companies have a program where your agent can pay certain types of small claims without specific approval from the insurance carrier. He or she can write you out a check on the spot for your damages. Ask if your agent participates in this type of program and what types of claims are eligible.

Obviously, it is very difficult to evaluate the quality of an insurance company's service until you deal with it directly. Companies will advertise that they provide excellent claim service. They promise catastrophy teams that rush to the scene of a disaster to settle your claim. They promise fast and fair claim service. Because you must take these advertisements with a grain of salt, you will have to rely on a company's reputation for paying legitimate claims.

Surprisingly, insurance companies do develop reputations, and bad ones at that. Spend a day or two asking friends and relatives about their experiences with insurance companies. You are bound to hear an abundance of horror stories, describing the service afforded by certain carriers. This is a good, informal way to do some price shopping, along with the information you will gather about service.

Unfortunately, a reputation for providing quality service to its customers only goes so far. Claim service at many insurance companies is cyclical. Carriers often go through periods where they attempt to cut costs by cutting service.

During those time periods, claim representatives are handling too many files to give your problem the attention it deserves. There might not be enough adjusters to come out quickly to inspect your damages. Carriers become convinced that customers will not pay for good service and feel that mediocre performance will suffice. During these periods, a company's reputation for good service won't reflect the treatment you'll receive if you choose them as your carrier.

Word-of-mouth isn't nearly as accurate as a formal survey. Periodically, *Consumer Reports* magazine will evaluate the service provided by insurance companies, along with other aspects of their performance. Many carriers do not score well in the magazine's evaluation of their claim service. In addition, there is often no correlation between the quality of service and price.

While surveys like this one can be extremely helpful in your evaluation of an insurance company, it is no guarantee that you will be treated well in your own dealings with the carrier. Your opinion of an insurance company will more than likely be based upon the individual who handles your claim or who discusses the problem you're having. Even a highly-rated company will have individuals who lack customer service skills.

In most cases, however, the results of surveys like this one will accurately reflect the type of treatment you can expect from a company. They often are indicative of a pervasive problem with customer service at that company. Perhaps, the company doesn't have the staff, equipment, training, or motivation to provide good service. The company might lack innovative programs to resolve claims quickly such as a drive-in claim center. Instead of waiting for an appraiser or submitting three estimates, this program lets you drive your car to the center, if possible, to have your damages appraised on the spot. This way, your auto claim can be resolved quickly and painlessly.

The insurance commissioner in your state might be an excellent source of data on insurance companies. The insurance division of your state government will probably keep records on the number of complaints filed against a particular company. Check to see if that office keeps meaningful statistics that reflect upon the customer service practices of a particular insurance company.

The Arizona Department of Insurance issues a report that can be quite helpful in your evaluation of a carrier. It issues the complaint ratios for the companies that are writing most of the personal insurance policies in that state. The ratio tells the consumer how many written complaints have been filed for each 1,000 policies that are issued. A ratio like this provides an excellent frame of reference, as opposed to a statistic, which simply gives the number of complaints filed for each company. With the ratio, a carrier writing a large number of policies is on the same footing as a small company that only writes a minimal amount of insurance.

Using this complaint ratio, the Arizona Department of Insurance can identify companies that are in need of regulatory action. Companies with a high complaint ratio can be subjected to an examination of their business practices. The report does not, however, look at the merits of the complaints filed.

In the 1990s, the family's insurance planner might have additional tools available with which to evaluate the service offered by a particular company. Carriers might be required to reveal how long they take to pay claims. The insurance department in every state might compile statistics that will assist you in your evaluation. Ideally, you will be able to find out the number of complaints against a company compared to the number of claims handled. Hopefully, these complaints will be broken down according to the line of insurance. If that distinction is made, you would know that a particular auto insurance carrier generates an excessive number of complaints in comparison to the volume of claims that it handles.

5

Before you get sued

"SUE ME." YOU MIGHT HAVE HEARD PEOPLE SAY THIS PHRASE IN JEST ON numerous occasions. It's not so funny when it happens to you, however. There's too much truth to it these days to find much humor in it any longer. The trauma and expense of litigation is nothing to laugh about.

If you listen closely, you can hear the sound of the litigation explosion in the distance. When you read the newspaper or watch the news, you will be amazed by the number of seemingly ridiculous lawsuits that are being brought each day. Perhaps the impact of this litigation explosion hasn't hit you directly . . . yet. The more fortunate reader will be reading this book before he is reading the suit papers that have just been served.

THE RISK OF BEING SUED

The popular perception is that people are suing their doctors and not too many others. In reality, it is important to realize that Americans are quick to sue anyone, for the flimsiest of reasons. You might still cling to the belief that people do not go to court without good reason. They do, and physicians have not been singled out as the defendants for these lawsuits. Individuals are suing their lawyers, their accountants, their teachers, their parents, their ministers and rabbis, and just about anybody else they can think of suing.

Most of these lawsuits are brought for valid reasons. These plaintiffs, the persons bringing a lawsuit, have been genuinely injured and often have little choice but to resort to litigation. The enormous damage awards they receive are well-deserved.

Unfortunately, there are many less-deserving plaintiffs receiving damage awards. Their injuries and the factual basis for their lawsuits are suspect, yet they have managed to convince a jury that they are entitled to compensation. Because evaluating injuries and estimating damages is no easy task, a sympathetic jury can arrive at almost any figure as it attempts to reach a fair and impartial verdict. There is no scientific formula that can be applied to a set of facts that results in just result.

Many lawsuits never go to trial. An insurance company or the defendant decides that the cost of defending the matter, or the uncertainties of the jury system, make a settlement desirable. Whereas the person bringing the lawsuit can usually find an attorney to handle the case on a contingency fee basis and pays no fee unless an award is received, the defendant has significant defense costs.

Chances are, you've read about unusual lawsuits in the newspaper. For each one of those cases, however, there is an unpublicized one that is even more unusual and disturbing. They never get to the point where a lawsuit is filed. Someone threatens to sue or hires an attorney, and the insurance carrier settles the case. It never reaches the newspapers unless the lawsuit is actually filed. At that point, someone from the newspaper or the wire service notices the unusual nature of the litigation.

The news reporters often make a common mistake, however, when reporting on these stories. You'll read that a lawsuit is asking for $20,000. As a result, you might think you have adequate protection for that situation. The newspapers often don't recognize that the lawsuit is asking for damages in excess of $20,000. This $20,000 figure is a common requirement to bring the case within the jurisdiction of a particular court and to guarantee a jury trial. Otherwise, the case might go before an arbitrator. Many attorneys feel it's worth a shot to roll the dice and bring the case before a jury, which could award any amount of damages, not just $20,000.

Jury Verdict Research, Inc., an independent statistical analysis company, has reviewed hundreds of thousands of jury verdicts over the years. According to their statistics as published by the Insurance Information Institute, million-dollar personal injury verdicts are becoming increasingly common. The first million-dollar verdict was recorded in 1962. Through 1982, 2,700 have been awarded. New York, Florida, and California lead the nation in million-dollar verdicts. Although medical malpractice and product liability cases accounted for a large percentage of these million-dollar verdicts, vehicular liability accounted for a significant number.

In making their awards, juries consider earnings, health care expenses, the severity of the injuries, and other factors. You would expect death, brain damage, quadriplegia, paraplegia, and amputations to result in large jury verdicts.

Surprisingly, Jury Verdict Research, Inc. found average verdicts for knee injuries to be almost $300,000 in 1986. While a million-dollar verdict is unlikely, your loss exposure is still significant.

The purpose of this book isn't to enrage you or to persuade you to become an advocate of tort reform. This background information is simply to make you aware of the legal climate in which you live. You are a member of a litigious society and consequently, you are at risk of being sued.

Because of the number of lawsuits being filed, the risk you face is significant. Corporations hire risk managers to analyze potential threats to corporate assets posed by lawsuits and other hazards. You need to be certain that you have sufficiently protected your own assets. Most families have inadvertently erected a layer of protection against lawsuits, but too much can go wrong with that approach.

Just as it's too late to write a will after you've died, it is too late to worry about litigation after you've been sued. If you have no assets at risk, you don't need to worry. No plaintiff will be able to collect a verdict against you. Nevertheless, if you do possess assets, an effective program to deal with potential lawsuits is imperative.

Although insurance is the foundation of that program, it is not simply a question of buying more to guard against lawsuits. An effective plan will use the right type of insurance. Even if you are swimming in insurance, coverage problems might emerge . . . after you have been sued. Therefore, your personal risk management program must utilize the right types of insurance to insulate your family from litigation.

LOSS PREVENTION

Any program to guard against lawsuits should also pay particular attention to loss prevention. You should constantly be on the lookout for problems that can lead to a lawsuit. All it takes is common sense and a thorough analysis of your family's conduct. It requires no special training or legal knowledge.

Let's look at a simple situation that is becoming more and more common. If you throw a party and a guest becomes intoxicated, you might be held responsible for injuries that your guest causes if he later becomes involved in an accident. For many reasons, you should be concerned with friends who are driving while intoxicated. When you take away their keys and find them another way home, that's a loss prevention technique and it can save you from a lawsuit.

You need to identify potential risks in order to avoid lawsuits. When your child has friends over to play, you might be toying with a lawsuit. Suppose your child has a set of lawn darts that you allow her to use. These lawn darts could be viewed as a "dangerous instrumentality" if an accident occurs, just as if you allowed the child to play with a BB gun. As part of your loss prevention program, you should be looking closely at the risks you are taking, knowingly or unknowingly.

You might be engaging in activities that can result in lawsuits. Perhaps you're a skier. You might expect that you'll someday do damage to yourself on the slopes. It's unlikely you're expecting that your skiing could result in harm to other people. When this occurs, the odds are quite good you'll be on the receiving end of a lawsuit.

The Colorado ski slopes have been the scene of several tragic skiing accidents. On one occasion, an eleven-year-old girl was killed when struck by an adult skier who was out of control on the slopes. Among other accidents, an eight-year-old boy had his leg shattered by a reckless skier. The boy was crossing a hill with his family.

Whether to prosecute these skiers in the same way you would prosecute a reckless driver has been debated. The criminal penalties are not our concern. We are more interested in the civil lawsuits that would be brought against a skier.

The appeal of skiing, it is said, is to take risks while trying to maintain control. Sports like this one can increase your risk of being sued. When you engage in any sport where you put yourself and others at risk of injury, check your health insurance and your liability insurance. Before you get sued, keep in mind that you might have to pay for the consequences of the risks you take.

CAUSES OF THE LITIGATION EXPLOSION

We all have this impression of greedy people causing the litigation explosion in this country. Perhaps, the rash of lawsuits is caused by desperate people not greedy ones. One of the premises of this book is that people do not have the right insurance to meet their needs. An injured party with inadequate medical insurance, who is looking at mounting hospital bills, is more likely to look for someone to sue. It is quite possible that this person would not have considered suing, had his insurance been adequate. Thus, someone else's insurance mistakes can result in a lawsuit for you. If that is the case, let's hope your own insurance is adequate.

It's not just desperate people who bring lawsuits. There might be situations where someone invites a lawsuit by behaving outrageously. A friend of mine's daughter was riding her bicycle in the neighborhood. She came out from between two cars and her bicycle was struck by a neighbor's car. Fortunately, she only suffered a few scratches. The man driving was relieved, as was my friend.

A few minutes later, the driver's wife came down to my friend's house. She proceeded to read him the riot act because her car had an almost unnoticeable dent from where it hit the bike. She demanded that he turn the claim in to his insurance carrier. You would think that an accident involving a child would put matters in perspective. The driver and his wife should have been relieved that the child was not hurt and should have been thankful there was no tragedy.

Instead, the wife was more concerned about who would pay for the damage to the car. No matter who was at fault, this was a situation that invited a lawsuit. The wife made a horrible scene, embarrassing both my friend and her own husband. My friend was still stewing over her conduct several days later. Fortunately for her, he was not the type to pursue a frivolous lawsuit.

It was not a tirade over teaching a child safety habits. This was not the ranting and raving of someone who had narrowly missed hurting a child and was upset over that possibility. This was someone who was concerned exclusively with the dent in her car. Who knows if those types of incidents don't lead to some lawsuits?

PROTECTION AGAINST LAWSUITS

There are three primary sources of protection should you get sued: your homeowners or renters policy, your automobile policy, and your personal liability umbrella policy. Problems that arise directly from your profession are not discussed here, only problems that concern the insurance coverage your family needs to guard against suits brought against you outside of the workplace.

Earlier, we talked about first-party claims and third-party claims. Your liability coverage protects you against third-party claims. The plaintiff in a lawsuit is actually a third-party claimant against your liability policy.

In subsequent chapters, we will discuss the liability protection available under the homeowners, auto, and umbrella policies. In creating a blanket of protection, my intent is not to make you nonchalant about a lawsuit. Even when you have the most comprehensive insurance, a lawsuit can do devastating psychological damage. Even when you're secure in the belief that you have the right type of coverage and in adequate amounts, you're unlikely to be blasé when faced with a lawsuit.

NEGLIGENCE

If your legal education consists of Perry Mason reruns and episodes of L.A. Law, some background information is in order. When you are sued for damages, a judge or jury determines if your conduct caused the harm to the plaintaff. We are talking here about the civil justice system, as opposed to the criminal justice system. Our concern is tort liability law.

A tort is a wrongful act, other than breach of contract, that the civil justice system tries to make right. The person who commits a tort either acts improperly or fails to act at all. A tort results in injury or property damage to others. When you commit a tort, you expose yourself to liability for these damages. The most common tort is negligence. In simple terms, negligence means you didn't act reasonably under the circumstances.

In opposing a negligence standard, the judge or jury looks at four elements of your conduct: duty, breach of duty, causation, and damages. Did you have a duty to act in a certain way, given the particular circumstances? Did you deviate in any way from that standard? Did that breach of your duty cause, with some degree of certainty, the injury to the plaintiff? Were there damages?

We are all careless from time to time. We've all had close calls when driving and narrowly miss having a major accident. If you weren't so fortunate, that same situation could result in a major lawsuit. The court will then look at whether you acted as a reasonable and prudent person would have in view of all of the circumstances. When we're driving, we must exercise due care. We have a duty to live up to certain standards. A deviation can result in a jury finding us negligent.

You can even be found negligent in a situation where you are trying to help someone. You see someone floundering in deep water. You swim to save him. You not only fail to rescue him, you cause further injury before the lifeguard saves you both. You can be found negligent. Although you had no duty to rescue him, once you attempt to do so, you can be held to a certain standard of conduct. In certain situations, the only reward you'll get for helping others is a lawsuit. In most jurisdictions, there is no duty to aid a stranger. Nevertheless, when you do become involved, you must act as a reasonably prudent person would under the circumstances.

Earlier in this chapter, we looked at the risk of a lawsuit faced by a skier. The lawsuit against a skier who causes a mid-slope collision would charge that the skier did not act as a reasonable person would have under the circumstances. A jury might view this conduct as anything from an innocent mistake to pure recklessness. If the allegations are pure negligence, the homeowners policy will provide a defense and cover the damages awarded up to the limits of the policy.

Obviously, these examples point out the need for seemingly high limits. A proficient skier can reach speeds of 30 miles per hour without losing control. When an adult, let alone a child, is struck by a skier at that speed or greater, the damage can be devastating as was the case with these two tragedies.

COMPARATIVE NEGLIGENCE

There is a rule of law that will allow plaintiffs to proceed against you, even when they are negligent themselves. Comparative negligence, as the name implies, weighs the plaintiff's negligence against the defendant's. The plaintiff's damages are reduced by the amount of his own negligence in a given situation.

Suppose a third-party claimant has damages of $10,000. If he is found to be 40 percent negligent, his damages are reduced by 40 percent or $4,000. Thus, a suit against you can be successful, even if the plaintiff is negligent.

The doctrine of contributory negligence has lost favor. At one time, it was the predominant rule of law. If the plaintiff was at fault in any way, the claim was thrown out and no damages were awarded.

The bottom line is that a suit against you can be successful, even if the party bringing it was partially responsible. Comparative negligence applies in bodily injury and property damage claims, whether the suit arises out of an automobile accident or in some other fashion. On the plus side, comparative negligence will reduce the amount of the damages that might be awarded against you.

JOINT AND SEVERAL LIABILITY

There is another rule of law that can leave you holding the bag in a lawsuit. Suppose you are involved in an accident where your own actions and the actions of others cause an injury. The plaintiff sues all of you, even though you are only responsible in some small way for the injury. Despite that fact, you could be totally responsible for the judgment if one is awarded.

The rule of law is called joint and several liability. If your action and the actions of those others caused a single and indivisible injury, you might be left to pay the judgment. Perhaps, the other parties don't have insurance or declare bankruptcy. If you are the only party with the financial means to pay the verdict, the plaintiff can come against you alone for the entire amount. Because of this legal doctrine, you can be held responsible for all of the damages, even though your negligence was slight in relation to the other parties involved.

THE COLLATERAL SOURCE RULE

The collateral source rule can lead to a much larger award than you'd expect. When juries award damages to the victim of a tort, not all of the information is out on the table. As a result, many assumptions are made, often incorrect ones. No mention can be made of insurance. Nevertheless, the jury assumes that the defendant has insurance. An award will often be made based upon that assumption. If you are the person being sued, you might not have nearly as much as the jury expects you to have. Their award might be a product of the plaintiff's injuries, your wrongful act, and their expectation of who will pay the damages. Undoubtably, their award would be a lot lower if they thought you alone were paying it.

The collateral source rule stipulates that no evidence can be introduced regarding other compensation received by the plaintiff. The jury will not know whether the victim received disability benefits from his employer or if health insurance paid off the medical bills. When awarding damages, the jury will allow for those lost wages and medical bills even though the victim has been fully compensated. Thus, a double recovery is possible in some jurisdictions

An even more troubling result of this rule is that you could be found liable for much more in damages than you would expect. These lost wages, medical bills, and other expenses could fall squarely on your shoulders. These damages, along with a potential award of pain and suffering, could exceed your liability limits. You might end up paying more damages than the person actually sustained.

COMPENSATORY AND PUNITIVE DAMAGES

There are two types of damages, compensatory and punitive. Compensatory damages are awarded to restore the individual to where he was before the loss. These include economic damages like medical bills, lost wages, and repairs to property. Noneconomic damages are those awarded to compensate the victim for pain and suffering, mental anguish and emotional distress.

Compensatory damages are awarded in the vast majority of cases. They put the injured party in the position he would have been had the loss not occurred, if that's possible. These compensatory damages make the victim whole again. He is given his lost wages and compensation for his pain and suffering. His medical bills are reimbursed.

Punitive damages are awarded infrequently. They are granted to a plaintiff to punish the wrongdoer for recklessly disregarding the welfare of others. Liability policies protect against claims for compensatory damages resulting from a tort but punitive damages are another story.

Punitive damages, although infrequently awarded, are designed to punish the wrongdoer. They are only awarded in circumstances where the negligent party has acted in a manner which society wants to discourage. In a number of jurisdictions, punitive damages are uninsurable. The theory is that by paying punitive damages owed by an insured, it would not be a deterrent to others. Consequently, it is against public policy to pay punitive damages.

Let's take an example where a drunk driver hits a small child. The courts are unlikely to view this tragedy in the same way they would a more typical negligence case. The judge or jury might be inclined to award both compensatory and punitive damages. Allowing the insurance company to pay the punitive damages would not achieve the purpose that the judge or jury had in mind. This is why many courts do not allow insurance policies to pay for punitive damage. The theory is that the public is made safer by punishing these drivers and by making certain that their insurance does not lessen the degree of punishment.

Punitive damages can also be awarded in other situations. A host who served liquor at a party could face an award of compensatory damages if an intoxicated guest injures someone in an auto accident. If that same host served liquor to a minor who became intoxicated and was involved in an auto accident, punitive and compensatory damages might be awarded to the injured party.

To look at the skiing example again, the situation where a skier acts with reckless disregard for human life might result in an award of punitive damages. These exemplary or punitive damages would be awarded to deter other skiers from acting without concern for others on the slopes.

Dog bite cases are common claims under homeowner policies. The law used to be that every dog was entitled to one bite. Until a dog had bitten someone, the owner was not presumed to know that the dog had a dangerous propensity. The law has changed, however, and now there are other ways to show that a dog owner knows of an animal's vicious propensity. Keeping a dog tied up might be one method. Previous complaints of the dog chasing the mailman or the posting of a sign could also show that the owner knows of the dog's dangerous propensity.

When a dog bites a child or an adult, the most common award is compensatory damages. The result might be different, however, if someone is bitten by a vicious dog that has attacked people on several occasions. If the animal's owner has done little or nothing to prevent this problem from reoccurring, punitive and compensatory damages might be awarded. The punitive damages, if not covered by insurance, will teach the dog owner a lesson and discourage him from future conduct of this type.

NO-FAULT LAWS

So far, we've discussed the traditional tort actions that might be brought if your negligence causes an accident. If you are in an automobile accident that was caused by your negligence, the chances of you being sued, and the amount for which you can be held responsible, are altered by no-fault laws. A number of states have no-fault auto insurance laws. While there are some similarities in these laws from state to state, it is difficult to generalize because they can be significantly different.

Before you get sued for the damages you cause in an automobile accident, it is vital that you recognize one thing that no-fault hasn't changed. You can still be sued. A no-fault law, no matter how strict it is, will not keep seriously injured parties from suing you. Smaller suits, while annoying to be sure, are likely to be guarded against by your current insurance program. It is a claim for noneconomic damages like pain and suffering that can devastate you. The theory behind the wide range of no-fault laws is that insignificant lawsuits will be eliminated. Thus, you can only be pursued in more serious automobile liability matters, and that is exactly what you need to be concerned about.

Therefore, it is not enough that you live in a state with a no-fault automobile insurance system. Although a no-fault system usually limits the right of an accident victim to sue, it won't necessarily make you immune from a suit if you cause an auto accident. In some jurisdictions, the no-fault law will restrict the victim's right to collect both economic damages and noneconomic damages.

Therefore, if a lawsuit is brought against you, your exposure is less because of the limited damages that can be awarded.

Some states have a variation of no-fault that does not place any restriction on the right to sue. There are no-fault benefits available, whether you are responsible for the accident or not. In these states, you are either permitted or forced to buy personal injury protection (PIP) benefits. PIP might cover your lost wages, medical bills, or funeral expenses in a fatal auto accident. The mere availability of these benefits is why it is considered to be a no-fault state, not because of any limitations on lawsuits.

Depending on which state you live in, and the type of no-fault law it has on the books, if any, an accident victim might have to reach a stipulated threshold in order to bring a lawsuit against you. In one state, the victim only needs to exceed a "monetary threshold" of $400 in medical bills. Obviously, even if medical costs were not skyrocketing, reaching a minimal monetary threshold would not in any way preclude a lawsuit against you.

The more rigid thresholds found in some no-fault jurisdictions requires that the victim in an automobile accident meet a "verbal threshold." In those states, the victim would have to suffer "severe injury" or death in order to recover non-economic damages. "Severe injury" is defined by law and could be anything from scarring to broken bones.

In states with no-fault automobile systems, the person injured in the accident turns to his own insurance company first for payment of bills. After meeting the threshold, if there is one, the injured party can turn his attention to the person who caused the accident. In theory, no-fault laws limit lawsuits to those who are seriously injured. In some states, having no-fault means that only seriously injured accident victims can pursue claims against you. Therefore, no-fault doesn't really eliminate the risk of being sued. Once the "monetary" or "verbal" threshold is met, the injured party can sue for pain and suffering.

Practically speaking, the no-fault thresholds can be easily surpassed by anyone with even modest injuries. When no-fault legislation is passed, there are generally compromises between the various groups with interest in the law. As a result, the thresholds are too weak to eliminate insignificant lawsuits. On the other side of the coin, you can legitimately question why any injured party should lose the right to be compensated for pain and suffering, simply because they did not incur a certain amount of medical bills.

You might wonder how money is saved with this system, even in theory. It appears, at first glance, that the injured party's own carrier simply pays what the third-party carrier would pay in a state without no-fault. The idea is that noneconomic damages like pain and suffering are eliminated in less serious cases. In civil cases, juries often award noneconomic damages based on the measurable damages, such as medical bills and lost wages. When settling cases, attorneys for the injured party often use a multiple of five or more in deciding how much to ask for to settle the case. These attorneys realize that the more economic damages they can show, the more pain and suffering they can demand.

In any jurisdiction, whether it has no-fault or not, it is those noneconomic damages that can lead to a monumental award. Chances are, you already have enough insurance to cover a situation where someone ekes over the monetary threshold and is allowed to recover noneconomic damages. Regardless of where you live, and whether or not your state has a no-fault law, you might receive a large judgment against you when you and your automobile are responsible for the serious injuries of someone.

NO-FAULT IN THE 1990s

Because of the clamor over high insurance rates, there has been a great deal of legislative activity in this area. In the 1990s, there will be additional changes that can affect your chances of being sued. You might have to choose between no-fault and liability insurance when you purchase your auto policy. Depending upon the legislation that is passed, those who choose the no-fault option will not be able to sue or their right to sue will be considerably restricted.

Those who choose the liability insurance option on their auto policy will still be able to sue without restriction. Under this system, if it gains acceptance, there will be unique situations that must be addressed. Suppose a person who chooses the liability insurance option is injured by someone who has chosen the no-fault option. In that situation, the injured party might collect from an expanded coverage in his own policy. Because of the political compromises that can be expected in passing legislation of this type, it is hard to say how this new auto insurance program will work if it is accepted.

LITIGATION IN THE 1990s

While your right to sue after an auto accident might be limited in the 1990s, it is unlikely that the rush to the courtroom will slow down in other civil matters. More and more, people are becoming less reluctant to sue. In years past, a lawsuit was a measure of last resort. Today, the idea of suing someone isn't nearly as repugnant as it once was. People are less likely to overlook any harm that they feel has been done to them. Despite the litigation explosion, you might have come through the 1980s unscathed. You might not be so fortunate in the 1990s.

Although you can expect the litigation climate to remain the same, you shouldn't live in fear that you will be sued. It isn't too difficult to guard against virtually every lawsuit that you could potentially face. Better yet, it shouldn't cost you any more than you're paying now to shield your family from a suit. While you can't eliminate the risk of litigation, you should be prepared to face it.

6

The risk of
defending a lawsuit

THERE'S MORE TO THE RISK OF BEING SUED THAN JUST THE POTENTIAL damages that might be awarded against you. The cost of defending the allegations can be far more expensive than any verdict that you might have to pay. A court of law is much more formal than the tribunal of television's People's Court. The cases are far more involved with procedural issues. The hours in the courtroom are preceded by months and years of pleadings, depositions, interrogatories, and other legal maneuvers. It's unlikely you could defend yourself.

The liability protection you get in a homeowners, auto, umbrella, or some other policy also includes defense costs. When you don't have the right coverage to indemnify you against a particular claim, you also might not be entitled to a defense. The cost of defending the lawsuit would be on your shoulders, not the insurance company's. The irony is that the party suing you only pays a fee if he wins. You pay from the moment you engage an attorney.

THE COST OF HIRING AN ATTORNEY

It's not unusual for defense costs to be higher than the amount awarded. Look at some of the expenses. An attorney's fee might range anywhere from $75 to $500 per hour depending on where you live. When you are fighting a lawsuit and don't have an insurance company to defend you, you might pay thousands of dollars in one day and over $10,000 in the course of the litigation. Before you even get to the courtroom, there might be several depositions. For just one of those depositions, you might pay over $1,000 for an expert witness, over $100 for the court reporter, and several hours of legal time at the hourly rate quoted above.

Obviously, litigation is an expensive proposition. A complicated lawsuit can drain you financially. Many cases are settled simply because it is so expensive to defend them. Insurance companies often view a lawsuit as having a certain "nuisance value." No matter how ridiculous the charges are, there are carriers that will pay several thousand dollars to settle the lawsuit as a way to save money on defense costs. That's why lawsuits are such a serious problem. Even when the allegations are nonsensical, you are forced to offer a defense.

Suppose you find yourself in a situation where your policy does not provide coverage for a lawsuit naming you as a defendant. You will have to ask yourself the same question that insurance companies ask on each case that they handle. You must decide if you should defend the case, which will cost thousands of dollars, or simply try to settle it. Even if you decide to defend the lawsuit, you could still lose the case. You will have spent a great deal of money and still have a verdict against you to pay. You must decide whether it's cost effective to settle the suit against you.

It is not just a civil suit for damages that can generate legal expenses. One incident can lead to a civil suit and criminal charges being filed against you. You might need an attorney to handle both of these legal problems. Similarly, an automobile accident might lead to both tort actions against you for damages and prosecution on criminal charges. While your automobile policy would defend the civil actions against you, it would not come to your assistance in the criminal matters. Your personal attorney in the criminal matter would coordinate the criminal defense with the attorney hired by the insurance company to defend the civil matter.

Therefore, the automobile policy would not guard against the risk of paying defense costs in a criminal proceeding. The insurance company might be responsible for any bail bonds from the auto accident but that would be the extent of its obligation.

In addition to these situations, you might have to hire an attorney in a tort action against you when your policy limits are obviously inadequate. In that situation, the insurance company must advise you that your limits are in jeopardy and should encourage you to hire personal counsel to guard your interests.

LITIGATION MANAGEMENT

When you're paying an attorney yourself, it's up to you to control the legal expenses. Insurance companies call this litigation management. When you reach this point, you have to become the litigation manager for your family in addition to your duties as insurance planner.

The first step is finding the right attorney. You not only want someone who is experienced in the legal matter you are facing, you also need someone whose fees you can afford.

You should gather the names of qualified attorneys through referrals from friends, relatives, and business associates. Make sure you ask about the basis for their recommendation. Did they see the lawyer in action or is the attorney simply an acquaintance? Your local bar association can also recommend attorneys who specialize in the legal area you need. After getting these recommendations, interview the attorneys. If you feel comfortable with one of them and trust one of them, then discuss fees.

Ask for an estimate of how much the legal defense will cost. Perhaps the attorney will agree to the payment of one fixed amount, no matter how many hours are involved. If not, find out the hourly rate. Request that the attorney use paralegals or lower-paid staff members whenever possible. Find out the hourly rates of those staff members. After choosing one of these attorneys, however, make sure that lawyer will handle your case and it will not be delegated to someone else in the firm.

Make certain that you get an itemized bill. Request that any major expenditures, such as travel or the hiring of an expert, not be made without your approval. Ask for a description of all services that are performed. Find out about any miscellaneous charges that you will have to pay such as photocopying or mileage. Review all bills to make certain that all of the charges make sense. If they do not, don't be embarrassed to ask. Insurance companies do when they hire a lawyer.

Ask about litigation alternatives. There are various alternative dispute resolution procedures. It might be less expensive to consider arbitration, mediation, or mini-trials, which let both parties make a trial run, so to speak, before they go to court.

Above all, at that initial interview, ask about your chances of winning. If they're not good, or you only have an even chance of winning, you should consider offering a settlement. Why put yourself through a lengthy, expensive trial that you are not likely to win and pay a substantial verdict against you.

THE INSURANCE COMPANY'S DUTY TO DEFEND

Even if you successfully control expenses, defending a lawsuit will be an expensive proposition. Therefore, it's vital that you avoid a situation where you must hire your own lawyer. The first step is to have the right insurance coverage and sufficient policy limits. When you have the appropriate coverage for a lawsuit, the insurance company will have a duty to defend you.

There are some courts which hold that an insurer's duty to defend is discharged when it has paid its policy limits in a tort action. In these jurisdictions, when the insurance company sees that your policy limits are far too low to resolve the claim or claims against you, it can simply pay the amount it owes and refuse to offer a defense on your behalf. The insurance company tenders the policy limits, which are held in escrow and applied toward any verdict that is rendered against you.

This action leaves you with two problems. You face a lawsuit in excess of your policy limits. You also will be forced to engage an attorney to defend you. If your policy limits are inadequate, you should hope you're in a jurisdiction that views the duty to defend as an independent one. Even if the insurance company has paid out its policy limits to settle claims against you, it must still provide a defense. The defense costs are not deducted from your policy limits.

Insufficient policy limits are not the only problem. You might find that you have no coverage for a lawsuit, which means you are not entitled to a defense. If you find yourself in this situation, you should try to find some basis for triggering the insurance company's duty to defend. An insurance company has an obligation to defend you, if any of the allegations are conceivably covered by the policy. If there are any facts brought out in the lawsuit that might potentially be covered by the policy, the carrier owes you a defense. The company should advise you to seek counsel on other matters in the lawsuit they do not cover, but it will undertake to defend you. Remember, though, the company won't necessarily cover the award if it pertains to noncovered damages. The insurance company is obligated to defend you until it is clear that there is no coverage provided under the policy.

If your standard policy doesn't cover your defense, you might find incidental coverage in less obvious places. The auto club you belong to might reimburse some of your defense costs, if the legal matter is related to the use of your car. When the situation is unrelated to your auto, you will either be paying for the defense yourself or turning to legal insurance, if you have it.

LEGAL INSURANCE

While there are currently no products on the market that provide a full defense when your liability insurance is inadequate, there are prepaid legal plans that can protect your family from unanticipated attorney fees. These prepaid legal plans can be a bargain. They do not, however, guard completely against the risk of being sued. Few, if any, will cover your defense costs in full when you are sued for an incident that is not covered by any of your insurance policies.

There are a variety of prepaid legal programs on the market. Some employers and unions are offering these plans at little or no cost. There are also individual prepaid legal programs being offered by banks and credit card companies. For a specified amount per month, you will have access to an attorney to work on your personal legal matters.

The concept that led to the development of prepaid legal insurance is preventive law. The idea is similar to preventive medicine. Many dental plans pay in full for six-month checkups and cleanings, to avoid a long-term problem that could be expensive for both you and the insurance company. The same logic applies to legal problems. If a lawyer helps you in the initial stages of the problem, expensive litigation can be avoided in many cases. The concept of loss prevention has been stressed throughout this book, and preventive law has a lot in common with it.

For the $8 per month that one such service charges, you will get unlimited phone calls to an attorney to discuss personal legal problems and a certain number of in-office consultations. A great many legal problems could be avoided by having a lawyer review a document before you sign it. Depending on the plan, you might get a free will each year and up to three contract reviews.

With most of these prepaid legal plans, you must pay for complex legal matters. You do, however, get these services at a discount rate. Even with a discount, you could still be on the hook for enormous legal fees if you become embroiled in litigation. In addition to the lower hourly rate that you will pay, there might even be less of a contingency fee if you are bringing an action against someone else. The fee might be 30 percent of the recovery rather than 40 percent.

Some programs pay up to $5,000 in lawyer fees during the first year, if you are sued for libel or are involved in any other criminal or civil matter. The amount increases each year until the fifth year when you are entitled to $25,000 in legal fees. You are entitled to two, 30-minute consultations during your first year, and this increases to four by the third year. The cost is $16 per month and is provided to additional family members at no extra charge.

While a plan of this kind sounds like the answer to all of your legal woes, it does not hold up under closer scrutiny. During the first year, it only covers up to $250 for legal services rendered before a trial. This would be unlikely to cover your attorney's response to the service of a lawsuit. The plan then covers trial expenses at a rate of $300 per day until the $5,000 is exhausted. The problem here is that $300 won't pay even half of a trial lawyer's fee for a day. Unless you have a trial that lasts as long as Ollie North's, you'll never use the $5,000 in benefits. When the reimbursement is increased each year, the per-day limitation renders those increases meaningless.

On the plus side, prepaid legal plans like this one do pay some legal fees in full. One policy will pay your attorney fee in full in a criminal matter, if it arises in the course of driving a licensed motor vehicle. Unfortunately, this limits the occasions on which you can use the coverage. It will not help you if you need to appeal a conviction.

When you are looking at a prepaid legal plan, remember that it covers attorney fees but not necessarily the other legal expenses you might face. There still might be court costs, court reporters, and a host of other legal charges that are not covered by the plan. You also cannot choose the attorney you want. Although the attorneys are evaluated by the sponsor of the plan, you won't be able to hire the leading specialist in a particular area of law or select the lawyer recommended by someone whose opinion you value highly.

Nevertheless, these plans can be enormously useful in resolving everyday legal issues that invariably arise. Whether you get this benefit free or pay up to

$200 per year for it, having an attorney on call can keep potential legal problems from arising. At $100 per hour or more, the plan will pay for itself in short order. Attorneys routinely see legal documents after it's too late to do anything about them. Legal insurance can help individuals avoid that problem.

The attorneys providing the service do not make much money on the premium you pay. Very little of the premium filters down to them. The attorneys hope to make money by handling more lucrative legal matters for you, such as bodily injury cases, where they will receive a percentage of the amount you recover in a lawsuit.

A prepaid legal plan is only a good investment if you use it. When a contract puzzles you, call the attorney. Have a will drawn up for your family. The plan won't fully cover any defense costs you incur in a tort action, but it can help you avoid lawsuits over contractual matters.

7

The small print

AFTER YOU'VE CHOSEN THE RIGHT COVERAGE FOR YOUR FAMILY, YOU still might be concerned whether you're fully protected. You're probably worried that there are exclusions in the policy that will destroy the protection you've worked so hard to create. Exclusions are the perils or property that are not covered by the policy. These exclusions eliminate coverage that would exist otherwise. If it were not for these exclusions, you would have protection against a particular risk.

POLICY EXCLUSIONS

Rather than living in fear of exclusions, it helps to understand the reasons for why they appear in the policy. While you might believe the exclusions are there to cheat you out of your premium, they do serve a purpose. The exclusions limit the amount of risk that the insurance company is assuming. The carrier cannot guard against every risk. The price of the policy would be unaffordable.

Let's look at liability protection. It won't cover an intentional act. To take an extreme case, let's say the insurance company sells a liability policy to a real hothead. If there were no exclusion for intentional acts, the insurance company would be responsible for the damages caused by this hothead as he brawls his way across America. Even though the purpose of insurance is to spread the risks of a few among many, it's doubtful that you would want to buy a policy to help share this hothead's losses.

Exclusions also keep you from buying coverage that you don't need. A health insurance policy will have an exclusion for bills related to injuries suffered in the course of your employment. You don't need to buy coverage for that risk, because workers' compensation laws dictate that the bills are the responsibility of your employer. Because of that exclusion, the carrier's risk is less, and the price is cheaper. It is up to the employer to buy coverage for medical bills pertaining to a work-related injury, not you.

When an exclusion eliminates coverage from one policy, it is usually picked up by another policy or added by an endorsement. As an example, there are many exclusions in the homeowners policy for losses that occur while operating a business out of the home. A person who operates a home business can add this coverage with a special endorsement to the homeowners policy. When the business expands and has more risks to face, a commercial policy and not a personal one is needed. The endorsement is no longer sufficient and a whole new policy is required.

If all of these losses were covered by the standard homeowners policy, the premium would have to be much higher. It would be unfair to charge the homeowner without a business the same rate as someone who is operating a business. The exclusion puts all of the homeowners on the same footing. Everyone gets the same amount of coverage. The business owner can then pay to add the necessary coverage.

Unfortunately, all of the exclusions in the various policies will not have a recognizable logic. As we examine most of the common insurance policies on the market, I will try to point out the exclusions that can be dangerous and can chip away at your family's protection package. Though you might not think so at times, insurance companies are not looking for ways to deny coverage. Their employees do not save money by stripping you of your coverage. If anything, denying coverage makes more work for them than simply processing the claim.

Coverage problems are difficult to accept. It is not like a third-party claim where you're trying to collect on another person's policy. You did not pay good money for that insurance. You are presenting a claim against your own policy, the one you've paid for year after year. Despite those years of payment, you find you're not protected. You find yourself being self-insured without the benefits of self-insurance that we've previously discussed.

INTERPRETING AN INSURANCE CONTRACT

You have at least one thing going for you in your dealings with an insurance company. The courts give you the benefit of the doubt when it comes to the interpretation of an insurance policy. Where policy language is unclear, it is interpreted in a way that is favorable to the insured.

If you keep rereading the portion of the policy that the insurance company is relying on to deny coverage, and it still doesn't make sense, remember that the courts will be on your side. When interpreting an ambiguous insurance contract provision, the courts will favor your interpretation. You won't be able to make a farfetched argument, but a reasonable interpretation will be looked on favorably by the courts. You won't necessarily have to go to court to force the insurance company to change its position, as you will see in Chapter 21.

When you're dealing with coverage questions, it always pays to put them in writing. A friend of mine who works for an insurance company proved that off-the-cuff answers aren't always correct. One day, a pipe in her septic tank system ruptured. All of her coworkers told her that the damage was not covered by the homeowners policy. She continued to read her policy and could find no exclusion eliminating coverage for this occurrence. Because she was insured by a company other than her employer, the woman called to ask if the damage was covered. Again, she was told that the loss was excluded by the policy.

Nevertheless, she formally submitted the claim. She didn't threaten to sue. She simply forced the company to quote the language in the policy that specifically excluded her problem. When put to the test, her insurance carrier paid most of the damage. Digging up the pipe was covered by her policy. The damage to the pipe itself was not. Submitting a claim forces the carrier to look at the specific facts of your loss in relation to the exclusions in the policy. A decision will always be more thorough when you force them to take a position in writing.

DENIAL OF COVERAGE

When an insurance carrier wants to deny coverage, it must tell you promptly and fully explain the reasons why. Some states have implemented legislation that specifically lays out the manner in which coverage must be denied. In New York, a denial of coverage must be made in writing as soon as is reasonably possible. It must set forth the grounds on which this denial of coverage is based.

Florida's law gives a carrier a specific time frame to comply with when denying liability coverage. Written notice must be provided within 30 days from the point in time when the insurance company knew or should have known there was a coverage problem. Within that 30 day period, they must let you know there's a problem. Within 60 days, they must either refuse to defend you, obtain a nonwaiver agreement, or obtain independent counsel that is agreeable to both parties. With a nonwaiver agreement, the insurance company defends you but can still deny coverage at a later date.

You also have responsibilities to the insurance company, which are not limited just to paying your premium. Just as the insurance company is contractually obligated to you, there are certain obligations that you must comply with so as not to lose the protection of the policy. In looking at your obligation to the carrier, there are two important time frames to consider. There is the time period before the contract is agreed to by both parties, and the time period after the loss occurs. You have commitments to fulfill before you enter the contract and after a loss occurs.

You needn't fear that the insurance company is waiting to seize upon some obscure technicality in the contract in order to deny coverage. The carrier will not be able to deny coverage if you fail to dot every "i" or cross every "t". There are legitimate reasons to require that you live up to these obligations. Your coverage will not be adversely affected if you act reasonably.

BEFORE YOU SIGN A CONTRACT

A contract can be nullified if you fraudulently conceal information. Because an insurance company must make a decision as to whether to insure you and how much premium to charge, you must disclose all material facts. Chapter 22 covers your obligation to act in good faith by disclosing all important information to the carrier. After the contract has been agreed to, there is no further obligation to supply information.

Misrepresenting any material facts in order to obtain insurance is fraudulent. To refuse to honor its obligations under the contract, the insurance company must show it relied on the misrepresentation and that it was a material one. The misrepresentation issue becomes moot in certain contracts after a period of time. Life insurance contracts have incontestability clauses which state that the insurance company cannot raise this defense after a stipulated period of time, usually two years.

The incontestability clause does not give you a license to lie on insurance applications and have the slate wiped clean after two years, however. There might be rare instances where fraud is so blatant, it will outlive the incontestability clause. Suppose a seriously ill woman wants to buy life insurance and sends someone to the medical exam in her place. It's a lot like sending a ringer to the college boards.

Even some lesser misrepresentations are not wiped clean by the incontestability clause. If someone lies about his age on a life insurance application, a claim for death benefits might be denied, even if it's beyond the two-year incontestability period. In some jurisdictions, the insurance company could deny that a valid life insurance policy exists. In other states, the heirs would be entitled to the life insurance coverage despite the misrepresentation by the deceased. The death benefit, however, might be reduced by the additional premiums that should have been paid. Obviously, an older person would have paid more for life insurance than a younger one.

A similar situation can arise out of a misrepresentation on an auto insurance application. Suppose you lie and say that your vehicle is kept at a relative's address, which is in a low-crime area. In reality, you keep it at your apartment, which is in an area where auto thefts are common. Your rates are lower because the insurance company believes the car is kept in a relatively safe community. In theory, the insurance company can deny coverage and won't reimburse you for your loss, if the car is stolen. In some cases, a misrepresentation such as this one won't invalidate your coverage. The carrier might simply deduct the amount you should have paid in premiums for the legitimate address of your vehicle.

You are asking for problems when you lie on an insurance application. These misrepresentations can come back to haunt you when you try to collect on your policy. Lying about your medical history on an application for health insurance can leave you without protection for medical treatment. When the insurance company obtains your medical records before paying a bill, these inaccuracies will be uncovered.

Concealing information and misrepresenting facts constitute insurance fraud. In the end, all of us pay for those individuals who cheat the system. Insurance companies are now taking vigorous steps to crack down on insurance fraud. Most companies have formed special investigation units staffed with experienced detectives. Their only job is to investigate insurance fraud.

At one time, carriers seemed content to look the other way at a certain percentage of insurance fraud and pass the cost along to their customers. The problem now is so large, however, that the industry seems determined to eradicate all fraud. Insurance fraud can't be rationalized as a way to strike back at insurance companies. It will simply destroy the foundation of your family's insurance program and can cut a hole in the safety net you're trying to erect.

REPORTING CLAIMS PROMPTLY

Virtually every insurance contract will have a provision that you report claims promptly. The reasons behind these provisions are obvious. The insurance company needs to investigate claims because it is going to be responsible for the financial consequences. The sooner it can investigate, the more thorough and accurate its investigation will be. The facts will still be fresh in the parties' minds. For the carrier to deny coverage, however, they must show that the failure to report the claim promptly prejudiced its position. There is also a prompt reporting requirement because insurance companies feel there is something inherently suspicious about claims that do not surface for a number of months after an incident.

Consequently, it is extremely important that you report the smallest of claims even if there is little chance that it will amount to anything. The most common example is a fender bender. There are thousands of instances where these seemingly insignificant accidents have escalated into major disputes over liability. Even if the accident appears to be of little consequence, you should go on record as having reported it. Quite possibly, the insurance company won't even investigate it and will simply file it away. Let that be the carrier's decision, not yours.

Obviously, if you are served with legal papers of any kind, it is extremely important to take them promptly to the insurance company. Lawsuits require answers within a short period of time, and any delay on your part could be extremely prejudicial to the carrier's interests.

You will find these time limitations even in situations where there are no readily apparent reasons for the constraints. Many medical insurance policies require that the claim be submitted within one year of the date of service. It's extremely important that you keep on top of bills from medical providers so that their charges don't slip through the cracks. Many good doctors are very bad bookkeepers. It's not unusual for them to neglect to send bills, and then send a large bill after considerable time has elapsed.

Don't let your own bad bookkeeping jeopardize your right to collect from an insurance carrier. I know a gentleman who waits until the end of the year to submit his medical bills for the year to the carrier. Not only does an insurance claim processor hate to see a year's worth of bills to review at one sitting, there is a risk of going beyond the one-year time limit.

Every policy has specific forms that detail how a loss occurred that you must complete in order to collect on a claim. A misstatement in a proof of loss does not justify the denial of payment unless it is viewed as a material one. Failing to give notice to an insurance company or to submit forms promptly won't invalidate your rights. Insurance companies must show your lack of timeliness prejudiced their rights and jeopardized their ability to act on your behalf.

COOPERATING WITH YOUR CARRIER

As the insured, you must cooperate with your carrier's efforts on your behalf by providing information, supplying records, appearing at hearings, and attending depositions. It is only logical that you help your insurance company. Suppose you cause an auto accident, and the driver of the other car is suing you for damages. Perhaps, you're not happy with the amount you got paid for the damage to your own car. You might even be disturbed that your rates go up at the time of your next bill. This does not give you the right, however, to be uncooperative in subsequent matters arising out of this accident. You would simply be cutting your nose off to spite your face. The insurance company's actions are in your best interest.

Even if you do fail to cooperate, it does not justify the insurance company denying coverage. The insurance carrier must show that it was prejudiced by your failure to cooperate. The insurance company would have to prove that your failure to cooperate caused it to suffer additional losses.

Technically, when you fail to comply with all of these obligations, you breach the contract. An insignificant breach of contract won't be held against you, only substantial breaches allow the insurance company to deny coverage. In most cases, the carrier cannot deny coverage if you offer a reasonable excuse for your failure to fulfill your responsibilities under the contract.

You can also assert the doctrines of waiver and estoppel against the insurance company. These legal doctrines are derived from very simple concepts. With a waiver, the insurance company is surrendering its right to refuse to honor the contract. When a contract has an incontestability clause, the insurance company says it will waive its defenses after a stipulated time period.

While an incontestability clause is an explicit waiver, an insurance company can relinquish its right to deny coverage through its conduct. If you breach your duty to the insurance company in some way, but the carrier ignores that act, the company implicitly waives its right to deny coverage. When you rely on that action which is inconsistent with an intent to deny coverage, the doctrine of estoppel prevents the company from following through later on that denial.

Fulfilling your duties under the contract is a far safer way to maintain your coverage than relying on these legal principles. Buying the wrong coverage is bad enough. Having the right coverage and then losing it is worse. It's like having the winning lottery ticket and then losing it.

AN AGENT'S LIABILITY FOR COVERAGE PROBLEMS

Suppose you have gone back and forth with your insurance company. The answer is still the same. You don't have coverage for a particular loss for whatever reason. There might be situations where the coverage problem is not your fault. If you relied on an agent for advice, you still have a remedy to cover your loss.

Insurance agents should carry an errors and omissions policy in case their mistakes lead to a coverage problem. Just as you buy insurance to cover the risks you face, agents buy insurance to guard against the financial consequences that can result from their mistakes. Errors and omissions coverage is a professional liability policy that the agent buys for protection against lawsuits based on his own mistakes. It's similar to a malpractice insurance policy that a doctor or lawyer would purchase.

There are many ways that an agent's conduct can cause you a coverage problem. He can fail to provide and maintain the proper coverage for your family. The agent might allow your coverage to lapse. If the insurance company he represents does not agree to write your business, you should be advised immediately. An agent might even talk you into cancelling a policy somewhere else, only to discover that he cannot find alternative coverage because you are a bad risk.

An agent can also be responsible for failing to recommend the proper coverage. If you ask for the best policy available and receive only minimal coverage, the agent might be liable for the losses you suffer that are not covered. It is up to you, however, to show that you relied on an agent's judgment and put no restraints on his recommendation, such as a price limit. When an agent is aware of your special insurance needs, you should be advised of the proper coverage to meet them. If your agent was aware of your home business and failed to recommend the appropriate endorsement or policy, you would have a potential claim against the errors and omissions coverage.

An agent is not permitted to misrepresent the coverage provided by a policy. This misrepresentation might occur during the agent's sales pitch. If you relied on an agent's statements and experience, and a coverage problem occurs, the agent can be held responsible for your damages.

In Chapter 4, I talked about the danger of an insurance company becoming insolvent. If an agent obtains a policy for you from an insolvent company, or one that is in financial trouble, he can be held responsible. In some jurisdictions, the agent will have a continuing duty to monitor the financial status of companies for whom he has sold policies. Despite the agent's duty in this area, you are without a remedy if you were aware of these financial problems. For example, you might have chosen a company that is a poor financial risk because it offered a higher interest rate or because it was the only company that would insure you.

An agent even has a duty to you after you make a claim. He must fully disclose all information you require pertaining to that claim. This information must be revealed, even if it forces the insurance company to make additional payments.

In virtually all cases, your agent wants your claim to be covered by the insurance company. When the insurance carrier denies coverage, it does not help the agent's image. It is bad for future business, which every agent counts on to help the agency grow. The only adverse impact of a claim is on an agent's loss ratio. This is the relationship between the premiums collected and the amount paid out in claims. An insurance agency's profits are tied to that loss ratio.

If this book raises any questions in your mind about the coverage you have, you should contact your agent. Keep notes summarizing your discussion, then follow up that conversation with a letter confirming the information you learned. This will document a situation where your agent has caused a coverage problem. Without this documentation, you will have no basis for presenting a claim against the agent's errors and omissions policy.

Homeowners insurance: Don't leave home without it

YOU'RE SEVERAL THOUSAND MILES FROM HOME, RELAXING ON A CRUISE ship in the Caribbean. You're having a drink by the railing with your spouse, watching the twinkling lights of St. Thomas. You reach to put your arm around your wife, and knock the drink off the railing. It falls on the head of another passenger on the deck below.

Naturally, your first instinct is to panic. Just when you thought your dinner companions were the worst thing that could happen on the cruise, you're about to bring home a lawsuit because of a momentary act of clumsiness. Before you panic, remember you already own a policy that protects you . . . even when you're thousands of miles from home. A homeowners policy covers a lot more ground than you might think. It can protect you from claims and lawsuits when you're on vacation or when an accident occurs on your own property.

Homeowners insurance provides much more than just protection for incidents that happen out of the ownership of your home. If your credit cards are stolen while you're on vacation or when you're strolling through the local shopping mall, you can count on a homeowners policy to pay for any unauthorized purchases that are imposed on you. It can even offer protection for the personal property you carry along with you when you're away from home.

Obviously, a homeowners policy has a lot more to offer than liability and property protection for your home. Nevertheless, it's still comforting to know it will cover an accident caused by your daughter leaving her skateboard on the front step and the mailman tripping over it. It's a protection package that will reimburse you when fire, tornadoes, or other disasters strike. Because there are so many hazardous situations that can arise, you should look closely at your homeowners insurance so that your family can take advantage of its far-reaching benefits.

LOSS PREVENTION

Before you begin looking at how to choose the best homeowners policy for the money, it's important to find ways so that you never have to use it. Although not all losses can be prevented, there are steps you can take to stop many of them from ever occurring. Using loss prevention techniques, which is what insurance companies call them, can save you money in the long run, and they can make your family a little safer now.

As a starting point, take a look at the security of your home. There are a number of precautionary measures to prevent burglaries. The best place to start is to install dead bolt locks. Make certain that the exterior of your home is well lit. The windows and doors should be secure when you leave. I know a family that has a button to operate the electric-eye garage door on the outside of the house in case the kids forget their key.

A security system is a step-up from these common sense ideas for preventing a burglary. Some more elaborate security systems can be linked to the local police station or to a private security firm that will monitor the alarm. More modest systems, which sell for less than $500, protect particular doors and windows that are most vulnerable to thieves. You can even buy a do-it-yourself kit at your local discount store.

Some people go with a less sophisticated loss prevention technique. They simply erect a sign that boasts that the home is protected by a security system, even though it isn't. Some stores even sell an electronic gadget that resembles a security system. None of these gadgets will deter the professional burglar, but they might discourage an amateur who is casing your home.

A neighborhood watch program could also be classified as a form of loss prevention. Using a safe in your home or even putting the lights on a timer when you're away are loss prevention methods you've practiced for years without realizing they warranted such a long-winded description. In a sense, the family dog might scare off a burglar and could be viewed as a type of loss prevention. In some communities, a member of the local police force will perform a security audit to see if your home is an easy target for a break-in.

To avoid sounding like McGruff, the Crime Dog, let's consider ways to avoid other types of losses. I know of a family that actually uses lighted candles on its Christmas tree for decoration. While most fire hazards are not quite so obvious, an inspection of the premises can reveal potentially dangerous conditions. You don't have to be an electrical expert to recognize unsafe wiring. You might notice defects in the heating equipment used around the house. Because cooking fires are often responsible for residential damage, you should make certain that fire extinguishers are operational and in an accessible location. Smoke detectors and alarms can be important safety features and an integral part of a loss prevention program. Finally, the connection between smoking and fires in the home cannot be disputed.

Loss prevention can be practiced to prevent other types of accidents from occurring. You should be checking your house and property on a regular basis for unsafe conditions that could result in accidents. If your local zoning ordinance does not require a fence around your swimming pool, put one in anyway. There might be an uneven step or a rotted tree branch ready to fall that you will discover in the course of your inspection. These checks can help you avoid lawsuits and prevent accidents in which family, friends, and visitors could be involved.

Loss prevention means making certain that accidents don't happen again. I know a claim representative for an insurance company who went to visit a policy holder whose dog had bitten a neighbor. The neighbor had presented a claim for damages against the homeowners policy of the dog owner. It was feared that the neighbor would sue for his damages. When the claim representative arrived to investigate the dog bite incident, he was bitten by the same dog. It doesn't take a genius in loss prevention to recognize that you should take steps to stop the dog from biting someone else, unless you don't mind having a number of lawsuits against you. You can be assured that your homeowners insurance carrier will mind, and won't look favorably upon your request to renew the coverage.

INSURANCE ROULETTE

As the person responsible for insurance planning in your family, choosing the right homeowners policy can make you look either very good or very bad. Of course, when it comes to insurance, you always are going to look good as long as you're saving money and you don't have any claims that aren't covered. Unfortuately, when you know very little about your homeowners insurance policy and probably haven't read it, you are playing insurance roulette. You are staring at disaster and waiting for someone to pull the trigger.

The typical homeowners policy does not cover all of the disasters your family faces. If disaster strikes, your claim to be reimbursed for your property damage could be struck down by an exclusion in the policy. Although you're more likely to mishandle a more common insurance issue, major disasters demand our immediate attention. When we discuss the particular policies that are on the market, we can look closely at the more common perils such as fire, lightning, and wind.

Many areas of the country have their own brand of disaster that could strike a homeowner. In California and Nevada, the danger of earthquakes must be guarded against with the appropriate insurance. Many areas in Pennsylvania are susceptible to mine subsidence. There is the threat of hurricanes during certain times of year in Florida. Tornadoes often strike in Texas and Oklahoma. Other areas of the country are not safe from similar disasters.

Even when your geographic area is not likely to be subjected to these calamities, you can't ignore them when you're handling the insurance for your home. Having coverage for major disasters is an important function of the family's insurance planner. Although the statistical likelihood of a disaster is small, the potential damages are enormous. Remember, the true purpose of insurance is to guard against financial catastrophes, not incidental damages that a family could afford to pay without the assistance of a policy. You must make absolutely certain that your homeowners policy covers the results of these events, even if they are uncommon ones.

EARTHQUAKES

Let's look specifically at some likely disasters. The standard homeowners policy doesn't cover earthquake damage. If you live in California or another earthquake-prone area, and don't have this coverage, you've left yourself open to a major financial disaster. Consequently, you should immediately purchase the endorsement to cover earthquake damage. In California, this endorsement will cost somewhere from $2 to $4 per $1,000 of coverage. The specific rate you pay will depend on whether your home is in a high-risk area that is near a fault or in a less risky area. The cost will also depend upon how sturdy your home is. For example, older, masonry homes are in more danger and would cost more to insure.

Despite the relatively small cost of this insurance, Californians have ignored the danger. The Federal Emergency Management Agency did a study of more than 17,000 homeowners who applied for federal disaster assistance after an earthquake struck the Los Angeles-Whittier area in October 1987. Although 97 percent of the applicants had homeowners coverage, only 15 percent had earthquake insurance.

You have to wonder what the insurance planners for those families were thinking. Perhaps, they were unaware that the homeowners policy did not cover the damage from an earthquake or simply thought that they would not be the victims of this type of disaster. That's not a good bet when some geologists are predicting that a severe earthquake will strike Southern California within the next 30 years. With these geologists predicting the odds at better than fifty-fifty, earthquake coverage would certainly be advisable.

To a lesser degree, other areas of the country are also in danger of earthquakes. It is not just California and Nevada that are in danger of earthquakes. The September 1988 issue of *Insurance Review* reported that seven states adjacent to the New Madrid Fault are in danger. Those seven states are Arkansas, Illinois, Indiana, Kentucky, Mississippi, Missouri, and Tennessee. South Carolina, New York, and the New England states also face the risk of an earthquake. In states other than California, the cost might only be 20 to 30 cents per $1,000 of coverage.

Earthquake coverage, however, comes with a very high deductible that can go from 5 percent to 15 percent of the amount of the coverage on the home. With such a high deductible, the small losses will be on your shoulders. Like it or not, this type of trade-off has to be made so that the insurance will not be unaffordable. Though an earthquake would cause a financial hardship because of the high deductible, it would not financially wipe out a family if the appropriate insurance is purchased.

A family with a high amount of equity in their home needs coverage for earthquakes to keep them from losing their house for financial reasons. Because many lenders do not require earthquake insurance, someone with little equity might walk away from an earthquake-damaged home, leaving the bank with the problem of selling it. You should be unwilling to accept that solution when coverage is available for your protection.

Keep in mind that some companies might be unwilling to renew your coverage if you are in a high-risk area. And if you decide to take the risk of not having earthquake insurance, there is a bright side. Although insurance companies won't cover quake damage without the appropriate endorsement, the basic homeowners policy does cover the fire damage that can result from this disaster. The earthquake in California on October 17, 1989, should have opened everyone's eyes to the danger.

HURRICANES AND FLOODING

The homeowners insurance policy contains other good news/bad news coverage situations. Policies will cover the wind damage from hurricanes but not the resulting flood damage. When hurricanes are brewing, the family's insurance affairs should already be in order. If not, you'll have to stick with boarding up the windows as your exclusive protection against the storm. That won't be much good against a hurricane like Frederic which caused an estimated $752,510 million in insurance losses in 1979. The insurance claims from Hurricane Hugo in September 1989 are almost $4 billion.

If your only protection is the standard homeowners policy, you'd better hope only the high winds from the hurricane do damage to your house. The wind damage will be covered, although your particular policy could have some limitations on this coverage. For example, your trees and shrubs might only be insured against limited perils and wind is probably not one of them. Strangely enough, it might not pay to replace the trees but it will pay to remove the fallen trees from the premises.

Although the damage from high winds to your house would be covered, floodwater damage is not. A hurricane can bring torrential rain and flooding along with it. Coverage for flooding from hurricanes and other sources must be obtained through the National Flood Insurance Program. You don't have to be near the coast to need flood insurance. You also don't have to be in an area with a high risk of hurricanes to be in danger of flooding. If you live in an area with poor drainage and excessive runoff, you should consider purchasing flood insurance.

Your insurance company is permitted to sell federally-backed flood insurance, using the guidelines and rates set by the government. To get further information about the National Flood Insurance Program, call your insurance company or the Federal Emergency Management Agency at 800-638-6620.

MINE SUBSIDENCE

The standard homeowners policy also does not cover damages caused by mine subsidence. In Pennsylvania and other coal-mining areas, there is a danger of underground mines collapsing and damaging your home. It is often easy to judge the risk of subsidence, because you can look at maps to determine if coal was once mined underneath your home. Any home that is located over or near an area that was once mined should consider the risk of mine subsidence. In Pennsylvania, for example, the insurance is normally bought from the commonwealth and isn't available from most companies. Unfortunately, it only covers structural damage and doesn't protect the property you own in the house. Furthermore, there is a ceiling on the amount of coverage you can buy from the state.

LETTER-PERFECT HOMEOWNERS COVERAGE

Up until now, I have sounded like Nostradamus with predictions of catastrophes for which you should have insurance. It's time to take a closer look at the more specific benefits and drawbacks of your particular policy. To do that, you first have to identify the type of homeowners policy you have. In most cases, it will be either an HO-1, HO-2, HO-3, HO-4, HO-6, or HO-8 policy. To make certain your policy is letter perfect, you must determine which of these policies you have.

This isn't as easy as it sounds. These policies were developed by the Insurance Services Office, an organization that serves the insurance industry. Most companies use its policy forms or some variation of them. Your carrier might use the forms exactly as they were originally written, or might alter them by adding different conditions. Some companies simply put their own name on the exact form provided by the Insurance Services Office. Your policy should indicate in some way that it is based upon a particular HO form.

You can't always bank on that fact, however. I spoke recently with a training supervisor for a large insurance company. As part of her duties, she teaches classes on homeowners insurance to new claim employees. She had no idea what an HO policy was. Her company uses its own homeowners policies, which make no mention of the HO forms. Despite this fact, her company's forms were quite similar to the HO series of policies.

Because of the different forms insurance companies use, one can never make unqualified statements about what is covered and what is not. Although generalizations can be made, there will always be some company that handles the situation differently. Examining the various HO policies will give you a clear picture of how most companies will handle important coverage questions, even though the policy conditions can vary.

HO-1 THROUGH HO-8 POLICIES

The HO-1 form is the most basic policy. It covers property against certain specified dangers, which are known as perils. There will usually be 11 of them:

1. Fire or lightning
2. Windstorm or hail
3. Explosion
4. Riot or civil disturbance
5. Damage from an aircraft
6. Damage from vehicles
7. Smoke damage
8. Vandalism or malicious mischief
9. Theft
10. Glass breakage
11. Volcanic eruption

The HO-2 policy is called the broad form policy. It has many similar features to the HO-1 policy, but your property is typically protected against six additional perils. They are:

12. Falling objects
13. Weight of ice, snow, or sleet
14. Freezing of plumbing, heating, or air conditioning systems
15. Accidental discharge or overflow of water or steam from a plumbing, heating, or air conditioning system
16. Sudden and accidental discharge from an artificially generated electric current
17. Sudden and accidental tearing apart, cracking, burning, or bulging of a heating, air conditioning, or sprinkler system

Naturally, the protection against these perils is modified by additional language in the policy.

The HO-3 policy is a special form contract that most homeowners buy. It's often referred to as all-risk coverage. The policy insures the homeowner's dwelling, and other structures on the premises, against all risks of physical loss unless specifically excluded by the policy. The contents of the house are not insured against all risks of loss with the HO-3 policy, however. A homeowner's personal property is only insured against named perils, which are clearly spelled out in the policy. These personal property perils are usually the 17 named above, except for glass breakage.

The HO-3 policy is probably called all-risk coverage for lack of a better phrase. It does cover the contents, but not on an all-risk basis. Furthermore, there are a number of exclusions that limit the risks it does cover. Two, in particular, are earth movement and water damage. These exclusions explain why earthquakes, floods, and mine subsidence are not covered by the basic policy and require special insurance coverage. Even though the HO-3 policy is labeled as all-risk, you still need to customize it with endorsements and separate insurance to plug many of the gaps.

Standing alone, the HO-3 policy should be called the "most risk" insurance contract. Nonetheless, it's probably right for your family as long as you are aware of its limitations. More than likely, unless you own a condominium or an older home, you probably have an HO-3 policy. If you can't tell from a careful review of your homeowners policy which type you have, call your agent or insurance carrier. If they don't know, ask them if your current coverage is all-risk for the dwelling and named perils on the contents. If it is, you probably have a policy that's comparable to the HO-3.

The HO-4 policy is for renters. The HO-6 is for the owners of older dwellings. These homes possess many unique features that cannot be replaced, and warrant special coverage. These policies are discussed later in the chapter.

PROPERTY COVERAGE

Whether you have an HO-1 or an HO-3 policy, your homeowners policy provides two broad categories of coverage. Every policy I've mentioned has this coverage. The type of policy you have, the limits of liability you've chosen, and the endorsements you've added will determine how broad these coverages are. Your role as insurance planner is to adapt the policy to meet the property and liability insurance needs of your family. To do this, let's start with the property insurance protection provided by the typical homeowners insurance policy. Because the HO-3 policy is the most common, we'll discuss the property protection it offers. You'll get the following coverages, subject to certain limitations, when you buy homeowners insurance of this type:

- You get Coverage A, which protects your house, and the structures attached to it.
- You get Coverage B, which covers other structures on the premises.
- You get Coverage C, which protects your personal property.

- You get Coverage D, which comes to your aid when you can't live in your house because of a loss.
- You also get a variety of additional coverages that protect you in the event your property is misused or if you suffer incidental damage that does not quite fall within the categories listed above.

PROTECTION FOR YOUR HOUSE: COVERAGE A

From our previous discussion, you should have a good idea what losses your policy covers. Nonetheless, you still need to find out how much coverage you have and how much you need though. A house is often the largest investment a family makes and, in your role as insurance planner for your family, buying adequate coverage is a high priority.

Your house must be insured for its replacement cost. Replacement cost is the price to replace damaged property with property that is similar in quality and value. If your house was damaged by a peril that the policy covers, the replacement cost would represent the price of rebuilding your home. Don't confuse replacement cost with the market value of your home. Replacement costs can increase even when the selling price stagnates.

You do not have to insure your house for a full 100 percent of its replacement value. Because total losses are very unusual, you can insure your house for 80 percent to 90 percent of its replacement value. You should never, however, allow the replacement-cost coverage to fall below 80 percent.

Replacement cost is determined by deciding how much it would cost to rebuild your house at today's prices. If houses are still being built in your neighborhood, this shouldn't be too hard to determine. Our builder is still building similar houses to ours in the neighborhood, and we cheer each time he raises the prices. This is a strong indication that the replacement cost has gone up.

When your home isn't newly built, calculating the replacement cost is a trickier proposition. Your agent or insurance carrier will work with you when you buy the policy to determine the home's replacement value. A good agent will personally inspect the home to make this determination. If the replacement cost coverage is handled by phone, you will be asked to answer questions about the house so that the insurance carrier can estimate the cost to rebuild your home.

Some companies send a cost evaluation form, which requires you to provide dimensions and draw diagrams of the house as well as describe the home in detail. There will be questions such as: Was the home custom built? Does it have custom cabinetry, hardwood floors, slate in the foyer, ceramic tile or unique ornamentation? Using this data, the insurance company will calculate the replacement cost of your home. You do not include the value of the land or the foundation when you calculate replacement cost.

As the years go by from your initial determination of this cost, keeping tabs on the replacement value becomes more difficult. You can automatically have the replacement cost increased by a certain percentage each year. You pay for the additional coverage that is added. Although these automatic coverage increases can help you keep pace with rising replacement costs, there is no guarantee that it will precisely match the actual replacement cost increase of your home.

You might want to hire an expert to help determine the replacement cost of your home. A contractor might be the best person to estimate the replacement cost. A builder in your area could also provide advice on this subject. An appraisal by your local realtor is not going to be of much help if he only provides the fair market value of the house. It must be stressed again that the market price of a home has nothing to do with its replacement value.

Some older homes possess many unique features, which really can't be replaced in today's building environment. It might be impossible to match the materials or to replace key fixtures. The HO-8 policy is designed for houses such as these. It does not provide replacement-cost coverage, because it is virtually impossible to determine what that replacement cost would be. Homes such as these are covered by the HO-8 policy form. The structure is insured at the market value rather than the replacement value, because it could not be rebuilt for less than an astronomical price. In other respects, however, it is much like the HO-3 policy.

THE MINIMUM REPLACEMENT COST REQUIREMENT

To avoid serious problems with your homeowners insurance coverage, you have to make certain that the replacement cost coverage remains above 80 percent of the replacement value. For someone who is unfamiliar with this requirement, there might be an inclination to lower the coverage on the dwelling. It might seem logical when you consider that a total loss is so unusual. You might think you are self-insuring for a portion of the risk which was suggested previously as a way to reduce your insurance costs. Your protection on the dwelling, which is usually found in Coverage A, must remain at 80 percent or higher to avoid one of the most severe penalties that an insurance company can impose.

Let's look at an example to see how this provision in the policy works. Suppose you own a house that would sell for about $250,000. Although the fair market value is $250,000, the replacement value is $200,000. It would cost you $200,000 to rebuild the house if it burned to the ground. Suppose your home is damaged by a minor fire. You would only receive a pro rata settlement from the insurance company if the replacement cost coverage is less than 80 percent.

In this particular example, you would have to buy a minimum of $160,000 in coverage to satisfy the 80 percent rule. Suppose you thought you'd save money by only buying $80,000 limits on your Coverage A, which protects the house itself. You then suffer a $10,000 fire loss. Seemingly, you should recover the full $10,000 in damage because it's under the $80,000 in coverage that you bought. It doesn't work that way.

The company would only pay a percentage of your damages, based on the amount you actually bought in comparison to the amount of replacement cost coverage that you should have purchased. Because you bought $80,000 worth of coverage and should have bought $160,000, you are only entitled to 50 percent on your fire loss of $10,000.

As long as you buy at least 80 percent of the home's replacement cost, you will receive 100 percent of your damages up to the maximum amount of coverage. If the full $160,000 in coverage had been purchased, any fire damage up to that limit would be paid in full. Although it's not advisable to buy the full $200,000 worth of coverage, it can't hurt to insure for more than the required 80 percent to avoid this harsh clause applying to your settlement. You might have read about this 80 percent requirement in your policy but not understood its dangerous implications. A typical clause reads as follows:

> If at the time of loss, the limit of liability for Coverage A is 80 percent or more of the replacement cost of the dwelling, the company will pay the actual cost to repair or replace the dwelling and other building structures without deduction for depreciation.

In essence, the insurance carrier is saying that if you underinsure your house by a certain percentage, it will depreciate your damages by that percentage. The carrier has inserted what amounts to a loss sharing clause.

This provision, which is sometimes called a coinsurance clause, was not inserted so the insurance company can hose you on a fire loss. If there were no penalty for insuring your house at less than its replacement cost, premiums would have to be set differently. There would have to be a higher premium for the first $20,000 in coverage and lower premiums as you buy more insurance. The rate structure would be disrupted, because too many policyholders would be underinsuring their homes.

You should never purposefully or unintentionally allow the replacement cost coverage to fall below 80 percent. The danger to your family is enormous. You are letting your family become a coinsurer with the insurance company. By underinsuring your house, you allow the carrier to share the risk with you. That's not worth the small amount you will save.

When you raise a deductible, you are coinsuring with the carrier to a certain extent. You are consciously deciding to assume $250 to $500 of a potential loss. On the other hand, you are placing your family at risk for thousands of dollars by not keeping the replacement cost coverage at 80 percent or higher. This is not an acceptable trade-off.

PROTECTION FOR OTHER STRUCTURES ON YOUR LAND: COVERAGE B

Coverage B of a typical homeowners policy covers structures on the insured premises that are separate from the dwelling. Again, remember that we are still discussing the property insurance protection available under the policy. This would protect a detached garage or some other structure on your land. Your policy will usually cover no more than 10 percent of the limit of liability applicable to Coverage A.

To stick with our previous example, let's say you decided to insure your home for its full $200,000 replacement value, even though you could have bought as little as $160,000 in coverage without fear of jeopardizing the 80 percent requirement. You would be entitled to $20,000 in coverage on the dwelling itself. If you sustain a major loss, which affects both your house and the unattached structures on your property, you can collect the full $200,000 as well as the additional $20,000. Utilizing Coverage B won't reduce the amount of protection available under Coverage A.

PROTECTION FOR YOUR PERSONAL PROPERTY: COVERAGE C

Coverage C of a typical homeowners policy covers the personal property owned or used by the insured anywhere in the world. This section of the policy is also known as the contents coverage. Whereas Coverages A and B protect the house itself and other structures on your land, Coverage C provides insurance protection for the contents of your house, garage, tool shed, and whatever structures might be found on your property.

It is generally recommended that you cover the contents of your house for 50 percent of the coverage on the home itself. To use our example again, the house with a $200,000 policy on the dwelling would be insured for $100,000 on the contents. The general rule does not stop you from customizing the policy to reflect the exact value of the contents. You should prepare a household inventory on a regular basis to take stock of the value of your family's possessions.

The fallacy of insuring the contents for 50 percent of the Coverage A limit can be seen when you look at a common occurrence. Someone moves up from a modest home, insured for $50,000, to a home which is insured for $200,000. As is often the case, the family has to scrimp and save to afford the more expensive house. They barely can pay for the new mortgage and down payment, let alone any new furniture. Conventional insurance wisdom would dictate that their personal property coverage should be increased from $25,000 (50 percent of $50,000) to $100,000 (50 percent of $200,000).

Obviously, the value of the family's possessions did not increase overnight from $25,000 to $100,000. Because of the steep mortgage and taxes on the new house, it might be a few years until their furniture and possessions are on equal footing with their expensive new home. In the interim, there is no need to buy more insurance than they require, no matter what the rule of thumb is pertaining to contents coverage.

The same logic should apply to those people who own modest homes, yet their personal property far exceeds the dollar value you might expect in homes of that type. The 50 percent rule of thumb on contents coverage might not provide adequate insurance for these people. Their personal property could be significantly underinsured. There's no law requiring the contents to be insured for 50 percent of the amount you purchased in Coverage A. It only makes sense if the 50 percent figure represents a fair approximation of the actual value of the house's contents.

I mentioned previously that Coverage C will normally protect you against only named perils, unlike the all risk coverage on the dwelling and unattached structures. Protection against named perils is more limited than coverage against all risks of loss unless specifically excluded. Nevertheless, some companies are broadening the named peril coverage by adding an endorsement to the HO-3. For example, one endorsement adds protection for food spoilage caused by a power failure. No more than $500 in food is covered.

Should a loss occur that is covered by the policy, you'll find that personal property is treated differently than the house itself. You learned earlier that a dwelling is protected by replacement cost coverage. Personal property replacement-cost coverage means the insurance company will repair or replace your damaged property with no deduction for depreciation if a covered loss occurs. Simply put, it means you will get the full replacement cost of an item damaged by some peril.

More than likely, your current policy will only give you the actual cash value (ACV) of property damaged by a covered peril. The actual cash value is the replacement value of the personal property less depreciation. After an insurance company has applied depreciation to your furniture, you'll be refurnishing at neighborhood garage sales. You won't be able to afford to buy elsewhere. A fire or explosion can result in a forced liquidation of your possessions. If you have actual cash value coverage, you'll only be entitled to garage sale prices on possessions that mean a great deal to you. The insurance check you receive will be insufficient to replace all of your furniture and personal items.

With apologies to Charles Dickens, I would like to tell you, "A Tale of Two Couches," to help you understand depreciation. We own two sofas, one in the living room and one in the family room. I live on the couch in the family room. I use that sofa for everything from eating to flossing. As for the couch in the living room, I haven't sat on it since 1982 when we had a party in there. The living room couch is in as good shape as it was when we bought it many years ago. In theory, the same amount of depreciation would be applied to both couches, since they were purchased at about the same time. The insurance company calculates depreciation by comparing the age of the couch to the expected useful life of that type of furniture.

If both of these couches were destroyed in a fire, we would be entitled to very little reimbursement. The insurance company would argue that these sofas have a minimal actual cash value. Their life expectancy is almost depleted. Some companies say furniture depreciates at a rate of 10 percent per year, so these sofas are worth very little.

It is important to recognize that depreciation percentages and ratios are not carved in stone. A property adjuster for a major carrier told me that he can be very flexible in making depreciation allowances. He often takes the type of treatment into account. The sofa in the living room might only be depreciated 30 to 40 percent, while the couch in the family room would have much more depreciation applied to it. The useful life of a sofa is another flexible area, depending on the brand and how well it was constructed.

Similarly, a video cassette recorder would depreciate differently depending on how it was used. This same adjuster told me that he talks with claimants to get a flavor for the amount of depreciation that should be taken. The VCR of someone who tapes the David Letterman show every night would depreciate differently from someone who infrequently uses the appliance. Even though your company's adjuster might try to apply rigid depreciation formulas to your personal property, make sure that you recognize that special circumstances can make a difference.

Because of depreciation, a policy that only pays the actual cash value can significantly limit your recovery. You should strongly consider adding an endorsement that offers the more desirable replacement cost coverage which does not apply depreciation. This way, you would be customizing your policy to more closely match your needs. Although this endorsement will increase the price of your policy, it will help you avoid the sometimes unfair application of depreciation to your personal possessions. While some endorsements are simply bells and whistles that add nothing to the substance of a policy, buying optional, replacement cost coverage for personal property is a worthwhile purchase.

PERSONAL ARTICLES FLOATERS

You might also need one other endorsement to make certain your personal property is fully covered. There are certain categories of property under Coverage C that will only be paid up to a maximum amount, regardless of the contents coverage you have selected. As a result, your coverage is likely to be inadequate on many of your most prized possessions. To avoid that problem, you need to buy a personal articles floater, which is sold as an endorsement to the homeowners policy, or in some cases, purchased separately.

These limitations on recovery exist, even when the limits of your personal property coverage are high. In our example with the home insured for $200,000, suppose you opted for the $100,000 in personal property coverage. Despite that high amount of coverage, there are severe restrictions on the recovery for certain items. The policy might limit recovery for losses involving jewelry, coins, stamps, fine arts, furs, watches, silverware, and firearms. If you own property of this type, there is a distinct possibility that you will be underinsured if certain losses occur.

Consequently, you have special limits for property that are far below the actual limits you chose. One explanation for these limits is that the insurance company is afraid of fraudulent claims. Although it is not difficult to verify that a couch was severely damaged in a fire, it is more difficult to challenge a policyholder who says that a coin collection was stolen in a burglary. There is also a question as to how much that collection was worth. In some ways, the insurance company avoids these credibility questions by establishing these special limits for certain types of personal property.

Remember, these special limits might only apply to certain perils. A policy might place a $2,500 limit on the theft of silverware, but if a fire destroys the silverware, you can still collect the value of the silverware without regard to the maximum. It's the theft of the silverware that's limited, not its damage by other perils. The rationale is there's no question that the silverware exists when it's damaged. With a theft, the company still has doubts that it was in fact stolen.

A personal articles floater, or personal effects floater, as it is sometimes called, can be used to supplement a standard homeowners policy. It also can be bought as an endorsement or rider to the renters policy, which contains similar limitations on this type of property. Usually, you must already have a policy with a company before they will sell you the personal articles floater. Companies like to have what they call an underwriting relationship with you before selling a floater, which has a greater element of risk for them than the run-of-the-mill insurance policy. You will probably see the same hesitation if you attempt to buy an umbrella policy that provides excess personal liability protection.

Scheduled Property

While your basic policy covers personal property in general, the personal articles floater covers "scheduled property." Scheduled property is listed separately and is described in great detail. When you purchase a personal articles floater, and schedule the property you want to insure, you and the insurance company are agreeing in advance as to the value of the property.

Listing property on a schedule can save you a great deal of grief if you need to collect from the company when a loss occurs. Normally, the carrier will adjust your loss (or calculate the damage) *after* it occurs. Some experts view the scheduling of property on a floater as a way of adjusting the loss *before* it occurs.

Even if you're not dealing with the type of property that insurance companies impose recovery restrictions on, it can be a good idea to schedule the property and cover it with a personal articles floater. Perhaps you own an antique that is one of your most prized possessions. The insurance company could view it simply as a used piece of furniture that is depreciating in value rather than appreciating. Listing items on a schedule helps you document the property's value.

A similar problem could arise if you have an expensive Oriental rug covering your floor. Once again, there is no internal restriction on its value other than the policy limit for personal property found in Coverage C. Despite this fact, the insurance company might dispute its value. Scheduling it on a floater policy circumvents that potential problem.

The personal articles rider to the policy is advantageous in other areas too. As we've emphasized, the contents coverage only applies to named perils. The floater covers all types of losses, unless specifically excluded. As a result, when you purchase a floater policy, you are buying much broader coverage. A mysterious disappearance of a diamond ring is not a covered peril, but would be paid for if insured under the personal articles floater. Another advantage with the floater endorsement to the policy is that it is not subject to the deductible.

Personal articles floaters require that you show recent appraisals of the property or sales receipts. These items should be appraised every three years to be certain that you are maintaining adequate coverage for property that has appreciated in value. Although hiring experts to appraise your property can be expensive, the price is small compared with the expense of proving an item's value after it has been damaged or lost.

It is not in your best interest to get an inflated appraisal. Some people believe this will result in a windfall if they must file a claim. Many policies give the insurance company the option of replacing an item with comparable property. Instead of paying the amount stipulated in the schedule, the company will simply replace it, because they can obviously do so at a lower price. The end result of your inflated appraisal is that you will pay higher premiums over the years, because you are buying more coverage than you need.

The price you pay for a personal articles floater will vary according to the area you live in and the insurance company's loss history for that area. Rates for different categories of property vary. Jewelry will be priced differently than stamps or coins. The personal articles floater can be very expensive if you have many items of extreme value that exceed the ceiling of the policy. One insurance executive told me he pays more for the property he schedules on the floater, than he does for his basic homeowners coverage.

One way to save money on a personal articles floater is to buy "in vault" coverage. A very expensive piece of jewelry can be kept in a safely deposit box. On the few occasions each year when you need to wear it, you must advise your insurance agent. You can also find less expensive insurance coverage through the collectors groups to which you belong. The American Philatelic Society, for example, offers low-cost insurance to stamp collectors.

Because a personal articles floater can be expensive, you might want to rely exclusively on the limited insurance under Coverage C in the homeowners policy. If you go that route, your decision should be based on your assessment of the risks you are facing. You should be relatively certain that the risk of loss is minimal. When your insurance is limited, you should be even more careful in your handling of that particular property.

The price of a personal articles floater should be taken into consideration when you buy personal property that is more expensive than the limits in the standard policy. It's like the salesperson who says, "If you have to ask, you can't afford it." In a similar vein, if you find the price of the floater to be prohibitive, you really can't afford the item. In addition, when you're investing in a collectible that falls within the restricted coverage classification, you should consider the price of a floater when calculating the return on your investment.

PROTECTION FOR LOSS OF USE: COVERAGE D

The loss of use protection under the homeowners policy is a natural extension of the property protection we've been discussing. If a loss covered by the property section of the policy causes your house to become uninhabitable, your family is entitled to additional living expenses. These expenses must be reasonable and must be necessary for your family to maintain its normal standard of living. Payment will be made for the shortest time required for your family to settle elsewhere.

You can compare this coverage to an automobile policy that provides for rental coverage in the event your car is damaged in an accident and is undriveable. The rental coverage won't pay for the rental of just any vehicle—it will pay the price of a reasonable substitute.

Suppose your family has to live in a hotel for a number of months or rent an apartment on a short-term lease. Not only would you need to be covered for that expense, but it would cost more to feed the family because dinners and other meals would have to be eaten at a restaurant. There would be other expenses as well, such as going to a laundromat because the family washer and dryer would be unavailable. Coverage D pays for these loss of use expenses.

When a fire or some other peril strikes your home, it could be a long while until things are back to normal. We've talked about how replacement cost is defined as the money it would take to rebuild your home. When you're calculating the cost, consider how long the process will take. Extensive remodeling can take many months.

A key phrase is additional living expense. You still have to pay your regular monthly bills. The meals you eat out would be paid for to the extent they exceed what you normally pay for food. If your children normally walk to school, Coverage D would pay the price of a cab or some other form of transportation. Your policy will place a limit on the amount of expenses that will be paid. Generally, your protection under Coverage D will be limited to 20 percent of your Coverage A. To use our example again, the $200,000 policy will have Coverage D limits of

$40,000. We can see again that the other property coverages are derived from your coverage on the house itself.

ADDITIONAL PROPERTY-RELATED COVERAGES

The loss of use of property isn't the only incidental damage you'll suffer when your house is damaged by some peril. There is a catch-all provision in the homeowners policy that can offer additional protection in a variety of situations. It will pay for fire department charges as long as the firemen are protecting property from one of the risks your policy covers. It will pay the cost of removing debris from the premises if a covered loss occurs. The basic hazard must be covered in order to trigger this additional coverage. For example, we talked initially about earthquake coverage requiring a special endorsement. If there is no coverage for the danger itself, this additional protection is not activated. There would be no payment for debris removal after an earthquake if the basic policy does not cover that hazard.

It's a lot like the lock replacement coverage which is often an additional property-related coverage. You are not entitled to lock replacement when you lose your house keys. The usual $250 in coverage is only provided when house keys are stolen in a covered theft loss.

Fortunately, there is no such limitation when your property is misused. We talked earlier about the protection for theft or unauthorized use of your credit card. Most policies will pay up to $500 when this occurs. The law permits credit card companies to charge a customer for up to $50 in charges if they were made before you notified them that the card was lost or stolen. If you carry a number of credit cards, you would have no trouble exhausting this coverage if your wallet is stolen.

LIABILITY COVERAGES

The most important of the liability coverages in a homeowners policy is the personal liability protection. Our earlier analysis of the HO forms has no bearing on this discussion. Regardless of the HO form you have, you are entitled to the protection offered by this section of the policy. The liability coverage gives you financial protection when you are held responsible for injury to others or for damage to their property, even if it occurs away from your home.

As discussed in Chapter 3, a third-party claim is a claim that is brought against the holder of liability insurance. As the insurance planner for your family, you must make sure that the liability protection you have in your homeowners policy is sufficient to resolve any third-party claims against you. We started off this chapter with an example of an accident that occurred far away from home. Remember how you knocked that glass off the railing onto the head of someone on the deck below. It's time we checked back on that passenger to see how he's doing.

Let's say the glass knocked him unconscious. If he wakes up with a headache and that's the end of it, there's no question your policy limits will be high enough to cover the damages. Suppose he has to be evacuated to a hospital in the States. Well, now we're talking about thousands of dollars in medical expenses and flight arrangements to transport him home. You'll, of course, have to compensate him for the loss of his trip. Don't forget about his wife's spoiled trip, and her special arrangements to get back to the States.

Suppose the scenario we are creating gets worse. His physicians discover brain damage. Since he's an engineer, there is some question if he'll ever be able to return to his high-paying job. Worse yet, he's a young engineer with a high-earning capacity that will be diminished for the rest of his life.

It's obvious by now that we're talking about damages of hundreds of thousands of dollars, not just a vacation ruined by a falling glass. Despite the unintentional nature of your act and the freakishness of the accident, you could be on the receiving end of a lawsuit. Fortunately, the liability section of the homeowners policy will cover any claim, except those excluded by the policy, for bodily injury or property damage. You have coverage whether the glass falls and causes the injuries I've described, or if it simply damages his sportcoat.

Because serious injury and property damage can result from silly accidents such as this one, you have to be sure your limits are high enough to cover any claim or lawsuit. Had you only purchased $100,000 in liability limits, a typical amount of protection in a homeowners policy, your insurance protection would be insufficient in our hypothetical situation. Even if you had raised your limits to $300,000, which is not that expensive, you still might receive a jury award against you for higher than that amount. We will see in Chapter 10 how the personal liability umbrella policy can be used to raise those limits even further.

Examples such as this one show that the homeowners policy offers much more than protection for home-related accidents. Because the liability protection is so broad, insurance companies want to reduce that coverage when they notice a dangerous trend on the horizon. In recent years, a number of people have charged that a sexual partner has transmitted a disease to them and have sued. In fact, a growing number of states now recognize the right to sue because of a sexually-transmitted disease such as herpes. In years to come, we will undoubtedly see lawsuits making similar allegations from AIDS victims.

In theory, the defendant's homeowners carrier would have to provide a defense and pay any damages awarded in a suit such as this. To avoid providing coverage, many insurance companies have added a Communicable Disease Exclusion. Because of this exclusion, the liability coverage in the policy would not apply to situations such as this one. Although these lawsuits will still be brought, homeowners insurance will not protect the party who is sued.

MEDICAL PAYMENTS TO OTHERS

A homeowners policy also provides coverage for medical bills when a person is injured in an accident on your property. This coverage doesn't apply to you or members of your household. It's not required that you be legally responsible for the accident which prompts the medical treatment. This coverage is available even when you are not at fault for the unfortunate event. Whereas you need personal liability coverage of at least $300,000, it is customary for the medical payments coverage to be about $1,000.

In some instances, an accident can occur off your property and still qualify for medical payments to the injured party. Suppose your dog goes after a neighbor and finally nails him several blocks from home. The neighbor could collect from the medical payments coverage if he incurs hospital or doctor bills. If the neighbor decides to sue you, your personal liability protection comes into play. In some respects, medical payments coverage provides an alternative to litigation. The neighbor would not have to show that you were negligent in any way in order to tap this coverage.

The policy will also make medical payment to others if your activities off the premises cause the accident. For example, an insured member of your household hits a golf ball that injures someone. The policy would pay the injured person's medical bills without addressing the issue of due care. We've already defined negligence, which provides the basis for a lawsuit, as the failure to exercise due care under the circumstances. It doesn't matter if the insured golfer was careful when hitting the shot. The only question is whether the insured's activities resulted in the injury that required medical treatment.

This same coverage could be used in a more unusual situation. The person who caught herpes from the insured could argue that the medical payments coverage should apply to that incident. Once again, a Communicable Disease Exclusion would defuse this argument. It states specifically that the Medical Payments to Others clause does not apply to the transmission of a communicable disease by an insured.

DAMAGE TO OTHERS PROPERTY

Many policies pay up to $500 per occurrence for property damage caused by an insured. Suppose you are invited to a cocktail party at your boss' house. In the middle of a boring story she is telling, you put your hand to your mouth to stifle a yawn. As you reach to cover your mouth, you knock over and break an expensive Lladro figurine that she values more than your service as an employee. Fortunately for you, your policy will pay up to $500 to replace the statuette.

This protection is similar to medical payments coverage because it does not require any proof that you were at fault for breaking the Lladro statuette. If this coverage were not available, your boss would have two options other than firing you. The first would be to submit the claim to her own homeowners carrier. If it's not covered or she has a high deductible, that option would be unpalatable. Her second option would be to submit a claim under your personal liability coverage. With that approach, she would have to show that you were negligent in the way you conducted yourself. The insurance company might argue that she did not act reasonably by placing an expensive figurine in a precarious position. If you have this particular coverage, however, these issues won't materialize. The damages aren't subject to a deductible and proof of any carelessness is not required.

This coverage can also help you or another member of your household. Say your son mistakenly throws a baseball through a neighbor's window. That property damage would be covered by this section of the policy. Even if a child (usually defined as under 13) deliberately throws a ball through a neighbor's window, this coverage would pay for the damages.

For yourself and family members who are aged 13 and older, the damage to the property of others must not be intentional. It also cannot arise out of a business pursuit. Another important exception to this coverage is that it cannot arise out of the operation of a motor vehicle.

As I have discussed on a number of occasions, it's useful to look at the logic behind coverage exclusions. If there were no motor vehicle exclusion, people would be using this homeowners coverage to pay for minor fender benders that they cause. That's not the purpose of the homeowners insurance policy and this coverage in particular.

COVERAGE PROBLEMS

As we've analyzed different homeowners insurance policies, a number of coverage problems have come to light. There are also additional problems you might encounter. With so many policy variations available, it's impossible to say how your company will treat these issues. When you run into these circumstances, you should be calling your agent or carrier for the specific policy guidance you'll need.

Suppose you're transferred and have to sell your present home. You move out and leave the house vacant and your pipes freeze. Your carrier might not cover the pipes, unless you can show you used reasonable care to heat the house and drained the water tanks. Vandalism might not be covered if the house has been vacant for more than 30 days. You will have to make special insurance arrangements when you find yourself in this situation.

Operating a business out of your home can trigger coverage problems. As the trend toward home-based businesses continues, the need for additional coverage under the homeowners policy increases. Your insurance company might view a money-making hobby as a business.

Business-related property might not be covered in full. Someone who falls when visiting your home business might present a claim. Your insurance company could argue that it falls within the business exclusion of the policy. Thus, your solid liability and property protection could crumble if a loss related to your business occurs.

You might not think you're even operating a business. Let's suppose you hold an occasional garage sale. Because the sales are so successful, you hold them on a regular basis. This could be construed as business activity that warrants additional coverage. It's doubtful that you would need additional coverage if you only hold your sale on one or two occasions a year.

You will always run into coverage problems with intentional acts. The one rare exception where payment can be made in spite of an intentional act we discussed is the damage to the property of others. A child under age 13 could commit an intentional act without jeopardizing the coverage. Normally, however, there will be no protection for losses caused by an intentional act.

Hiring domestic employees also presents another coverage problem. If a maid or baby-sitter gets hurt on the job, your liability coverage won't necessarily protect you in the way discussed previously. You might be obligated under your state law to provide workers' compensation benefits. Some policies require a special endorsement to add workers' compensation protection.

I mentioned earlier that there is a motor vehicle exclusion in the homeowners policy. Suppose you run over the greenskeeper with your golf cart while you're brooding over your last shot. In most cases, you won't have to worry about the motor vehicle exclusion. The typical homeowners policy will extend coverage to this situation. Look at how your policy defines motor vehicle or if it specifically provides coverage for golf carts. You might, however, need to buy special coverage for snowmobiles and other recreational vehicles.

Whenever your housing situation changes, you should check with your agent or carrier to see if your property and liability protection needs will be met. Adding new features to your home might mean additional coverage requirements. When you rent your home to others, you open the door to problems with your homeowners coverage. The theft coverage becomes worthless, when you rent the house to someone who is not a family member. A rental situation also creates liability problems and the policy must be endorsed to cover these contingencies.

RENTERS INSURANCE POLICIES

On December 13, 1987, a Florida newspaper reported the unfortunate story of a Tampa couple who were trying to save money to buy a new bed. Until they could afford a bed, they bought a $39 air mattress to use in their bedroom. They were using a blow dryer to fill their queen-size mattress. It blew up, causing an estimated $6,000 in damage to their apartment.

Because legal action could be brought against them for the property damage they caused, my first reaction was to hope they had renters insurance. Unfortunately, I wasn't very optimistic that they had purchased a policy. I assumed, and I hope I was wrong, that you won't be buying renters insurance when you can't afford a bed. Although it's too late to help the couple in Tampa, I am hopeful that others can learn from their experience.

According to the Insurance Information Institute, 95 percent of the nation's homeowners have household insurance but less than 25 percent of renters have insurance on their dwelling. Statistics compiled by the Institute show that a significant percentage of the renters were unsure if they had insurance. Most homeowners must show proof of homeowners coverage to get a mortgage, but there is really no safeguard to encourage renters to buy comparable insurance on their housing. Nevertheless, it is one thing to be unsure if your policy covers a particular peril and quite another matter to be unsure if you have insurance at all.

A renters policy is usually the HO-4 form in the grouping that was discussed previously. Like the homeowners policy, it's divided into two sections—property protection and liability protection. In the case of the Florida couple, liability protection would cover any damages they caused to the landlord's apartment. The landlord could come after them for the damage to his building, an amount that would be far in excess of their security deposit. A renters policy provides coverage for claims and lawsuits such as these, as well as the more common liability problems. Your defense costs would also be covered, just as they would be in a homeowners policy. Even if the landlord has his own insurance on the building, his insurance carrier can still pursue the party that caused the damage.

Had this Tampa couple bought renters insurance, there is some question whether their own property would have been paid for by the policy. A renters policy usually covers "named perils," which means their own property is only covered against specified dangers. Depending on the language of the policy, this accident might be classified as an explosion, which is a named peril and is protected by a renters policy.

As the story of the Tampa couple suggests, a renters policy can be indispensable for handling some of the common, and even bizarre, problems that life has to offer. The mere fact that someone isn't a homeowner doesn't mean they don't have assets that need to be protected. Even newly-married couples have personal property they've accumulated from wedding gifts and other sources. After years of having their personal property covered under their parents' homeowners policies, they might not recognize the need for renters insurance when they are out on their own. Their personal property might also be valuable enough to require a personal articles floater, which was mentioned previously.

Newlyweds aren't the only ones who need a renters policy. Students, especially perpetual ones, might need their own policy. The personal property of students, who are still members of their parents' household, is covered under their homeowners policy with certain limitations. It might be subject to a 10 percent limitation on contents coverage of the parent's policy. In some policies, theft coverage will only be afforded if the student was present at the dorm room or apartment during the 45 days prior to the loss. To be covered under the parents' homeowners policy, the student must still be a resident of the parents' household. This requirement could be questioned if your child has established residency somewhere else to qualify for in-state tuition or financial aid.

Property protection is not the only compelling reason to buy a renters policy. Claims and legal action can be brought against you even when a lease places responsibility on the landlord's shoulders. Suppose you rent a duplex, where the landlord lives in the other unit. Although the lease clearly states that it is the landlord's duty to keep sidewalks free of ice and snow, you could be sued if someone slips on the icy path. Attorneys often sue everyone associated with an accident, so that all of the potentially liable parties are named. The attorney bringing the lawsuit would not necessarily know who was responsible for cleaning the sidewalk. Without a renters policy, you would be responsible for your own defense costs and any damages that are awarded.

With a renters policy, you still have the same protection as a homeowners policy for accidents you cause that occur off the premises. You would also be covered for the theft or authorized use of your credit cards. A good policy will provide coverage for food spoilage, lock replacement when keys are stolen, and loss of use benefits when the rental property becomes uninhabitable.

You can make your policy even better by buying options to afford broader coverage. You should consider replacement-cost coverage on your personal property to avoid depreciation problems. Most policies will only give you the actual cash value of personal property that is damaged.

You can buy a personal computer endorsement to cover the personal computer you use at home, work, or school. If you've stepped up from an air mattress to a waterbed, you should consider the special coverage needed in case your waterbed leaks and damages someone else's property. Some apartment managers will require proof of this coverage before renting a unit to you.

The insurance planner for the family that rents can still utilize loss prevention techniques. It is often more difficult to prevent losses in an apartment setting because you usually aren't allowed to make structural changes in order to make the premises safer. The landlord is responsible for building security, and will often shirk his duties. Finally, more people have access to the premises than to a private home.

Despite these problems, many of the loss prevention techniques we discussed earlier can be applied to a rental situation. There are still steps that you can take to reduce the risk of crime, fire, or accidents around the home. Although you can't control the activities of your neighbors, your family can still do its part to minimize the need to call upon its renters insurance policy.

CONDO AND CO-OP INSURANCE

The HO-6 policy is the most common coverage used for condos and co-ops. Many of its features are the same as other policies we have discussed. It contains property protection, credit card coverage, and pays loss of use expenses. It also provides the same type of liability protection.

What is different is that it doesn't provide insurance for the dwelling itself. The condo or co-op association will carry insurance of that type, as well as liability insurance on the common areas. Generally, the interior of the unit is your responsibility. Your policy should cover you for loss assessments needed, because your association's insurance coverage has been exhausted.

PREPARING FOR A CLAIM

With any type of homeowners insurance, you should be taking preparatory steps in the event a loss occurs. You should be preparing an inventory of the household goods you own. A separate copy of the list should be kept in your safety deposit box.

You might also want to videotape the contents of your home, apartment or condo in case you need to prove your damages at some point in time. Take photographs of the more valuable possessions and keep them in a safe place. Sales receipts and appraisals should be stored in a safety deposit box rather than in the place where the loss is likely to occur.

In Chapter 21, how to process your claim if a loss does occur is discussed, and you will be able to see how these preparatory steps can help bring the claim to a satisfactory conclusion.

HOW TO SAVE MONEY

Throughout this chapter, I have suggested ways to improve your homeowners coverage. Although these endorsements and floaters only add to the price of your policy, they can be worthwhile investments. But there are ways to reduce the cost of your policy without sacrificing the quality of your coverage.

As is the case with any insurance purchase, there are good and bad ways to save money. Let's start off with the worst way to save money, and that's to skimp on your house's replacement cost coverage. Although you don't necessarily need to buy 100 percent of the structure's replacement value, falling below 80 percent is the worst mistake you can make.

It also makes no sense to save money by not paying insurance to cover earthquake damage and flooding problems if your home is at risk from these disasters. The minimal savings do not justify the substantial risk you are taking.

As with any insurance purchase, shopping around can produce the biggest savings. The prices for comparable coverage can vary from company to company. The operative word is "comparable." You should write down exactly what coverage you want and price that precise coverage from company to company. This can be difficult, because many companies are now pushing premium policies supposedly tailored to the needs of the affluent homeowner. These policies eliminate many of the restrictions we've talked about in this chapter. In these deluxe policies, many features that are optional in most policies are standard in these.

One policy of this type combines homeowners coverage, a personal articles floater, and a personal liability umbrella in one package. It also offers replacement cost coverage on personal property as a standard feature. There also are higher limits for some of the property that is usually restricted in a typical policy. Silverware theft coverage would be $10,000 not $2,500. Jewelry, furs, and watches would be covered up to $5,000 not just $1,000.

Another of these deluxe policies covers perils that are normally excluded. In Pennsylvania, a nationally known insurance company is providing mine subsidence coverage for the full value of a home, not just the $100,000 available through the state. It also offers higher limits and broader coverage for property that is normally limited in conventional policies such as guns and jewelry.

These deluxe policies are usually targeted at homeowners whose homes are valued at more than $200,000. Though they offer much more, they are not necessarily a better bargain. Not only will these policies make price comparisons more difficult, they will often give you much more coverage than you need. To use one seemingly insignificant example, one of these deluxe policies gives $1,000 coverage for food spoilage rather than the $500 found in the typical policy. If you never have more than $50 worth of food in the refrigerator, you're getting no additional benefit from the more expensive policy.

Similarly, you might not need more coverage for guns, silverware, furs, and jewelry. If you own one ring that exceeds the ceiling in the policy, you can buy a floater. In some respects, these deluxe policies offer a shotgun approach to meeting your insurance needs. They scatter a number of additional coverages in your direction, and hope that a few meet your needs. You would be better off buying only the coverages you need, and then comparing prices for that amount of and type of protection.

In addition to shopping around for the best price, you can also save money by installing a security system. Most companies will give you a discount on your premium for fire and burglar alarm systems that are connected to the police station or to a monitoring station. Installing dead bolt locks and smoke detectors can also reduce your costs.

At least one carrier is offering a discount to homeowners who don't smoke. Careless smoking habits can lead to fires, which explains the rationale behind the discount.

Raising your deductible can also reduce your premium. It is important to assume a reasonable amount of risk, because you should not be buying insurance to cover the small annoyances of life. Depending on your income, raising your deductible from $250 to $500 would lower your premium and not cause you financial harm. Keep in mind, however, that the tax law changes have made it tougher to claim these losses as a deduction, which is discussed in Chapter 20.

If you own a new house, you might be entitled to a new-home discount. When your home is less than five years old, some companies offer a discount on your base premium. Unfortunately, this discount often decreases each year. On the other hand, you might qualify for a discount as your age increases. At some companies, homeowners who are aged 55 or older qualify for a discount.

Insurance companies also have their own version of a volume discount. If you purchase both your homeowners and automobile insurance from them, you can qualify for a discount. Be sure you're satisfied with the individual rates of both policies before you agree to buy both car and home insurance from them in order to get the package price—it might not be such a great buy. These are called cross-sell discounts and encourage a policyholder to buy both policies from the same carrier.

Finally, you often can save money by paying your premium in full at the beginning of the policy year. Paying for your homeowners insurance on the installment plan can result in additional charges.

9
Automobile insurance

AS THE INSURANCE PLANNER FOR YOUR FAMILY, YOU'LL NEED TO TAKE A crash course on automobile insurance. Learning more about car insurance can help you save money and get the most coverage for your premium.

The stakes are high with automobile insurance. When you see the highway death toll after a holiday weekend, you'll recognize that driving the family car is not without risk. Your car insurance can help you guard against the financial risks that go hand in hand with the use of your automobile.

If you look at just the premium, the stakes are also high. The average car insurance premium in New Jersey is $1,000 per year. When you consider that car insurance is only a portion of your insurance budget, we're talking about a significant amount of money. If you clear $20,000 per year, your auto insurance might represent 5 percent of your net income. With so much at stake, it is worthwhile to learn more about car insurance so you can decrease that percentage.

WHY INSURANCE RATES ARE SO HIGH AND WHAT TO DO ABOUT IT

Everyone has an opinion about why auto insurance rates are so high. Some people blame greedy insurance companies, others blame greedy lawyers. A number of experts blame the skyrocketing cost of medical care. Some say fraud is causing the increase in insurance rates. Others attribute the high cost of automobile insurance to the steep price of automobiles and the parts used to repair them. The Insurance Information Institute says the price of personal auto insurance is rising because there are more accidents, which cost more than they used to. These accidents are likely to result in lawsuits. In addition, the Institute believes the increasing number of automobile thefts are responsible for the increase in prices. Consumer groups believe that high car insurance rates are caused by waste and inefficiency on the part of insurers.

Just as most people have an opinion as to the cause of high insurance rates, they also believe they know the solution. They opine that if you reduce repair, medical, and litigation expenses, you can lower the price of automobile insurance. There are those who believe that making cars more crashworthy will lower expenses and reduce rates. Another idea is to upgrade the safety of highways. Some advocate a lower speed limit and improving the safety of trucks on the highway.

Many knowledgeable people are suggesting changes in the no-fault system as a way to reduce litigation and indirectly lower the cost of auto insurance. Some believe that additional regulation of insurance companies is the key to lowering auto insurance premiums. Others believe that less regulation will achieve this goal. There are those who advocate a more direct legislative approach that forces the price of insurance lower, similar to Proposition 103 in California. Whatever the root cause of high-priced automobile insurance, you must work within the existing framework to lower the price you are now paying for auto insurance.

LOSS PREVENTION

Buying insurance does not end your responsibility to your family. You should be taking steps to minimize the risks that you are facing. Start by insisting that your family wear seat belts at all times. Some companies are even offering extra coverage at no cost if you are injured or die while using a seat belt.

You can take steps to safeguard the family car from theft. Although a locked car won't deter a professional thief, it will discourage amateur criminals. Assuming you don't live in "Mayberry," where there hasn't been a car theft since Opie was a pup, you can install one of the many antitheft devices that are on the market. Using one of these devices can result in a discount on your auto insurance premium. If you can't spring for the antitheft system, try a substitute. One insurance company has sent its customers stickers to place on their vehicles that warn that the car is protected by an antitheft device, even though it has none.

When your automobile policy comes up for renewal, you probably only look at the bottom line. That bottom line, depending on what state you live in, can be staggering. Knowing what you are paying for is a starting point in your effort to pay less for more coverage.

Essentially, an automobile policy consists of personal injury coverage and physical damage coverage. Personal injury coverages include the liability, medical payments, uninsured motorist, and personal injury protection (PIP) coverages. The physical damage coverages include collision, comprehensive, towing and labor, and rental reimbursement.

BODILY INJURY LIABILITY COVERAGE

The liability section of an automobile policy is the most important coverage you can buy. The liability coverage covers the injuries and property damage you might cause to others. It also provides a legal defense and indemnity should you be sued as a result of an automobile accident. The liability coverage also handles any injuries you cause to pedestrians, other cars, the occupants of those cars, or to someone else's property.

Depending on the company that insures you, your liability limits will be written either as a single limit or split limits. The single limit will have a maximum amount of coverage, such as $300,000. No matter how many people are involved in the accident, or how much property damage is caused, the maximum amount paid out is that $300,000.

A comparable split-limit policy might be written as $100,000/$300,000/$25,000. This policy would pay a maximum of $100,000 per injured person and a maximum of $300,000 per accident. The maximum property damage paid is $25,000. With the split-limit policy, there are ceilings on the amount that can be paid to each individual injured in the accident, as well as the internal limit on property damage.

Although you can still choose the right coverage with either split or single limits, the single limit has some advantages. It offers flexibility in resolving claims against you. It is difficult enough choosing the right policy limits. Split limits increase the odds that you'll make a mistake.

For example, suppose your negligence causes injuries to two people in another car. One is injured very seriously, and the other sustains only slight injuries. The single limit would allow the company to settle the serious claim for up to $290,000 and the other for a nominal amount. With the split limit, you would only have $100,000 with which to settle the serious claim.

With a single limit, there is a large pot available to protect you from lawsuits. With split limits, you have to be far more accurate in your assessment of how bad the accident will be. A single-limit liability coverage in a large amount is preferable to split limits because it covers the gamut of problems that can occur.

PROPERTY DAMAGE LIABILITY COVERAGE

A single-limit policy can also provide flexibility in resolving claims against you for property damage that you cause. You're driving past a Porsche dealership on a beautiful sunny afternoon. Your Chevette purrs as you try to convince yourself that you'd rather have the economy and reliability of your current car instead of that ostentatious sports car. Then it happens. A bee flies through your open window, your substitute for air conditioning, and attacks. Because of your inordinate fear of bees and your impression that it's a South American killer bee, you panic.

You lose control of the car and crash through the showroom window of the Porsche dealer. Four Porsches and a semiconscious salesman lie in your wake.

This is as close as you'll ever come to buying a Porsche. You've done $60,000 worth of damage to the cars, and $10,000 worth of damage to the dealer's window and showroom. Let's not worry yet about the Porsche salesman you hurt, even though he makes more money than you do and certainly drives a nicer car. Here you are with an auto policy that pays $25,000 for damage caused by you to the property of others.

Farfetched? Maybe. Nonetheless, based upon your increasing skill in risk analysis, you can see that certain coverages are woefully inadequate. It doesn't take a rocket scientist to recognize that $25,000 won't go very far if you demolish a BMW or a Mercedes on a day when your driving skills aren't up to par.

There is more to liability coverage than just injuries to other people. Even in a more realistic situation than this one, you can still cause property damage that exceeds your policy limits. You don't have to crash into the top-of-the-line Mercedes to exceed a $25,000 property damage limit. Although you might be driving an inexpensive car, you can still do major damage to the property of others.

When driving the family automobile, you risk causing bodily injury or property damage to others. Whether your company offers a single limit or split limits, you should make certain that your coverage is sufficient to guard against the serious damage you might cause. Because companies offer liability protection in these two forms, price comparisons are a little tricky. The single-limit liability coverage should be slightly higher in price than split limits. A single limit of $300,000 would be slightly higher than split limits of $100,000/$300,000/$25,000. No matter which coverage your company sells, you can raise those limits for a small amount of money.

CHOOSING THE RIGHT LIABILITY LIMITS

There will be situations where the largest liability limits won't help. In a recent Pennsylvania case, two sisters were waiting in front of a grocery store for their mother. She was getting the car, while they watched their grocery cart. A car struck them, causing both girls to be pinned against the wall of the store. Their brother was injured also, but not as badly as the girls were. Sadly, each sister had a leg amputated below the knee.

The jury awarded $7 million in damages to the older sister and $5 million to the younger sister. Their brother received $35,000. The driver of the car was drunk, which probably influenced the jury's award of damages. The point of this sad story is that the driver only had limits of $100,000/$300,000.

Perhaps, you are not worried about inadequate policy limits, since you don't intend to drive while intoxicated. While that's certainly a good idea, it doesn't necessarily mean your policy limits will be adequate to cover any auto accident you might cause. This verdict was from a jurisdiction which is not reknowned for high verdicts, such as California.

What would you do if this happened to you? Would you start transferring assets in the hope of avoiding the collection of this debt? Chances are, it's too late at this point. Any attempt to put assets in another family member's name would be considered a fraudulent conveyance.

So what do you do? Where do you start? You must evaluate your risk. Do you drive a lot? Do you have a number of close calls? Do you drive around with the neighbor's children in your car? Have you had a number of minor accidents? Do you drive with a temper? These events might be clues that a more serious accident is in your future.

The personal liability umbrella policy, which is discussed in Chapter 10, can increase those liability limits and raise them to a level that will cover almost any tragic circumstance. The umbrella policy will increase your limits of liability on an automobile policy and in other potential areas where you might face a lawsuit.

Although an umbrella policy can save you from financial ruin, it is no substitute for the appropriate limits on an underlying automobile policy. An umbrella policy underwriter will require that you have a liability limit of several hundred thousand dollars in your standard auto policy before agreeing to write it. Even if you don't buy an umbrella policy, your liability limits can be raised by hundreds of thousands of dollars for a comparatively small amount.

The minimum coverage required by financial responsibility laws is inadequate for your purposes. The limits you choose for the liability portion of your policy won't limit the person suing you. If you have assets worth pursuing, the party bringing the suit won't quit when your insurance runs out.

MEDICAL PAYMENTS COVERAGE

The next part of an automobile policy to analyze is medical payments coverage. Medical payments coverage pays the expenses of anyone hurt while riding in your car, regardless of fault. Under some policies, it can even pay your medical bills while you or your family members are riding in someone else's car. It can cover you even while you're walking and are hit by someone else's vehicle. Unlike most health insurance plans, medical payments coverage is "first dollar coverage." "First dollar coverage" pays for virtually all the medical bills incurred from the very first dollar billed, unlike your health insurance plan, which probably has deductibles and copayments on most forms of medical treatment.

Personal injury protection (PIP) is similar to medical payments coverage but is generally broader. It can cover lost income and expenses from an accident such as a death benefit. In states that have some variation of no-fault, PIP in some amount, is usually required.

CATASTROPHIC MEDICAL EXPENSE COVERAGE

If a family member is severely injured in an automobile accident, there is a significant risk of incurring medical and rehabilitation bills of immense proportion. The injured party might face hundreds of thousands of dollars in bills. In addition to the hospital and physician charges, there could be significant expenses for wheelchairs, physical therapy, and training. These costs won't necessarily be covered by your personal medical policy.

Some insurance companies are now offering catastrophic medical expense coverage. Before you consider buying this, however, you should first look at the amount of medical coverage your own health insurance will pay. You should also look at the types of medical care that will be paid for, and whether therapy and rehabilitation are covered. You might need this coverage if your regular health care policy is limited. In addition, the medical payments coverage, or PIP protection, often limits the amount of medical reimbursement you can collect. Instead of this coverage, consider beefing up your regular health care policy, which will pay for any medical problem, not just an auto-related one.

UNINSURED MOTORIST COVERAGE

The uninsured motorist coverage in an auto policy comes into play when there is an accident with an uninsured or a hit-and-run driver. Obviously, the other driver must be at fault for the accident, but your own insurance company settles your claim on behalf of the driver without insurance. This coverage pays the damages you are legally entitled to recover from the owner or operator of that vehicle. If you can't reach a resolution of the claim, the policy provides for arbitration.

Although collision coverage pays for the damage to your car caused by the other driver, uninsured motorist coverage pays for the other damages you might suffer when involved in an accident with an uninsured motorist. It would pay for pain and suffering, lost income, permanent disability, and other damages you suffer.

You might question the value of uninsured motorist coverage because most states have financial responsibility laws requiring minimum amounts of auto insurance. As insurance rates go up, drivers will circumvent these laws and drive without insurance. In some cities, it is estimated that 50 percent of the cars have no insurance.

Consequently, you are faced with another difficult decision in choosing how much uninsured motorist coverage to buy. Consider what you can lose in an accident with an uninsured motorist. Look at your other sources of protection. Do you have disability and good health insurance? Even if these plans are adequate, they will not reimburse you for the pain and suffering that would result from an accident involving an uninsured motorist.

Uninsured motorist coverage protects your right to sue. If that right is important to you, make certain your uninsured motorist coverage is adequate to cover the equally-tragic accident where someone else has caused injury to you. It's almost like buying a liability insurance policy for the other guy.

UNDERINSURED MOTORIST COVERAGE

Underinsured motorist coverage operates on the same principle as uninsured motorist coverage. Suppose a family member is injured by an individual who didn't read this book and only purchased minimal liability limits. The coverage protects your injured family member if the other driver has insufficient insurance to cover the injury. Like uninsured motorist coverage, you proceed against your own insurance company for recovery. Underinsured motorist coverage is an alternative to pursuing the other driver in court. If the other driver has assets that are worth pursuing, you can still go after him to collect the appropriate damages that result from the injury.

COLLISION COVERAGE

So far, I have discussed personal injury coverages, but you also need to analyze your physical damage coverages. Collision coverage pays for the damage to your vehicle when you collide with another car or some stationery object. It also pays the damage if your vehicle overturns in an accident. You are entitled to that payment, regardless of who caused the damage. This type of coverage almost always has a deductible, which requires you to pay a stipulated dollar amount.

COMPREHENSIVE

Comprehensive coverage protects you against fire, theft, vandalism, and other potential perils such as glass breakage. Surprisingly, a collision with a deer falls under the comprehensive coverage rather than the collision. Since comprehensive coverage is usually written with a lower deductible than collision, insurance people joke that insureds are quick to blame deer as the source of their collision rather than revealing how it really happened.

There will be unusual instances where no deductible is applied. Suppose you're driving along the road and another vehicle kicks up a stone which damages your windshield. This damage would be covered by your comprehensive coverage. You would have little success going after the driver that kicked up the stone, because this is considered to be a road hazard.

You would be able to file a claim under the comprehensive coverage in your automobile policy. While you normally will have a deductible under that coverage, your insurance carrier might waive the deductible if you agree to have the windshield repaired rather than replaced. There is a process, which costs about

$50, that can repair chips in a windshield. If the damage to the windshield is in the driver's line of vision, a repair is usually not permitted. The windshield must be replaced. The cost of replacing it runs from $200 to over $1,000, depending on the make and model of the car. This windshield replacement is covered by the comprehensive coverage and is subject to the deductible.

If the chip is not in the driver's line of vision, it can be repaired. If for some reason the repair does not last, and the windshield must be replaced, the glass shop should apply the cost of repair toward the cost of replacement. In some states such as Florida, no deductible will be charged even if the windshield has to be replaced.

Don't forget that a theft involving your car might impact your other insurance policies. You might have personal property items that are covered by your homeowners insurance.

ADDITIONAL PHYSICAL DAMAGE COVERAGES

Along with these basic coverages, additional protection is available. You can buy coverage to pay for towing and labor in the event of an accident or breakdown. You might be surprised to know that you don't need to have an accident to use the towing coverage under the policy. This coverage might be superfluous if you belong to an auto club, however.

You can also buy rental coverage to reimburse you for the cost of a rental vehicle while your car is out of action. If you have other cars at your disposal, you needn't buy this option. In many areas of the country, it usually won't pay more than $15 a day toward the rental. If this seems especially low, remember you won't be using one of the rental agencies that business travelers use. There are car rental companies that cater to people involved in auto accidents. A temporary substitute vehicle that you rent while your car is in the shop is covered by your own auto insurance policy and, therefore, is less expensive to rent than the one you rent on vacation or for business trips.

When you are without the use of your vehicle because of another person's negligence, you should ask that person's carrier to authorize your use of a rental car. If the liability is clear, it will send you to one of these special insurance rental agencies and pick up the bill.

Insurance companies can be inflexible in their rental reimbursement coverage. Some companies will only reimburse you up to a maximum of $15 per day. They will not pay mileage costs. Although that sounds unfair, it really isn't. When you drive your own car, you don't pay mileage per se, but your car does depreciate at a rate of at least 25 to 35 cents per mile. Although you are not paying mileage when you drive your own car, it does lose value. Therefore, you are not losing money by having to pay the rental car company for each mile you drive. It's offset by the depreciation you save on your own car.

One customer of a large insurance carrier ran into problems, even though he had rental reimbursement coverage under his automobile policy. He rented a car from a rental agency that specialized in ugly but functional cars. He only paid $11 per day, thus saving the company $4 over the going rate. Nevertheless, he was not paid for his mileage even though it still would have been less than the $15 charged by other rental car companies. The insurance company's policies won't always be logical.

HANDLING YOUR AUTO DAMAGE CLAIM

Claim department employees often joke that people are more concerned about the damage to their cars than they are about injuries they've sustained in an accident. They will argue more about the value of their damaged automobile than the value of their injuries. People accept that accidents happen. For some reason, they are more possessive about their cars and become more agitated over the damage to their vehicles.

Let's look at the auto damage claims you might have. You might have a first-party claim against your own carrier under the collision or comprehensive coverage, or a third-party property damage claim against the driver who caused the damage to your car. Some involve both types of claims. You present a claim against your own collision coverage, while proceeding against the other driver's insurance.

ACTUAL CASH VALUE

No matter which type of claim you have, you are sure to be inconvenienced and aggravated. It's the wrong time to learn about actual cash value. If you own an older car, there's a good chance you'll get a first-hand look at this method of measuring damages and won't like the way it applies to your car.

When you have an automobile accident, you won't necessarily get the cost of repairing your vehicle. You will receive the repair cost, or the actual cash value, whichever is lower. The operative word is "lower," and this can cause you problems. Suppose you own a 1981 compact car with over 70,000 miles on it. It runs perfectly, because you've changed the oil regularly and have done all the required maintenance. When you go to collect, the insurance company wants to give you $2,000 for it, less your deductible. The cost of repairing it is $4,000. It doesn't matter how dependable your car was before the crash, $2,000 is all they're offering for it. Welcome to the world of actual cash value, or ACV as the insurance people like to say.

Try replacing that same car today with the $2,000 you got from the insurance company. It might cover your down payment on a new car. It is of little consequence that you haven't experienced a day's worth of trouble with your old car. The insurance company isn't going to give you new for old.

Obviously, this imposes a hardship on the innocent victims of car accidents who own older vehicles. They're going to get very little compensation for their cars, because the ACV will often be less than the cost of repair. When the insurance company declares a vehicle to be a total loss, it means that the cost of repair is greater than the actual cash value.

When the damaged car is considered to be "totalled," the insurance company will calculate the ACV. To do this, they will usually use two valuation guides. The two guides used are the *Automobile Red Book* and the N.A.D.A. Official Used Car Guide. The carrier will often take an average price for your make and model from those guides to arrive at the ACV that you will receive.

Paying the "book value" for your car is perfectly legitimate. Nevertheless, it won't necessarily put you in the same position you were before the accident occurred. With the insurance company's check, you might be unable to find a car that was as lovingly cared for as the one you've lost. The ACV is often far less than the car is worth to you. If the book value of your car is low, you might want to consider dropping the collision coverage. In the event of an accident, you are going to get very little for the vehicle. Therefore, it is not cost effective to pay for collision coverage because the payback will be small.

The reality of the ACV problem is that most cars depreciate each year until their value is quite low. With a newer car, you run into this problem less often. The cost of repairing the vehicle is usually less than the ACV. Even if your car is declared to be a total loss, you can generally find a comparable car for the money you receive. To avoid the depreciation problem entirely, you can buy replacement cost coverage as an endorsement to most auto policies. The carrier will give the replacement value of your vehicle without applying depreciation. This option is only available on newer cars.

Remember, you can challenge your carrier's calculation of the ACV. On a total loss where the cost of repairing the vehicle exceeds its value, the amount of money the insurance company says your car is worth is still subject to negotiation if you do not feel it is fair. You should double-check its figures by reviewing the valuation guides, which are available at many libraries. Make the appraiser aware of any special features in the car, such as air conditioning or a bigger engine that raises the value of your car. If your car has been reconditioned or is exceptionally clean, make that fact known to the appraiser. These are only estimates and might be adjusted by getting quotes from a car dealer.

REPAIRS

Even when your car is being repaired, it is important to realize that there is no definitive estimate of the damages. Some companies still require that you get three estimates and you will be paid the lowest of the three estimates as your damage. Most companies have their own staff or independent appraisers who will either come out to inspect the damage or will ask you to bring the car, if possible, to a specified facility where the car will be inspected. The damage appraisal is not carved in stone. The appraiser will need to readjust the figures if the shop can't make the repairs for the amount of money stipulated in the appraisal.

You might hear about policies that pay for "hidden" damage. This is not some special coverage that should influence your choice of policies. It is simply a marketing ploy to make you believe you are getting the most wonderful automobile policy ever written. Even after your car is appraised by your own company or the other driver's, you are entitled to additional reimbursement for any damage discovered while the work is being done.

It is very common at insurance companies to pay more than the damage shown on the original appraisal. When additional damage is found at the body shop while repairing the car, the appraiser is made aware of the so-called "hidden" damage. A supplemental appraisal is written and virtually all policies pay for the damage.

You might even have a situation where additional damage is not found until weeks or months later. Perhaps, as an example, no one realized that the power steering was damaged in the accident. You can present a claim for this additional damage, and the only question would be whether the problem was caused by the accident.

Although appraisals are flexible to some extent, some individuals think they can demand a higher payment by claiming they suffered injuries in the accident that caused the damage to their car. This form of leverage usually doesn't work too well. Insurance companies have seen this ploy thousands of times. The person appraising the car is usually not the one who is handling the injury claim, and this not-so-subtle coercion doesn't work too well.

AFTER-MARKET PARTS

After-market parts are those not manufactured by the original equipment manufacturer. If people aren't agitated enough when their car is damaged, the thought of getting inferior parts infuriates them. In advertisements, original equipment manufacturers claim these parts are substandard. They contend that the use of these parts in repairing your car can invalidate your warranty. General Motors sponsors a number of commercials stressing that you should insist on genuine GM parts. Car makers question whether the after-market parts offer the same fit, performance, and quality of the original parts. When writing an appraisal, the appraiser makes a judgment call as to whether after-market parts are suitable. On an older car, where there is no lifetime warranty against rust, the after-market parts would be satisfactory and would undoubtably be an improvement over the equipment in the car before the accident.

On newer cars, there would be more reason to use the original manufacturer's parts. In fact, there is legislation on the horizon to address this issue. The National Association of Insurance Commissioners (NAIC) has drafted a model bill that states could follow to enact legislation in this area. This regulation would require that the after-market parts carry a manufacturer's warranty. An independent testing laboratory could be used to determine if the quality is at the same level as the original part. The after-market parts, if the prototype regulation is adopted, would have to be identified with the name of the manufacturer in an accessible spot.

You can expect your state to enact legislation dealing with this issue of after-market parts in the near future if it doesn't already have one. Some states have already dealt with this subject, with laws and regulations patterned after the NAIC model. Generally, these laws require the insurer to notify the claimant that the estimate is based on the use of after-market parts. Some states permit the refusal of after-market parts. Conceivably, the use of after-market parts might leave the consumer in the middle of a warranty dispute at some point in the future.

COMPARATIVE NEGLIGENCE

I mentioned how comparative negligence can be used to reduce a claimant's damages by a percentage based on the amount of his own negligence. You might not be overly concerned with comparative negligence until it is applied to the claim you are making. In the jurisdictions where comparative negligence is the law, many insurance companies are taking advantage of this defense on claims that are seemingly clear-cut. Suppose someone runs a red light and slams into your vehicle. Fortunately, you're not hurt but you do suffer $2,000 damage to your car. Some companies might argue that you should have looked in both directions, before entering the intersection. If the light had just turned from yellow to red, the claims person for the other driver's insurance company would argue that you were partially responsible for the accident.

Your being 10 percent responsible can mean a large hassle. Instead of getting the $2,000 you need to fix your car, you might only recover $1,800 instead. If the other driver's carrier decides you were only 5 percent responsible, you would be paid $1,900 for the damage that's costing you $2,000 to repair.

There are some companies that are adding more staff so they can raise issues like comparative negligence. They feel the additional staff members will save them money on claims in the long run. In the past, claim departments were far too busy to argue the point. While you should expect a claim problem such as this, you don't have to take it lying down. The insurance company must have a rational basis for using that argument after making a thorough investigation of the accident. Remember, comparative negligence has no bearing on your collision claim. It would only be used if you are presenting a claim against the other driver's carrier.

HOW PREMIUMS ARE DETERMINED

Before looking at ways to save money on your car insurance, it helps to understand how premiums are set. Insurance companies use a number of elements in determining how much you should pay. Depending on the particular insurance company you're dealing with, the underwriters will look at your driving record, loss history, type of vehicle, the age of the drivers, expected usage of the car, and other variables. Some state courts have ruled that gender cannot be used as a factor in calculating the premium. In those jurisdictions, male and female drivers would not be evaluated differently in the underwriting process.

Because of the complex factors that affect your premium, it pays to shop around. Companies weigh these variables differently in determining insurance rates. Their experiences vary, even with comparable groups and geographic areas. If the companies' statistical data is different, different rates will be charged.

There are also different surcharges applied from company to company. These surcharges are applied if you receive a ticket or have an accident. You would be well-advised to consider the impact of a drunk driving conviction on your insurance premiums, along with the many other compelling reasons for driving sober. With one carrier, a drunk driving conviction can cost you over $2,000 more per year in premiums than you would pay otherwise. Furthermore, the surcharge remains on your record for three years. Another insurance company won't accept customers with drunk driving or drug-related convictions within the preceding five years.

Your state of residence can mean a great deal in the way your premium is calculated. A state like New Jersey is one of the most expensive places to buy car insurance, while certain midwestern states rate near the bottom of the list which is a very good place to be. It isn't always a no-fault law that makes the difference in premium. It's simply a question of how well the insurance system of your particular state works.

HOW TO SAVE MONEY ON AUTO INSURANCE

No matter where you live, you can still shop around for the best deal on car insurance. There are approximately 1,000 property/casualty companies in the United States that sell automobile insurance. These policies are offered in a variety of ways. There are companies that market through direct mail. Others offer their product through single-company agents, independent insurance agents, and others who use a brokerage system.

Insurance agents can help you shop around for the best price on auto insurance if they have access to the rates from a number of companies. A single company agent will only have access to the rates of one particular company. If your agent only represents one company, it's up to you to call a number of companies to compare prices. Ask your friends who they buy their car insurance from and whether they're happy with the price and service they receive. Unfortunately, the rate for a driver in your classification might not be as inexpensive as the price your friend gets.

Your state's insurance department can help you save time shopping around for the best deal. Often it will publish a consumer's guide to car insurance, which compares the prices for insurance offered by the companies operating within the state. Nevertheless, the rates vary among classifications within each company. A lower rate in the guide might not mean that your rate will be lower with that company, but the odds are in your favor and much of your homework has been done for you.

Although shopping around is important, a slightly lower premium might not warrant a switch to a different company. You might not qualify as a new customer because of some driving indiscretion. Furthermore, finding a quality company with good service and financial strength is more important than saving a few dollars. With so many companies to choose from, you should choose a company that has an A+ or A rating from the A.M. Best Company. You will not want to select any company that has a reputation for bad service.

On the other hand, you don't always get the best service from the most expensive company. Many insurance companies with high rates brag that their service more than makes up for the higher premiums. *Consumer Reports* magazine, which does consumer surveys, found that there is often no correlation between price and service. The mere fact that a company is more expensive won't guarantee its service is better.

There are good and bad ways to save money on car insurance. Cutting corners on your liability limits is no way to save money. It's a sure-fire method for putting your family's assets in jeopardy. In your own mind, you should be performing a balancing test. You should weigh the cost of increasing the policy limits against the severity of the consequences if you are underinsured. Liability limits can be raised significantly for a modest amount.

A better way to save money is by raising the deductibles on collision and comprehensive coverages. Depending on your financial position, you should consider carrying a $500 to $1,000 deductible. At first glance, you might be appalled at the thought of paying out that much if an accident occurs. Consider, however, how reluctant you are likely to be to report a small accident that is only slightly higher than your deductible. Carrying a high deductible counteracts that reluctance and makes it pay off. You save money now. In the long run, you save money by maintaining a good driving record. You are more likely to take extra precautions, such as where you park your car. You won't be reporting small claims that will jack up your premium.

Dropping collision and comprehensive coverage on an old car is another excellent way to save money while limiting the outside risk that you are taking. If you are driving a car that has depreciated significantly from the time you bought it, you should begin considering this alternative when a car reaches five or six years old. If your Jaguar is still fetching $50,000 at the five-year mark, stick with collision and comprehensive coverage. If your car isn't of high value, the coverage might not be worth keeping.

When you choose a higher deductible, or drop the collision coverage on an older car, keep in mind that the tax laws will no longer cushion the impact of a casualty-property loss. Casualty and theft losses must exceed 10 percent of your adjusted gross income in order to be deductible. If your adjusted gross income is $50,000, your cumulative casualty-theft loss would have to be above $5,000 to be deductible. This certainly won't help you on a deductible even a large one, nor will it be useful with a collision loss where you have no coverage.

When you raise your deductible or drop your collision coverage, you are self-insuring up to a point, which is something corporations do to reduce their insurance costs. To take a higher deductible or to assume the risk that comes with dropping collision coverage is consistent with the true purpose of insurance. It is designed to guard against financial catastrophe, not to eliminate the smaller risks that you can afford to carry on your own. Unfortunately, there will be readers who raise their deductible, or drop their collision coverage, and will have an accident soon thereafter. While they're unlikely to be happy with their decision, the vast majority of readers will benefit from this cost-saving advice. In the long run, the savings will more than offset your loss if you do have an accident.

Another possibility is to consider a deductible on PIP coverage where permitted. PIP coverage potentially duplicates other insurance coverage you have such as medical and wage loss protection.

This duplication can occur in other areas of the policy. Towing and labor coverage under an automobile policy might be a carbon copy of the protection and benefits you get from an auto club.

Dropping medical coverage is another way to save money on your car insurance. If you or your family are injured, the medical coverage under the auto policy might duplicate your health insurance benefits. Consider, however, that it might not just be family members who are in your car. It might be friends who aren't blessed with good medical coverage. To get their bills paid, they might be forced to sue you.

You should not be paying for options unless you absolutely need them. If you are a luxury-car owner, some riders offered are geared toward the special needs that insurance companies think you have. One insurance company offers an option that permits a customer to have the car repaired at a brand name dealership and not a body shop. It will pay the expenses that result when the car is stolen while away from home such as lodging, meals, transportation, and phone calls. It also offers unique rental coverage, which allows the rental of a luxury model.

You must decide if these perks are worth the money. If you can't bear the thought of riding around in your everyday rental car while your auto is in the shop, you might fall for the snob appeal approach of this type of insurance offering. Although you might suffer damages if a car is stolen while away from home, is it really necessary to pay extra for an insurance company to assume the risk of this problem occurring? Shouldn't you be able to afford renting your own luxury car?

If you have the assets that make this coverage appealing, you would be better served by buying extra liability coverage, because you are, undoubtably, a target defendant. That risk is far more dangerous than the more remote possibility that you will need to use an option such as this one. Instead of purchasing this policy, buy a bumper sticker that you can attach to that sub-par rental car that says, "My other car's a Mercedes."

When the time comes to buy a new car, you will have another opportunity to save money on your insurance. While you won't want to revolve your automobile purchase around the cost of insurance, you certainly should consider this issue. Naturally, you expect your insurance premium to go up when you buy a more expensive car. A higher price tag, however, is not the only factor that is considered in setting your new premium.

The claims experience is one variable in setting the premium. If your new car is more easily damaged, expensive to repair, or a likely target for theft, the physical damage coverages we discussed will be assigned a surcharge. The underwriters look at the severity and frequency of claims for each model. Thus, when you shop for a car, keep insurance in mind if you want to save money. This might not be a bad idea for one other reason. You might be able to afford the monthly payment on the new car, but the insurance premium could put it beyond your reach.

Discounts

Insurance companies offer various discounts that can help you lower the cost of your auto insurance. Companies offer multicar discounts, special rates for good drivers, and lower prices for customers who take defensive driving and driver-training courses. There are price reductions for good students, for drivers who participate in car pools, and for those whose cars are equipped with passive restraint devices.

A cross-sell discount might lower your insurance costs, where companies will reduce your auto insurance premium if you carry your homeowners policy with them. If you have already bought the homeowners policy after price shopping, and you're satisfied with the company's service, it won't hurt to see if you can get as good a deal with that same company on your car insurance. Don't tie yourself to that company just because you're getting a package deal on all of your insurance. It is a bad idea to assume that the company with the least expensive homeowners coverage automatically gives the best price on car insurance. You still need to shop around.

There are a host of other discounts that can be found. They won't, however, make a silk purse out of a sow's ear. Most discounts apply at all companies in one form or another. Some companies give age discounts beginning at age 50, while others require you to be 55 or older.

When looking at discounts, remember that you are normally only getting a discount on a particular coverage, not taking a percentage off the total price of the policy. The 5 or 10% discount for drivers of cars equipped with antilock braking systems won't always reduce the price of both your collision and liability coverage. Similarly, the discount on comprehensive coverage for installing anti-theft systems and for etching windows with the Vehicle Identification Number won't lower your liability premium. Together, however, these discounts can add up to significant savings.

You can also save money on your automobile insurance in an indirect way. Except in rare instances, you should not be buying extra insurance through the rental car company.

COLLISION DAMAGE WAIVERS

It's 11:30 at night and you're dead tired. You've just spent six hours in the air, and all you can think about is getting to your hotel. You climb aboard your third form of transportation that day, and doze as the bus takes you to the rental car counter.

Then the real fun begins. You hear the pitch encouraging you to upgrade to a larger and more expensive car. You resist those attempts to sell you on a more luxurious model. Then the insurance sales pitch begins.

In his most grave voice, the rental car agent suggests that you buy the collision damage waiver, that costs $12 per day. The consequences if you don't are outlined in detail. You will be responsible for any damage done to the automobile. Worse yet, you can't remember if your own policy covers rental cars. Buying the collision damage waiver is promoted as a hassle-free way to drive a rental car, but it's certainly not a hassle-free or inexpensive way to buy insurance. The insurance you get via the collision damage waiver can add up to over $4,000 per year. You won't be renting a car every day, but it's still an expensive form of coverage.

It's not just your exhaustion that might prompt you to purchase the collision damage waiver at the rental car counter. There are some truly scary problems that might arise when you damage a rental car. In addition to the damage to the vehicle, you can be held responsible for loss of use of the rental car. When the car is being repaired, the agency is not able to rent the vehicle out and make money. You can be required to pay for that down time.

Even when you're not exhausted, it's difficult to determine if your own insurance protects you when you're renting a car. Not all auto policies cover the damage you might do to a rental car. Even if your auto insurance does cover damage to the rental vehicle, it won't necessarily pay for the down time of the vehicle. You could have a situation where your policy will pay for repairs to the rental car, but won't pay for the rental agency's loss of use.

There are other problems that are difficult to resolve, even when you've had a good night's sleep. Your policy will normally pay for damage to the rental car under the collision coverage. The collision coverage on your vehicle is simply transferred to the rental car. When the damage is paid under your collision coverage, you owe the same deductible that you would be responsible for in an accident involving your own car. If you've dropped the collision coverage on your car, you have a problem.

Aside from exhaustion, there are other reasons for your confusion over whether to buy the collision damage waiver. In rare instances, the damage to the rental car is paid under the liability section of the auto policy, which pays for damage to the property of others. If your state treats rental car damage this way, you would not have to pay a deductible, and indirect damages such as loss of use would be covered. You would not have to worry if you've dropped collision coverage since your liability coverage takes care of it.

Because of these confusing issues, you might simply break down and buy the collision damage waiver. In theory, the collision damage waiver takes you off the hook for any damages to the car that you cause. The rental car company waives its right to collect the damages from you. Even when you purchase the waiver, however, you can still be held responsible for the damage if you abuse the vehicle in some way.

The collision damage waiver is one of the worst insurance purchases you can make. It is a form of insurance, no matter how vehemently the rental car companies argue that it is not. The collision damage waiver violates many of the rules we've discussed for buying insurance. It is a policy of limited duration that you would never buy if you calculated the price on an annual basis. In many instances, it will duplicate coverage you already have. Finally, it is another situation where you are buying insurance against a risk that you can deal with on your own.

Depending on where you're renting the car, you might not have to worry about the collision damage waiver. On January 1, 1989, Illinois became the first state to eliminate the waiver. If you were to rent a car in Illinois, you would be unable to purchase a collision damage waiver. This is part of an action, taken by the attorney general in many states, to eliminate this costly form of insurance. In Illinois, renters are required to pay the first $200 of damage to their rental car, whether from a collision or vandalism. New York followed with a similar law, which makes the renter responsible for the first $100. Other states are expected to enact legislation of this type. Naturally, there will be exceptions in these laws when the driver is guilty of wrongdoing of some kind, such as drunken driving.

The New York law goes even further in eliminating the confusion over your need to buy a collision damage waiver when you rent a car. The law requires that personal auto insurance policies contain coverage for cars rented in the United States or Canada. Therefore, even the most exhausted New Yorker knows that his policy will cover the car he rents in another state. If you are a resident of another state that doesn't have this requirement, you will have to determine in advance if your auto policy covers rental cars. If you can't tell from your policy, ask your agent or insurance company for clarification and confirm the answer in writing.

Where does this leave the renter who doesn't own a car or who doesn't have insurance that applies to a rental car? If you are in that unfortunate group, you have a problem. You also have a problem if you own an older car and have dropped collision coverage on it. There is no collision coverage to transfer to the rental car.

Aside from buying the collision damage waiver, one answer is to rent the vehicle using one of the credit cards that now offer coverage. Many of the premium credit cards, in order to increase usage, extend free collision damage protection. The coverage varies from company to company, however. Find out precisely what coverage your credit card company offers in this situation. It might pay for collision damage but not for vandalism and theft. Make certain it covers every vehicle rented and doesn't exclude certain types of luxury cars.

If you are renting a car for work, find out if your company has a corporate agreement dealing with collision damage waivers. Some corporations have specific guidelines instructing you to decline the waiver. The waiver might be automatically afforded as part of the corporate rate.

PERSONAL ACCIDENT INSURANCE

Personal accident insurance is one coverage you can definitely avoid at the rental car counter. No matter now much they charge, it's no bargain. A typical personal accident insurance policy sold by a rental company will pay for accidental death or dismemberment, along with emergency medical care. This coverage will undoubtably duplicate protection that you have through other policies. It is another example of a policy of limited duration. Although it might cost a small amount each day, the coverage is very narrow. It is always sobering to calculate how much this coverage would cost on an annual basis. Although you are only paying a few dollars per day, you are getting very little coverage.

10

Personal liability umbrella policy

IT'S YOUR FRIDAY NIGHT POKER GAME. YOU'RE LOSING, AND LOSING BADLY. Herman Munster, a regular at the game, is cleaning your clock. He's won virtually every hand. Suddenly, you can't stand it any longer. You scream at him and accuse him of cheating. Munster storms out, and the five other players drift out after him.

You hardly give the incident another thought until five weeks later, when you're served with suit papers charging you with defaming Munster's character. You aren't too concerned at first. After all, you have a deluxe homeowners policy with very high limits. You call your agent to make certain that slander, a form of defamation of character, is covered under the policy. After hanging up, you feel you're getting another bad deal. Your agent tells you that slander isn't covered under the homeowners policy.

For this reason and many more, you should take a good, hard look at a personal liability umbrella policy for your family. The umbrella policy raises the limits found in your homeowners and auto policies. It also provides coverage independent of those policies. It expands your liability protection to cover a wide variety of third-party claims and lawsuits. The umbrella policy can eliminate any question of whether your liability limits are high enough.

Though your Friday night poker partners might set a limit on bets and raises, there's no end to your potential liability when you're sued by someone. Perhaps, you've already given thought to raising your auto and homeowners liability limits after reading this book and hearing about the problems that can occur if a policyholder's liability limits are too low. Depending on how high those limits are now, you might be able to buy an umbrella policy to achieve the same purpose. Even if they are high already, you still might need a personal liability umbrella policy.

Today, million-dollar lawsuits are a reality and might be only a starting point in a trend toward even higher liability awards. An umbrella policy provides excess liability coverage over and above the amount you've selected in your automobile and homeowners policies. Usually, the personal liability umbrella runs anywhere from $1 million to $5 million.

An umbrella policy provides an extra layer of protection. Your primary protection against claims and lawsuits is derived from the liability coverage in your homeowners, renters, or auto policy. When these underlying limits are exhausted, the umbrella policy kicks in to resolve the claim against you. In Chapter 9, I discussed split limits under the auto policy. The split-limit policy forces you to make several choices and, unfortunately, gives you ample opportunity to choose inadequate liability coverage. An umbrella policy picks up where the split limits left off.

The umbrella policy gives your insurance plan the layered look. You have the first layer of protection afforded by your primary policies, which we've seen can be quite broad. You then get a second layer of protection to further insulate you from a suit for damages that can put a chill on your financial situation.

Naturally, you need to maintain adequate limits on your primary liability policies. The umbrella can't be used to get around buying the basic coverage under your auto or homeowners policies. The underwriter for the company selling the umbrella will require certain limits before you qualify for the policy. The bodily injury limits under your auto policy would have to be at least $100,000 per person and $300,000 per accident. The property damage liability coverage would have to be $25,000 or greater. The liability limits under the homeowners or renters policy would have to be at least $100,000. Another underwriter might insist that your underlying liability limits are much higher than these figures.

The premium for the personal liability umbrella would depend upon these underwriting requirements. A million-dollar umbrella policy should be under $200 per year. You might think it's cheaper to simply raise your limits on those underlying policies rather than buying an umbrella. By doing this, however, you are not protecting your family against the wide range of problems that the umbrella will guard against. Comparatively, umbrella policies are inexpensive, because most of the risk is assumed by the underlying policy.

EXPANDED COVERAGE IN AN UMBRELLA POLICY

With a personal liability umbrella, you're not just getting an increase in your liability limits. You are also getting expanded coverage. The insuring agreement in the umbrella policy states that the insurance company will pay damages on behalf of the insured due to bodily injury, property damage, or personal injury. It is primarily in the personal injury area that the umbrella offers additional protection.

Personal injury is usually defined as injury caused by false arrest, false imprisonment, malicious prosecution, libel, slander, defamation, invasion of privacy, or wrongful entry or eviction. Personal injury is usually distinguished from the bodily injury protection you get in your primary policies. You'll get protection for both in the umbrella.

Depending on the umbrella policy you buy, you might also get coverage in other circumstances. You can get protection if you're serving as a trustee or board member of a civic, charitable, or religious organization.

In addition to these expanded areas of coverage, an umbrella policy will cover the defense costs you might incur if allegations are made against you that must be defended in court, which can be significant. If your underlying policy does not afford coverage for the occurrence, it will not pay the defense costs either. In our example where you called Herman Munster a cheater, your homeowners policy would not cover any damage award against you. It also wouldn't cover the cost of defending the suit. Slander actions, however, would be covered by an umbrella policy.

Even with the umbrella policy, you cannot protect your family against every type of problem. There are exclusions in the umbrella policy that limit the reach of its protection. Some losses are excluded because they are normally covered under a different policy. Other expenses are considered uninsurable.

The typical umbrella wouldn't cover bodily injury, property damage, or personal injury arising out of a business pursuit. You would be expected to have a business insurance policy to guard against those problems. A lawyer who calls someone a thief in the course of representing his client would properly look to his professional liability coverage rather than to the protection of an umbrella policy.

Some expenses are considered uninsurable, so the umbrella policy won't cover them. Punitive damages are an example of this. Punitive damages are awarded to punish wrongdoers for their conduct. Your behavior might be so outrageous that it warrants additional damages beyond those that simply make the victim whole again, which was discussed in Chapter 5. This is conduct society wants to discourage. If you were able to buy insurance to cover these damages, people would not get the message that this behavior will not be tolerated. Punitive damages are only awarded in the most extreme and outrageous situations, where someone was far more than just negligent. They must have acted with reckless disregard for the safety of others. Courts have ruled that by allowing an individual to have insurance against punitive damages, public policy is not served. As a result, even your personal liability umbrella will not cover these damages.

An umbrella policy will also not, as a general rule, cover intentional acts.

Had you smacked Herman Munster in the kisser when you thought he was cheating at cards, your umbrella would not provide coverage nor would your underlying homeowners policy. You should look for an umbrella, however, that makes allowances for extenuating circumstances. On one hand, there will be a clause saying the insurance does not apply to bodily injury or property damage expected or intended by the insured. It should apply, however, when you are using reasonable force to protect your family and property.

Despite an umbrella policy's many advantages, there is one minor drawback. Unlike most liability coverages, a deductible might have to be paid by you before the damages are covered by the policy. Usually, this only applies when the loss is not covered by the underlying policy. For example, I mentioned that personal liability is covered by the umbrella and not by the homeowners policy. Therefore, you would pay a deductible on a personal injury loss. The deductible might run from $250 to $1,000, which is a small price to pay if you are hit with a major personal injury lawsuit.

11

Life insurance

IN HIS MOVIE, "LOVE AND DEATH," WOODY ALLEN SAID SOMETHING LIKE this: "There are worse things in life than death. If you ever spent an evening with an insurance salesman, you know exactly what I mean." You might think that reading a chapter on life insurance runs a close second, but as the family insurance planner, you must make these sacrifices. Most adults need life insurance in some form to protect their loved ones from the financial consequences of death.

TERM INSURANCE

In a nutshell, there are two types of life insurance: term insurance and whole life. Unfortunately, it's not quite that simple. There are dozens of variations of each. It would appear that the insurance industry looks at the policies already on the market and mixes them with their own to create new ones.

Term insurance is pure protection against the risk of dying. The term in term insurance indicates the period during which the premium remains constant. When you renew a term insurance policy, the premium will usually be higher during the next term. This is logical, since you are older at the time of renewal.

The premium for a term insurance policy is based on your age, your health, whether you smoke or not, and the amount of coverage you're hoping to buy. Term insurance prices are easier to understand than the other life insurance policies I will be discussing later and in the next chapter. You will pay a specified price for each $1,000 of death benefits. Because you pay a set annual fee which is tacked onto every purchase of term life insurance, it often pays to buy larger amounts.

You have to watch out for companies that offer inexpensive term life insurance during the first few years, but the prices increase markedly during the later years. This type of rate structure attracts new customers at the expense of existing policyholders. Theoretically, it is simple enough for these existing policyholders to go elsewhere to buy from some other company offering lower rates on term insurance. Practically speaking, however, many people do not price around for life insurance each time the premium is raised.

In general, term insurance prices have decreased for a number of years. Although this downward spiral cannot continue indefinitely, longer life expectancies have helped fuel this trend. Some experts are predicting that the AIDS crisis will stop that downward movement. Because more men are likely to get AIDS than women, the rates for men buying term insurance could get higher.

With term insurance, the death benefit is paid if the insured, the person whose life is the subject matter of the policy, dies during the policy period. The term can last one year, five years, or ten years.

RENEWABLE TERM INSURANCE

Renewable term insurance means that the policy can be renewed at the end of the term, without evidence of insurability. The right to renew is optional on the part of the policyholder. The right to exercise this option continues for a limited number of successive terms, but usually continues until age 65 or 70. The fact that the term insurance is renewable doesn't mean the price remains the same. The premium normally goes up at each renewal because the insured keeps getting older.

If term insurance is not renewable, the company selling the policy can require a new medical examination when each new contract period begins. It is certainly risky to assume that you will always be healthy enough to buy insurance. Although a one-year renewable term is the least expensive, you can buy other periods, such as five-year renewable term.

The latter is considered to be level term insurance, because the premiums stay the same for five years. Naturally, it will cost more because you are averaging the normal premium for the insured's age when the policy begins and the insured's age during the last year of the policy. When the five years are over, the policyholder can renew for another five years at a higher rate.

When you are given that option to stay insured, you pay more than you would for nonrenewable term insurance. It costs more because the insurance company is agreeing to accept you, no matter what your health is at the time. Although you might be in perfect health at the end of a particular term, you are paying for the privilege of buying insurance should you want it. It's a great deal like an option to buy a piece of property that is kept open for a certain period of time.

CONVERTIBLE TERM INSURANCE

With convertible term insurance, the policyholder is granted an option. He or she can convert the term insurance policy into a permanent one. This conversion privilege might not sound like any big deal, unless you find yourself in poor health and unable to buy life insurance. The permanent policy can be purchased with no questions asked. You will, however, pay the going rate at the time of the conversion.

EMPLOYER-PROVIDED INSURANCE

As we've seen with other types of insurance coverage, sometimes your best deal on a policy can be found through your employer. Most benefits packages, the conventional ones and the flexible programs, offer a number of life insurance options. Many companies provide basic life insurance. The amount you get will usually be based on your annual salary. Even better, the life insurance that your employer buys for you isn't included in your taxable income, unless more than $50,000 worth is purchased. In that case, the premium paid for life insurance in excess of $50,000 is viewed as taxable. With the new cafeteria benefit plans that employers are offering, choosing free life insurance might be at the expense of other benefits. Therefore, consider buying it elsewhere.

Even if you get a significant amount of life insurance through your employer, don't bank on having that life insurance forever to meet all of your needs. The amount you receive through work might decrease as you get older. If you lose your job, you can usually convert that life insurance to a permanent policy. When you convert to an individual policy, you need not submit to a medical examination, which can be a blessing if you are in poor health. You will, however, pay the rate for an individual, not a group, at your age when the policy is converted. Depending on your age at the time of the conversion, the cost might be enormous. If you are in good health, it would pay to price other policies before converting your existing one.

Your employer might also offer term insurance at reduced rates. Depending on your employer's benefits plan, you should be able to buy life insurance at very modest rates. Although there is usually a restriction on the amount of life insurance you can purchase through your employer, you might be able to buy life insurance at these low rates for other family members. Keep in mind, however, that the deal you get through your employer on this additional insurance isn't necessarily better than the price you'll get from some other source.

Don't confuse the term insurance you get through work with the more limited life insurance benefits that will be paid in certain situations. Your employer might provide an Accidental Death and Dismemberment policy, but it pays only in very limited circumstances. There has been considerable litigation over what constitutes an accidental death, and you might be surprised at the number of circumstances that aren't considered to be accidental death.

Your employee benefit book might delineate those situations that aren't considered accidental deaths. One handbook makes it clear that you don't have an accidental death if it results from:

- Treatment of an illness.
- An infection, unless caused by an external wound resulting from an accident.
- Suicide or attempted suicide.
- Self-inflicted injury.
- War or warlike actions.

Remember, too, that you can't count on the large amounts that most employers pay when you die while on work-related business.

WHOLE LIFE INSURANCE

We've been discussing term insurance, which gets its name because you buy it for a particular time period. We've also looked at a few of its offspring or mutations, depending on your point of view. Now let's take a look at whole life insurance and its many variations. Whole life is so named because it lasts for the insured's whole life. The premium stays the same forever. Protection lasts for a lifetime, unlike term insurance which lasts for a specified term.

In some respects, it's not fair to make the distinction that term insurance isn't permanent while whole life is. You can continue to buy term insurance in later years, although the prices become prohibitive. On the other hand, whole life insurance premiums remain constant for a lifetime. The critics of whole life would argue that the policyholder overpays for that protection during the insured's younger years, which negates the savings during later years.

Traditional whole life is different from term insurance because it offers both protection and cash value. On a whole life policy, the cash value builds slowly. Life insurance companies stress its value as a savings account. The cash value is the money that would be paid to a policyholder when the policy is surrendered. It is sometimes called the surrender value of the policy. Universal life and variable life policies, which are discussed in Chapter 12, are simply variations of a whole life policy.

With whole life, part of the premium buys the insurance and part goes toward the cash value. The sales commission hinders the cash build-up during the first few years. It also earns interest at a low rate. The interest is tax-deferred and remains tax-free if you never utilize the cash value before your death.

In addition to these variations of whole life, there are a number of different names for insurance products that are really whole life in one form or another. The following terms are often used synonymously with whole life:

- Permanent insurance
- Ordinary life
- Straight life
- Level premium life
- Cash-value insurance

Straight life has fixed payments for the lifetime of the policyholder. Limited payment life is the same as straight life, except that the premiums are only made for a limited time. The policy would be paid for completely in 20 or 30 years, or by some specified age.

The term "participating" refers to whole life policies that pay dividends. These dividends can reduce the actual cost of your life insurance policy and are nontaxable. The IRS views them as a return of your own capital and not income. The dividends can be used to purchase additional insurance or can be taken in cash.

FORCED SAVINGS FEATURE

When an agent sells any whole life policy, he will stress the forced savings feature. The premium payments, which the policyholder is required to make, build a cash value that can be tapped at some later point. Proponents of whole life insurance would argue that the money spent on term insurance is frittered away, whereas the premiums made on a whole life policy grow. With term insurance, the policy does not build up any cash or loan values.

When deciding on a whole life policy, you must decide if this forced savings feature outweighs the relatively low interest rate that you will be receiving. Traditional whole life pays about 5 percent. Maybe you need whole life, just as some people need Christmas Club accounts. They pay either no interest or a low rate of interest, but there are people who swear by them.

It is this forced savings feature that might sell you on whole life, but only if you are the type of person who can't put away money any other way. The price is not cheap, however. You are getting less than the market rate on your money and you are paying a high, up-front commission. You are overpaying for insurance protection, just so you can be forced to save.

I have purposefully kept this discussion of whole life segregated from the topic of insurance as an investment. You can't view whole life as an investment. There's no investment where you would accept not knowing what your interest rate actually is. It's no more an investment than a Christmas Club account. It's a place to park your money, because you don't trust yourself with it. Buying whole life is an admission that you can't save, unless someone sends you a bill for the amount you owe.

I will discuss more attractive forms of whole life that can be looked at as an investment in Chapter 12. Some of these insurance policies, however, lack the forced savings feature because they offer flexible payment schedules. These hybrid forms of whole life let you skip payments, which is obviously not a good idea for the person who lacks the discipline to put away funds willingly without being prompted by a bill. When you buy traditional whole life insurance, you are given an ultimatum. You must make your premium payment on a regular basis, or your life insurance policy will lapse.

Rather than having the insurance company hold a gun to your head, consider sticking with term insurance and looking for other financial vehicles that offer forced savings. You could set up an automatic investment plan to transfer money from your checking account to a mutual fund on a regular basis. Before considering whole life, you should also make certain that you are exhausting all of the automatic savings plans at your place of employment, because your employer will probably add to your contributions.

CASH VALUE

I've talked about the build-up of cash value. You might question the utility of any cash value policy when you realize that it's not yours to keep. When you die, it reverts to the insurance company. Some critics of cash-value policies have argued that you essentially are paying your own death benefit.

If you borrow against your policy, you can tap the cash value. It's then subtracted from your death benefit unless it's paid back before your death. Still, it's a good source of ready cash if you run into trouble. By law, the death benefit must exceed the cash value. As a result, when you've held onto the policy for a considerable length of time, the death benefit grows.

The cash value build-up is slower than you would expect because of the sales commission on whole life. This might be as much as 100 percent of the first year's premium. The commission is smaller in later years.

Dividends are different from cash value. Dividends, which are paid on participating whole life policies, are a refund of your premium. The dividend declared by a company is based on its investment success and whether the company correctly forecasted the number of insureds who died. Once again, whether you take them in cash or use them to buy additional insurance, dividends are not taxable because they are simply a partial return of your own money.

You can't discuss cash value without talking about inflation. Critics of cash value policies point out that although cash values build, they are worth less every year because of inflation. Consequently, the actual growth is very small.

You also have the issue of inflation in one other respect. With a term policy, you are paying less now. With a whole life policy, you are spending more in today's dollars to build cash value that will be worth little later because of inflation. On the other hand, proponents of cash value policies could argue that a whole life policy lets you lock into a particular premium now, which you will be paying for later with cheaper dollars. Your premium will look less expensive because of inflation. Of course, inflation will also make the death benefit look smaller. Nevertheless, if you anticipate needing life insurance throughout your life, whole life can satisfy that need at a cost that will remain the same forever.

LOANS ON WHOLE LIFE POLICIES

I've discussed how the forced savings feature can be just right for some individuals because they have such a hard time saving. You can still circumvent that feature, however, by borrowing against your cash value. The loan rate will normally be lower than the going market rate for loans. On older policies, the interest rate can be especially attractive. Any loans outstanding at the time of your death are deducted from the amount paid to your beneficiaries.

The cost of borrowing against your cash value is more expensive than it first appears. As the loan is repaid, your death benefit grows. The loan, however, can still cause long-term damage to the policy. Your cash value grows much more slowly because of the loan. Before borrowing against your policy, check to see if there are any hidden charges and if the loan adversely affects your cash value.

You might also find that you have very little cash value to tap during the early years of the policy. I have mentioned previously that the commissions on whole life policies are enormous. Still, borrowing against your cash value has its advantages. The loan does not have to be repaid, although it will be subtracted from the death benefit. There is no credit check. Nevertheless, don't expect to be able to borrow during the initial years of the policy. You also won't get a tax deduction on the interest paid.

WHOLE LIFE AS A TAX SHELTER

Whole life has great appeal as a tax shelter. The cash value of the policy generates interest. The interest is quite low, but it does grow without being ravaged by taxes. The interest is tax deferred. In other words, if you never tap the cash value, it would be tax free. This growth within your policy is called the inside buildup. The problem is that a very large portion of your premium payment isn't going toward the tax-sheltered cash value. Instead, it is going toward a sizeable agent's commission and other expenses. If you must look at whole life as a tax shelter, look at it as a very long-term tax shelter. The cash value will not grow much during the early years.

Remember that the tax advantages of whole life are always vulnerable to legislation. Some forms of whole life have lost their appeal because of tax code changes. An example of this is discussed in Chapter 20.

DECIDING BETWEEN TERM AND WHOLE LIFE INSURANCE

Despite the tax advantages of whole life, most people are better off with term insurance. An annual renewable term policy will let you buy more protection at an affordable price. Your money will go exclusively for life insurance and not towards significant commissions. Assuming you have the discipline to bank your savings, you will be far better off in the long run than you would by buying whole life. You'll get a far better rate of return than you will with traditional whole life.

The National Insurance Consumer Organization (NICO) recommends annual renewable term, and I find their reasoning to be persuasive. NICO believes it offers the most protection for the least cost. This form of term insurance is affordable for young families on limited budgets or others on a limited budget. NICO also feels that annual renewable term benefits those people who must drop the policy after a few years because of changes in their personal situation.

Although I also recommend annual renewable term for most people, I believe some families can benefit from a whole life policy. Once you buy a whole life policy, stick with it. A whole life policy will have no advantage whatsoever if you drop it after a few years.

Whole life can turn out to be a wise purchase in certain situations. After you have reached age 40, the price of term insurance begins to rapidly increase. If you anticipate needing a great deal of insurance when the price becomes prohibitive, it might pay to turn to whole life insurance at an earlier age. You will then pay that premium throughout your lifetime. Because term insurance costs increase in later years, you might find yourself unable to afford the insurance you need to buy.

Every life insurance purchase is based on the needs of your family in the event that a loved one dies. An insurance agent will be happy to discuss those needs with you, because that discussion will often lead to the sale of more insurance.

ANALYZING YOUR INSURANCE NEEDS

According to author Dave Barry, if you accidentally say the words "life insurance" aloud, you might awaken the insurance agents who hang by their feet from your eaves. This would cause them to swarm upon you until you agree to let them review your financial needs.

When they're not hanging by their feet from your eaves, insurance agents use other methods to gain your attention. They might offer you a free gift of nominal value. The catch is that you have to meet with them in order to take possession of the gift. You then become a captive audience as the agent explores your insurance needs.

You can bet that your financial needs will always be in excess of the amount of life insurance you have. I'm convinced you have to give up your life insurance license if you ever tell customers they have too much insurance or just the right amount. The amount of life insurance you should have is on a "needs to know" basis. You must examine your family's needs in order to determine how much life insurance you should have.

Let's assume you are healthy enough to buy all of the life insurance you need. There are brokers who specialize in obtaining life insurance for individuals who are difficult to insure. I'm concerned with the individual who has enough insurance and is getting pushed to buy more. Make sure it's you who needs the life insurance policy rather than a situation where the agent wants you to buy it.

The agent would like to sell you whole life more than term insurance because, in many cases, the commission on whole life might be as high as 100 percent during that first year. The commission on term insurance isn't as high. The commission structure might motivate an agent to sell a particular policy, even though it isn't what you need.

Whether you opt for term insurance or whole life, how much you buy will depend on your needs. Determining your family's needs isn't easy, and to make matters worse, your needs change constantly. For example, the birth of a child increases your need for life insurance. Conversely, when your child graduates from college, your life insurance needs would decrease.

THE IMPACT OF AGE ON LIFE INSURANCE NEEDS

Your life insurance needs are tied to your financial situation more than your age. age. You can't isolate your insurance needs without looking at your other assets and liabilities. At first glance, it would seem that an older couple with significant assets and few liabilities would have little need for life insurance. Upon death, their assets could be sold or used to produce income for any dependents. On the other hand, if those assets aren't liquid, or if there are estate taxes to consider, life insurance might be necessary.

A younger family with a large mortgage and little equity in their home would have a different set of needs. Where one spouse is the sole breadwinner and younger children are involved, a compelling case for life insurance in large amounts can be made.

The purpose of life insurance is to protect against financial harm caused by you dying before your time. As you get older and approach that time when dying wouldn't be such a big surprise, your need for life insurance decreases. Still, you cannot make a blanket statement that life insurance becomes less important as you grow older.

There is a growing trend toward earlier retirements. It is not uncommon for men and women their late fifties to retire, willingly or unwillingly. Therefore, they lose the group life insurance coverage they've had for so long through their employer.

There is also inflation to consider. Even though your life insurance needs diminish as you get older, the $100,000 life insurance policy that seemed ample before could look paltry to you now.

It is not uncommon to see older people with young children. I know someone who recently retired in his late fifties. His youngest child is ten-years-old. Obviously, with rising divorce rates and with more couples waiting to have children, one can't state categorically that there are no life insurance needs for individuals of retirement age. Even having a child who is in college or graduate school can drastically alter the insurance needs of parents—at any age.

HOW MUCH LIFE INSURANCE DO YOU NEED?

Analyzing your needs is difficult. For that reason, you'll run into rules of thumb to help you determine how much life insurance you need. You might only have two thumbs, but there are dozens of formulas. One magazine suggests buying life insurance to replace 75 percent of a wage-earner's salary. In other words, if your family's breadwinner makes $40,000 per year, you would look for an amount of life insurance that replaces 75 percent of that income. Therefore, to calculate your life insurance needs, you would ask what lump sum would produce $30,000 ($40,000×75 percent) at a reasonable rate of interest. A family would need a $375,000 life insurance policy to pay out that amount using an interest rate of 8 percent.

This would assume that all of the funeral costs and other expenses would be paid for from other savings and wouldn't deplete the $375,000 needed to generate $30,000 in income. Formulas like this one don't seem to take inflation into account or that the family might require additional money for college expenses.

Obviously, you should look at whether a spouse has an earning potential to pick up the slack for the wage-earner who dies. Still, these rules of thumb persist. Many authorities suggest four to five times your annual income if you have dependents.

Humorously enough, companies selling life insurance often contradict themselves in the same brochure. I received one brochure that stressed the need for an annual review of one's life insurance coverage. It talked about how the cost of housing, education, and medical care is increasing at rapid rates. It implied that your life insurance might be inadequate to meet those costs. Obviously, the company was making the point that as your needs become greater, your life insurance should be raised accordingly.

I expect this type of sales pitch in a life insurance brochure. In the same breath, however, it proceeded to give a rule of thumb. It encouraged customers to buy life insurance of at least six times their annual salary. This rule of thumb contradicts the previous discussion of the impact of changing needs.

There were thousands of people receiving that literature all with a host of different needs, yet the simple answer was buying six times their salary. The answer was the same even though the brochure was received by DINKs (Double Income, No Kids), traditional families with children, single parents, and couples who are living together. A rule of thumb would hardly make sense.

You can bet that a life insurance agent's rule of thumb will suggest you need much more life insurance. Recently, a life insurance agent was on a talk show and suggested that the average family usually needs six to seven times their gross income in life insurance.

These same salespeople will even have pseudoscientific formulas to demonstrate that you need more life insurance. Many of these formulas have great names like Capital Needs Analysis or a Financial Needs Analysis. The calculations take hours of your time, but might be just as speculative as using a rule of thumb. For example, the Financial Needs Analysis looks at how many children you have and whether you expect them to go to college. Then you have to predetermine whether they'll go to a state school or a private one. You estimate the costs per year depending on your choice. By the time you get through with this analysis, you'll find you need a great deal of life insurance.

You end up with a string of "if's." *If* I happen to die, and *if* my five-year-old decides to go to college, and *if* she decides to go to Harvard rather than Penn State, how much life insurance would it take to satisfy all of those contingencies? You would wind up with enough insurance to keep your agent happy for years. While some assumptions are certainly necessary to calculate your needs, keep in mind that an agent might use them to prove that you are underinsured.

This same agent was asked to compare a renewable term policy bought through a group association with a private policy bought from a nationally recognized company. The group association policy was several hundred dollars cheaper. He spent five minutes telling the caller how the service you get through an agent more than makes up for the hundreds of dollars. You shouldn't overpay for a life insurance policy so that your beneficiaries will get better service upon your death.

In fact, special service might be afforded even when an agent is not involved. USAA Life Insurance Company of San Antonio, Texas, does not sell through agents. Nevertheless, it provides a Beneficiary Assistance Program that offers help when a loved one dies. It advises the surviving spouse or family member of the organizations and agencies that should be contacted. The program sends information and publications designed to help deal with the loss of a family member.

When deciding if you have enough life insurance to meet your family's needs, you should not even consider any policies that only pay for death in speci-fied circumstances. For example, assume you purchase an accidental death pol-icy: Your $50,000 policy through your employer might pay double that or $100,000 if your death results from an accident. If you've calculated that you need a $375,000 policy, only $50,000 of that need has been met by your policy through work. Keep in mind that your needs won't be permanently met by a work-related policy if someday you get the axe.

After you have determined what your needs are, you don't necessarily have to meet them with either whole life or term insurance. There are situations where a combination of term insurance and whole life will be the best solution.

INSURANCE FOR CHILDREN AND NONWORKING SPOUSES

Even though life insurance on children is inexpensive, they do not need life insurance. Unless your child is making commercials or starring in a television sitcom, no one is dependent on that child for income and there is no estate to protect. Even if you believe that life insurance is an investment, it makes no sense.

The spouse who contributes a small portion of the household income would need life insurance to replace that income if necessary to support the family's life-style. A nonworking spouse who is responsible for child care should have a policy to cover any child care expenses that would result from the death of that person, as well as any other services performed by the nonworking spouse, such as shopping, cooking, or housekeeping.

MORTGAGE LIFE INSURANCE

As you're computing your needs, you should be taking all of your obligations into consideration. Once you have determined how much life insurance you need, you don't have to address particular areas where life insurance might be appropriate. If your bank does not require mortgage life insurance as a condition for getting the loan, don't buy it. The amount you owe on your mortgage should be consid-ered when calculating how much life insurance you need. Mortgage life insur-ance is decreasing term insurance. You pay the same amount each month, even though the amount of death benefit is decreasing. The insurance premium is normally added to your monthly mortgage payment. Many banks require this insurance in order to approve a mortgage.

We've established that your life insurance needs should be looked at on an annual basis, and the mortgage on your house is just one of many debts that should be looked at in the evaluation process. Because a mortgage is such a large debt, you might think that your family can't lose with the mortgage paid off when you die. When you have mortgage life insurance, the loan is automatically paid off, but depending on the interest rate of your mortgage, this might not be the most desirable course of action. Instead of having that loan paid off at death, the insurance proceeds might be used for other purposes. With mortgage life insurance, you won't necessarily have that option. An 8 percent fixed-rate mortgage might be better left unsatisfied rather than paid off, especially if interest rates have increased significantly. You can buy decreasing term insurance from a source other than your bank, which avoids this problem.

Do not let convenience dictate your insurance decisions. Your bank might encourage you to include the mortgage life insurance in your monthly payment. If your current mortgage is set up this way, find out exactly how much you are paying. You should be allowed to cancel that life insurance once you have built up significant equity in the home.

Mortgage life insurance is a bad deal for most people. If you are healthy and would have little trouble buying insurance elsewhere, the mortgage life insurance is going to be more expensive through the bank. A nonsmoker should be able to find better rates than the bank will offer. This is especially true in the early years of the loan, because few people will hold the mortgage to maturity. They will not reach the point where the prices are comparable to other term insurance policies.

As the years pass, it can become an increasingly bad deal. If you pay ahead on that mortgage, you are making matters worse from a life insurance standpoint, even though you're doing yourself a favor because of the interest you'll save on the loan. The insurance company will only pay off the remaining portion of your mortgage, which is smaller—thanks to you. Nevertheless, your premium remains the same.

Instead of mortgage life insurance, you need a policy that addresses all of your needs. Mortgage life insurance does not even take care of the expenses associated with being a homeowner. You still have taxes, maintenance, and a host of other expenses that your family must keep paying. While a mortgage might be your largest debt, many financial obligations will still exist long after it is paid off.

Buying a new house or vacation home is one of those events that should prompt you to reevaluate your insurance needs. Obviously, taking on an additional financial responsibility might mean that more life insurance is in order so that those obligations can be met in the event of your death. Simply buying mortgage life insurance through the bank where you got the loan is definitely not the answer, even though it's the most convenient one. In the next chapter, we'll discuss universal life insurance, which lets a policyholder increase or decrease coverage without purchasing a new policy. You might consider universal life as a way to adapt your current insurance to meet those changing needs.

On the other hand, you might be strapped for cash when you buy a new home. The last thing you'll want is an insurance policy that combines protection with a savings element. You might have tapped all of your investment capital to buy the new dwelling. Accordingly, you might be better off with a term policy where you pay for pure protection, which is all you can really afford in view of your significant investment. You hardly need to make a life insurance investment when you are already spending most of your discretionary income on real estate.

If you own several homes, the problem of mortgage life insurance can be an even bigger one. These are separate insurance contracts on each loan. The amount you owe on any outstanding mortgage should be considered when you calculate your needs. Buying one life insurance policy to cover those needs is definitely better than one mortgage life insurance policy, let alone two.

Assuming your bank doesn't require you to buy a mortgage life insurance policy, you might decide your life insurance needs aren't any different despite the new home. The logic would be that a vacation home is not an integral part of your family's life-style. Therefore, it's not necessary for you to buy insurance to pay for it. The vacation home can simply be sold in the event you die.

CREDIT LIFE INSURANCE

If you're a person who has a lot of credit cards or uses a personal line of credit, there's a good chance you've bought credit life insurance and don't even know it. When you got your credit card or line of credit, you might have agreed to the insurance. Similarly, when you took out a car loan, you might have bought credit life insurance. It added very little to the monthly payment, and you probably thought, "What the heck!"

Unfortunately, you're probably paying a *heck* of a lot more for life insurance than you should. When you buy credit life insurance, it's usually a decreasing term life insurance policy just as mortgage life insurance is. As is the case with mortgage life insurance, you're buying life insurance on a piecemeal basis instead of satisfying all of your life insurance needs. The debt you owe on your car or your personal life of credit is just part of the obligations that you should plan for when you're buying life insurance.

When you buy credit life insurance, you really have no idea how much you're paying for it. If you're young and in good health, you're probably paying a great deal more than you should. Buying credit life insurance often protects the creditor more than it does you. The policy might be superfluous if you already have sufficient life insurance to meet your needs. This would be especially true if you're single and have no dependents.

BURIAL INSURANCE

When you have a handle on your needs, you can avoid purchasing life insurance to address specific purposes. You might hear a pitch for burial insurance. Playing upon your fears, the insurance company offers burial insurance of $10,000 or a similar amount. With a funeral costing between $5,000 to $10,000, it might seem like a good idea. In reality, you would be far better off with a term insurance policy that addresses all of your family's needs, not just burial expenses. Instead of buying that burial insurance policy that you see advertised, stick with a term insurance policy. Remember that buying term insurance in larger amounts is less expensive.

"DREAD DISEASE" INSURANCE

I have continually stressed that comprehensive policies are far better than those that only pay under limited circumstances. The last thing you need is a life insurance policy that only pays if your death was caused by a specific illness. A "dread disease" policy might only pay benefits if your death results from cancer. Even if you risk getting that disease, you would still be better off with a life insurance policy that pays for any reason. You do not need policies that limit the situations in which you can collect benefits. A "dread disease" policy might be interpreted narrowly, limiting your protection even further. The policy might not cover pneumonia, even though you can easily catch it when you are weak from cancer surgery.

RIDERS

Just as with the riders on homeowners policies, endorsements to a basic insurance contract can add significantly to the price of the policy. Although riders are not available on all policies, you must decide whether the benefits they add are worth the additional cost. The president of American Airlines tells the story of how he cut the olives from the salads served on flights and saved $40,000. Some of the riders to insurance contracts add little more than those olives.

If you're a movie buff, you have probably heard of the double indemnity rider. In the 1944 film, *Double Indemnity*, Fred MacMurray hoped to take advantage of a rider of this type. This endorsement stipulates that your beneficiary receives double the policy limit if the death is accidental. You have to look at your life-style and age bracket to determine if this rider is a good investment. Younger people are more likely to die in an accident than by any other means. If you are engaged in a hazardous occupation, it might also be worth considering. When you don't live life on the edge and are at the age where sickness is more of a threat than an accident, it's not worth the extra money. No matter, double indemnity riders for accidental death are not nearly as good as they seem at first glance. You might think you're doubling your coverage for a minimal amount of money. As I have pointed out before, the accidental death requirement eliminates a great many causes of death.

Also, as I've said before, your selection of life insurance should be based on your family's needs. You should have purchased this life insurance policy after calculating how much your family requires. You don't need to supplement that with an accidental death rider. It's a great deal like flight insurance. You should be going to the airport with your insurance needs satisfied, without having to buy additional insurance out of a machine or over the counter.

Guaranteed insurability riders are worth the extra expense. Too many times, people overbuy on insurance for fear that they will need more at a later date and won't be healthy enough to buy it. But an endorsement that guarantees your insurability keeps options open for you at a minimal cost. It certainly beats buying much more insurance than you need at a time when you can ill afford it.

The guaranteed insurability rider gives you the option of buying more insurance at a later date without having to go through a medical exam. This rider is normally available with whole life policies. Find out how much you will be able to buy at that later date, and how much it will cost. This rider won't mean much if you can only buy a small amount.

You can also buy a rider that automatically increases your insurance. This endorsement purportedly guards against inflation by automatically increasing the coverage each month. No matter how bad inflation gets, your insurance needs are not increasing each month. A rider like this one could put you on the hook for more coverage than you need. You pay for both the rider and the increased life insurance coverage you purchase.

Insurance companies also sell riders that cover additional persons. With this endorsement, you can add your spouse or children to the policy. I have mentioned previously that purchasing life insurance for these other family members still hinges on whether you are dependent on them for income. If not, the coverage is unnecessary.

You'll have the opportunity to buy a waiver-of-premium rider, which helps you out in the event of a disability. With this endorsement, the life insurance company will waive the premiums you owe in the event that you suffer a qualifying disability. Make sure you know what the rider is giving you. If this is an endorsement to a whole life policy, the company might only be waiving its right to collect the premiums on the life insurance portion of the premium. This might only be a small portion of the premium, so the disability waiver might save you very little.

With a waiver-of-premium rider, you run into many of the same issues that you do when evaluating a disability policy. How long must you be disabled before the rider relieves you of your duty to pay premiums? Is total disability defined as being unable to work in any occupation or your own occupation? You would want a broader definition of total disability. If the definition of disability is narrow, you might be paying for a rider with little value.

LIFE INSURANCE POLICIES THAT PAY BEFORE DEATH

It sounds like a headline from a supermarket tabloid. "Man collects on his own life insurance policy." Strange as it sounds, there are now whole life insurance policies that pay benefits prior to death. In essence, a living benefit rider is added to a whole life insurance policy. You can collect a specified portion of the policy prior to your death. You get a percentage of the death benefit without dying.

There's only one catch. Something very bad must happen to you. Some policies have a long-term care rider that requires that you be committed to a nursing home. Others require a life-threatening, catastrophic illness. In some policies, this is defined as a heart attack, stroke, coronary artery surgery, life-threatening cancer, or renal failure. When one of these events occur, you are entitled to accelerate the death benefit. Some policy riders combine both features.

The theory behind this benefit is intriguing. The benefit is advanced to the policyholder at a time when the benefits are needed most. If it's a long-term care rider, there would be nursing home expenses that require payment. Other riders seem to be based on the assumption that you'll want to live life to the fullest after a catastrophic illness is diagnosed or occurs. Therefore, you'll need money to do it. You might decide to use the advance on the death benefit to take a dream vacation or to finance extraordinary medical treatment.

Let's look at a typical rider that prepays a death benefit for nursing home care. It pays 2 percent of the death benefit per month while the policyholder is confined to a nursing home. Suppose you purchase a $100,000 life insurance policy with a long-term care rider. While you are in a nursing home, you receive $2,000 per month. If you are in the nursing home for 50 months or more, the entire death benefit would be exhausted. Other riders will place a ceiling on the amount you can collect.

To evaluate a living benefit rider, you should first consider the cost of the endorsement. Often, this process will be confusing. With one company, a life insurance policy with a living benefit rider is 10 percent higher than one without it. The company, however, claims that the higher cash value of a policy with this rider will offset the additional cost.

Another company charges $105 per year premium for a nursing home rider on a $50,000 policy purchased by a 55 year old. This is not much money. As I indicated previously, this should be a clue that you are not getting very much in the way of additional coverage. On closer examination, you might find that there is a long waiting period before you can take advantage of the rider.

You might question whether the insurance company is giving up anything when it attaches a living benefit rider to your life insurance policy. After all, it is only paying you the death benefit that your beneficiaries will eventually receive. With a living benefit rider, you can collect a portion of that death benefit far earlier than the life expectancy table would suggest. A 50-year old male might have a life expectancy of 25 years. By adding this rider, the insurance company exposes itself to the risk of making payment years earlier.

You might also question whether a policy loan would satisfy the same purpose as a living benefit rider. When you have one of these riders on your policy, you can collect the specified benefit without regard to the cash value that has accrued. If one of the provisions in the rider has been met, you can tap into the policy. A policy in which little cash value has accrued would not permit the same withdrawal.

In some respects, these riders let you kill two birds with one stone. You guard against more than one risk. Some riders resemble disability policies in that they permit payment triggered by some catastrophic illness. In theory, you could use the payment from your policy to make up for a loss of income. With riders of this kind, there is no requirement that you be off work to collect the accelerated benefit.

It is more common for the insurance company to suggest that you are satisfying both your life insurance and long-term care needs in one policy. The living benefit riders, which offer partial payments when long-term care is needed, are not the solution to your nursing care needs. You should still be buying a long-term care policy. It should not simply be an afterthought when you are buying a life insurance policy. A family can still be devastated by a long nursing home stay, even when it has life insurance with a living benefit rider.

There is something troubling about these life insurance riders that pay benefits before your death. Tapping the death benefit while you're still alive reduces the payment to your heirs. If you've properly analyzed their needs, and bought life insurance in the appropriate amount, there would be inadequate cash to support their life-style. A long-term care rider can conceivably reduce the amount of life insurance your family has to go forward with their lives. On the other hand, these nursing home expenses would have to be paid for in some way, and a life insurance policy with a long-term care endorsement would be one source of funds. Otherwise, the family might have to sell other assets to meet those expenses. Although a long-term care rider is a shabby substitute for a solid long-term care policy, it can increase a family's options when faced with this dilemma.

In the 1990s, policies with living benefit riders will become increasingly common. You might be offered this option on all whole life policies. If so, it is the underlying policy that should be the focus of your attention. If it meets a genuine need and compares favorably with other policies of the same type, you should consider purchasing it. Once you have made that comparison, you can then take the additional step of evaluating the living benefit rider. The attractiveness of that rider should not alter your original decision.

TRAVEL ACCIDENTAL DEATH INSURANCE

It used to be that you pulled out a credit card, and tried to remember how much you had left on your limit. Otherwise, you'd get a nasty letter chastizing you for exceeding that credit limit. Now you have a bigger choice. One card gives you frequent-flier mileage. Another gives you cash back. A third donates money to your favorite charity. On top of that, some of them give you travel accidental death insurance.

By itself, accidental death insurance is a long shot. It's definitely a coverage you would not want to go out of your way to buy, no matter how small the amount. Through your credit card, it might get thrown in anyway. The Discover Card, for example, gives $100,000 in accidental death insurance when an injury occurs while in the process of being a fare-paying passenger on a common carrier. The fare must be charged on the Discover Card. Though the insurance is free, keep in mind how limited the circumstances are. You must die in an accident on the bus, train, or plane, and that trip must be on your Discover Card.

When you have to pay for it, however, it's a bad deal. Rental car companies love to sell you personal accident insurance. Maybe you've bought it by mistake. Just as we saw with collision damage waivers, the few dollars you spend adds up to too many dollars per year. When it's late at night and you're tired at the rental car counter, don't buy that personal accident insurance policy.

There are other policies that provide accidental death protection. J.C. Penney Life recently sent a brochure that promised up to $250,000 in accidental death protection. The first clue that the protection is limited comes when you look at the price—it's too cheap. For $7 a month, you aren't going to get far-reaching coverage.

As you examine the promotional literature more closely, you find that the $250,000 in accidental death protection is only for accidental deaths while traveling by plane, train, taxi, bus, or other forms of public transportation. That certainly limits the likelihood of your collecting. The coverage gets smaller for more likely occurrences. You only get $50,000 if you're killed while driving or riding as a passenger in an automobile or while walking.

The actual amount of the coverage, however, is $40,000. This is the amount the carrier will pay if you are killed in some other kind of accident. This is a far more likely possibility than your being killed while riding on a bus or taxi, no matter how bad a driver you happen to have at the wheel.

The amazing part of the literature for some of these policies is that you don't have to read the fine print to recognize how little they cover. The brochure boasts that there is guaranteed acceptance, no age limit, and no medical exam is required. It doesn't matter if you're 10-years-old or a hundred, you still have to die in an accident. Your health and age are a moot point.

It might be useful to look at one lawsuit involving an accidental death policy.

In a letter to the Travel Editor of *The New York Times* on June 4, 1989, an attorney discussed a problem his client had. He represented the widow of an executive. The executive was a healthy, 43-year-old who flew from New York to South Korea. During the very long flight, a blood clot developed. The executive died three weeks later from a pulmonary embolism.

The executive had purchased an accidental death policy from a major insurance carrier. The company denied payment on the policy, contending that it was not an accident. A pathologist was called as a witness to show the relationship between the blood clot and the executive's death. The jury decided that the blood clot was triggered by the long flight and not by natural causes. Because of that verdict, the widow was able to collect the face value of the policy as well as interest.

Had the policy paid a death benefit for any reason, no litigation would have been needed. Insurance against accidents is too limited to protect your dependents. When you recognize that the insurance company will have a narrow definition of "accident," you'll see that it offers little protection for your loved ones.

SHOPPING AROUND FOR LIFE INSURANCE

To get the best life insurance for the money, you are going to have to shop around. This is the same advice I have given for virtually every other type of policy. Unfortunately, shopping around for life insurance is like shopping around for a car. After spending hours at the dealership, you can't bear the thought of going through the process again at another car dealer's showroom. The process is so painfully slow, they count on you giving up after one or two experiences.

Pricing life insurance involves the same painful process. No salesperson will simply give you a price without explaining the policy at length. Invariably, you will spend hours hearing the sales pitch. You are likely to buy the insurance out of boredom and frustration rather than looking further for the right policy.

Despite the time involved, there are ways to make shopping around a little easier. You should know exactly how much insurance you need, before speaking with the salesperson. Never let the agents do the arithmetic for you. With their formula, you will always need more than you already have and much more than you really need.

You must also know the type of policy you want. Once you understand the basic concepts, you should be comparing only that type of policy through several agents. Don't be distracted by the new, improved policies they will try to show you. Every day, insurance companies offer new policies and the agent might try to sell you on the merits of those offerings, rather than the policy you initially wanted to buy.

Shopping around isn't always easy. You won't always be able to compare the price of one life insurance policy to another that has the same coverage. Price comparisons can become complicated because some companies will give you additional coverage without charge, which is tacked onto the amount you've already purchased. This is usually done because of favorable claims experience and as a way to encourage continuation of your insurance policy. These insurance companies will send policyholders a rider that increases the coverage already in force. The coverage bonus might be 20 percent or more. These increases are granted with no additional required contribution. These coverage bonuses make it difficult to determine how much insurance you are getting for your money.

You might also start your shopping trip with a call to USAA Life. The National Insurance Consumer Organization and many consumer magazines recommend USAA as a bench mark when comparing other policies. USAA is a direct writer of life insurance and its representatives do not earn sales commissions. When you shop around for the right policy, you can compare the price and fees against those charged by USAA. Its toll free number is 1-800-531-8000.

INSURANCE QUOTING SERVICES

We've talked about how you're buying pure protection when you purchase term insurance. You would hardly think that there would be a significant difference in the price of this coverage, because you're not buying the extras as you are with whole life. You still have to shop around for the best price, however. As I indicated in Chapter 2, there are services available to help expedite your shopping for term life insurance. Some of these services can provide price information on other types of policies, and are not limited to quotes on term insurance.

Insurance Information, Inc. of Lowell, Massachusetts, bills itself as an insurance information shopping service. You call the toll free number (1-800-472-5800) and receive the names of five of the lowest cost insurance companies. The company operates by charging a $50 fee. It guarantees that you will save at least that much on the policy you buy. In its promotional brochure, it states that term insurance rates can vary by as much as 300 percent. Insurance Information, Inc. doesn't sell insurance, but merely provides information on which companies offer the lowest price.

SelectQuote (1-800-343-1985) deals with 18 companies, all rated A or A+ by the A.M. Best Company. Whereas Insurance Information, Inc. charges $50, there is no charge for SelectQuote. The figures supplied by SelectQuote give a price comparison over a number of years, so you can make certain you are not just getting an introductory bargain price on the term insurance. InsuranceQuote (1-800-972-1104) also has no charge, but is in the brokerage business.

LOSS PREVENTION

Throughout this book, I have talked about the concept of loss prevention. You can reduce your need for insurance by taking steps to prevent losses from occurring. This concept applies, even in the life insurance context. You can't avoid dying altogether, but you can make certain choices that might extend your life expectancy.

You don't need to be reminded again that a healthy life-style can add years to your life. The rates for life insurance depend on your risk classification. You can't change some aspects of your risk classification, such as age. The older you get, the greater risk you become. You can, however, change your classification by not smoking. It will make a significant difference in the rates you pay for life insurance. There are health risks that can cause you to be rated up by the insurance company.

HOW TO EVALUATE A LIFE INSURANCE POLICY

You shouldn't need to be an actuary to buy life insurance. You can however, have an actuary review of the policy you own or plan on buying. The National Insurance Consumer Organization will evaluate cash value life insurance policies. The organization calculates the rate of return on a policy for $30. It will charge $20 for each additional policy. This rate of return service is worth the investment and will quickly pay for itself. Remember too, the actual rate of return will differ from that which the life insurance company claims to offer.

This rate of return would not be applicable to a term insurance policy. The rate of return is an estimate of the interest rate you're getting on the investment portion of your cash value policy. You can calculate this rate of return yourself by getting James H. Hunt's book, *Taking the Bite Out of Insurance,* which is available from the National Insurance Consumer Organization. Its address is 121 N. Payne Street, Alexandria, VA 22314.

STOCK VERSUS MUTUAL COMPANIES

When you buy life insurance, you will have a choice between a stock or a mutual company. It is commonly believed that you will get the best deal from a mutual company, because it is not being operated for the benefit of its stockholders. You might also get a good deal from a reciprocal company such as USAA Life. A reciprocal company is owned and operated by its members.

The stock insurance company, as its name implies, operates for the benefit of its shareholders. The stockholders are the main concern when the company sells a life insurance policy. The more profit they make on a policy, the better the stockholders like it. This does not necessarily mean you can't get a good policy from a stock insurance company. Having a good product that sells is good for the stockholders too. Generally speaking, a stock insurance company sells nonparticipating policies rather than policies that return surplus funds to policyholders.

A mutual insurance company has no stockholders to consider. Excess earnings are returned to policyholders. These dividends reduce the insurance premiums that you pay.

INSURANCE BY MAIL

You might think that insurance by mail would be a great deal. You're not dealing with an agent. We've talked before about hefty sales commissions, and mail-order insurance would seem to eliminate these problems. Despite this seemingly advantageous method of buying insurance, it can often be a bad deal.

If you feel you do have a need for more insurance, the mail-order policy isn't going to help unless you outlive the first few years after you buy it. During that time frame, benefits are extremely limited. If you die, your dependents might only get back what you paid. These policies that guarantee acceptance are good for those who are considered to be rated risks. They have health problems that make life insurance companies shy away from them. When you're looking at policies like these (and you can save yourself a lot of time and money by not even looking at them), look for language like "graded death benefit." This is the language the life insurance company uses to pay you very little benefits in the first few years.

When you consider the impact of the graded death benefits, you're really paying a lot more than you should. The policy isn't inexpensive if you're getting very little protection from it. You're paying for coverage that you're not getting. It's like buying an automobile policy that will not pay during the first half of the policy. It's doubtful you'll sleep better with policies such as these.

Once you have calculated the amount of insurance you need, and reevaluated those needs when changes in your life demand it, you can ignore all of the solicitations to buy more. When you get a proposal in the mail or hear a celebrity encouraging you to buy more, rip up the letter or punch the channel selector. On too many occasions, people feel it couldn't hurt to get more.

Not only can it hurt, it does hurt. It just hurts in smaller doses. Buying additional death or "dread disease" policies increases the amount of money you're spending on insurance. They do not offer that much more in the way of coverage. Your chances of collecting are slim. You would be better off with either term or whole life insurance than you would with policies that bleed you to death. Remember, buying policies for pennies a day is a good way to nickle and dime yourself to death.

It helps to explore why these policies are so expensive. One answer is that the association endorsing the insurance is likely to get a percentage on each policy that is sold. It gets a cut and the insurance company must still make its profit. A second reason for these high costs is that the insurance companies are buying a pig in the poke. They are accepting you as a risk, sight unseen. They know very little about you, other than what their demographics tell them. They only know that you landed on one of their mailing lists.

A third reason is that poor insurance risks are more likely to respond to these direct-mail offers. You might expect that when the brochure proclaims, "Guaranteed Acceptance," a healthy person would not be as attracted to the offer as much as one who does have trouble getting insurance because of physical problems. Therefore, the death rate will be higher than a more typical sampling of the population. It is no wonder then that the premiums take that into account.

We've talked before about how buying larger amounts of life insurance is less expensive than purchasing smaller amounts. These mail-order offers are usually for small amounts of life insurance. Because of the risk they are taking, these direct-response companies will not put their necks on the line for life insurance in larger amounts. Therefore, you can only buy small amounts, and you won't get as good a deal as you do when you purchase larger policies. It's similar to buying a larger size bottle of shampoo and getting a better deal.

Once again, the pennies-per-day solicitation disguises the comparatively high cost of this life insurance. Not all mail-order insurance is a bad deal, however. Companies like USAA hold up well against all life insurance companies, not just those that sell their product through the mail. The bottom line is you must carefully analyze what is being offered before considering any policies, the same as you would when dealing directly with a company or an agent.

SHOULD YOU SWITCH LIFE INSURANCE POLICIES?

It's bad enough that you will be encouraged throughout the course of your lifetime to buy more life insurance. Once you've bought a whole life policy, you are often encouraged to switch policies. It would have to be an exceptional situation to warrant your switching policies though. Why? The major reason is that you're going to have to pay a new sales commission. We've already talked about how large those commissions are. You would immediately be in the hole on the new whole life policy because of that commission. The size of that commission should also make you question whether the salesperson has your best interests at heart.

A second good reason for not switching is that it opens a new period of contestability. As I indicated in Chapter 7, many policies have a two-year contestability period. During this period, the insurance company can question any statements you made on the application or can argue that your death was the result of suicide. You could be opening a can of worms for your beneficiaries. You also will have to go back to square one on your cash value when you switch policies. It's like a mortgage. On a 25-year mortgage, you hardly put any money toward the principal during the first few years. Because of the large commission, you would see very little growth in your cash value during the initial years of the new policy. There might also be surrender charges to consider.

You might find there are some overwhelming reasons to switch policies, however. You might own a nonparticipating whole life policy which means you receive no dividends. This reason alone would not be enough. You should find out if your policy has been improved either through interest-rate hikes or a reduction in premiums. If you own a participating whole life policy, it would be worth holding onto even if the interest rate is lower than you can get elsewhere. The dividend is likely to increase when interest rates are going up.

You might want to switch from whole life to term insurance. It could be that pure protection is all you really want from a life insurance policy and you now realize it doesn't meet your needs. Despite my preference for term insurance in place of whole life, changing policies in midstream isn't necessarily a smart move. You might be reaching the age when whole life is more of a bargain. Since a term insurance policy becomes more expensive as you grow older, the price of a whole life policy might look good if you bought it when you were much younger. If you've had the whole life policy for many years, the bulk of the commission has been paid and the cash value should grow more rapidly. In any event, be wary of any agent who aggressively courts you and urges you to switch policies. Changing policies is in their best interest not yours.

If you are healthy and have no trouble getting insurance, you might even want to move from one term insurance carrier to another. Over the years, the price of term insurance has decreased and you might be paying too much.

If you do decide to replace one policy with another, do not cancel the old one until you are certain that the new coverage is in place. You could be left with a surrender charge on the old policy and a rejected application on the new one. You could lose all of your life insurance, and your health might not permit you to buy more.

HOW TO SAVE MONEY ON LIFE INSURANCE

There are a number of steps you can take to save money on life insurance. Much of the advice I have offered in previous chapters is also applicable to life insurance. Once again, it must be stressed that you should shop around for the best price on life insurance. Use a rate shopping service to help you. Buy only the life insurance you need. Once you have met your needs, don't buy any more. If no one is dependent on you for support, don't buy any life insurance. You don't need to buy life insurance for your children.

If you do have a spouse or children who depend on you for support, buy life insurance but don't buy more than you need. Your beneficiaries should be able to maintain their standard of living if you die, but life insurance isn't supposed to enhance their life style. And unless your kids are helping you make ends meet by giving you money, you don't need to buy a policy on their lives.

Unless there are special circumstances, buy annual renewable term insurance. Invest the money you save in some alternative savings vehicle. When you have needs that require large amounts of life insurance, use annual renewable term insurance to satisfy those requirements at a reasonable price.

You can also save money by purchasing life insurance in larger amounts. Cover all of your needs in one large policy. Avoid piecemeal purchases of life insurance to handle one specific purpose. If you're not required by a lender to buy it, stay away from mortgage life insurance, credit life insurance and other policies of that type.

Save time and money by ignoring the insurance solicitations you receive in the mail or watch on television. These policies will only be of value in the most limited of circumstances. Avoid "dread disease" and accidental death policies.

Once you have decided on a policy, be selective in your choices of the riders that are available. These riders can generate significant revenue for the insurance company at your expense.

Pay your annual premium in full rather than on the installment plan. Often, there will be extra charges when you pay the premium over the course of the year.

Finally, try to become the best risk for the company to insure. That means giving up smoking and losing weight because these factors are looked at closely by the insurance company in setting your premium.

12

Life insurance
as an investment

UP TO THIS POINT, I HAVE BEEN DISCUSSING TRADITIONAL WHOLE LIFE insurance. Over the years, different forms of whole life insurance have evolved. These newer varieties of whole life insurance possess investment characteristics. At best, traditional whole life provides both protection and a savings feature. More recent forms of whole life offer protection against the risk of dying, along with an investment element.

Even as you're reading this, insurance companies are developing new types of whole life insurance policies. These new varieties are a far cry from the plain vanilla whole life insurance that stood alone for many years. You can choose from a host of products. The primary products are universal life insurance, variable life insurance, and variable universal life insurance.

When you begin to look at life insurance as an investment, you run into many of the same issues that you did when we discussed the forced savings feature in whole life policies. Many experts would argue that you are far better off buying term insurance, and investing the difference in something other than a life insurance product. With traditional whole life, the argument is a compelling one. Whole life policies pay low rates of interest and cannot be classified as investments. I mentioned in Chapter 11 that the forced savings feature might support your choice of whole life over term insurance if you're the type of person who can't put away money on a regular basis.

The same arguments exist when you deal with the newer forms of whole life. Undoubtably, there are better investments around. Adding the forced savings element to these whole life products makes them more appealing, however, for those who find it hard to save. Although some of them do allow the flexibility to skip payments, there is the tendency to continue making them. Thus, you would be more inclined to continue with this investment program. Whereas a traditional whole life policy would be a forced savings plan, these newer products would be forced investment programs for those who lack the discipline to act on their own.

Unfortunately, advising you to buy term insurance and invest the difference is too simplistic. Even if you do faithfully invest your savings from buying term insurance, you might not choose your investments wisely and would gain little from your decision.

ANALYZING YOUR NEEDS

The mere fact that certain life insurance policies have investment characteristics does not mean that you should ignore the needs analysis that determines the amount you should purchase. You should be buying the same amount of coverage, whether you buy term, whole life, or a policy that has some investment potential. The best method for satisfying those needs depends on your comprehensive financial plan. Depending on your financial situation, off meeting your needs with universal life rather than with term insurance or a more traditional whole life policy.

Universal life is a form of permanent life insurance. It offers the death benefit that we expect to find in any life insurance policy, along with an investment component. The policy accumulates cash value and can be adjusted to meet your needs as they change throughout your life.

UNIVERSAL LIFE—HOW IT WORKS

Universal life has been called the ideal policy. It was created to remedy many of the problems associated with whole life insurance. You start off with a renewable term policy, with no cash value and premiums that go up each year. It's combined with an investment account that's a lot like a money market fund. You have the flexibility to adjust either the term policy or the investment account. You can earmark the amount you want for insurance and the amount you want in savings.

You don't have to be an insurance expert to guess the first step in how universal life works. You pay a premium, and the insurance company deducts expenses from that premium. The remainder is then placed in your investment account within the policy, which is the cash value. As interest is earned, it is added to the cash value. Each month, the portion of the premium allocated to the life insurance coverage is deducted.

You might see universal life called by another name. In some states, it is known as Flexible-Premium Adjustable Life. This describes many of its benefits. You can stop paying the premiums temporarily. The cash value pays for your insurance, and it is not considered a policy loan. You can increase the amount of life insurance as you need it without buying a new policy.

This flexibility might work against you if you're the type who needs forced savings. You might circumvent the forced investment feature by taking advantage of the flexible payment schedule.

Proponents of universal life view that flexibility as a major selling point. It will let you pick your own premiums, depending on your financial situation at that time. You can boost your payment or pay less than you normally do. You can even skip payments if your cash value is large enough to pay the policy expenses. You're not locked in, because you can actually pay your premium out of the cash value you've accumulated.

The policy is flexible enough to meet your changing needs. During a lifetime, a family's needs change at various stages, and your life insurance coverage should go hand in hand with those needs. Universal life offers flexibility in your choice of coverage. You can even buy additional coverage, if you qualify. Each policy will have medical criteria that must be met to increase that coverage, however. You can also reduce the amount of coverage, as long as it doesn't fall below the minimum limits of the policy.

Universal life can be a useful tool to meet your changing needs. It can also be useful if your income fluctuates from year to year. You can vary your premium if you have a year with lower income. When you vary your premium, your death benefit will fluctuate along with it.

Universal life tax advantages

In any sales pitch for universal life, you will always hear about its tax advantages. The investment value grows without current taxation. The tax on the interest is deferred while the policy is in force and until the funds are withdrawn. Traditional whole life has that same tax advantage. The sales charges and administrative expenses on these policies might offset some of the tax advantages, however.

Many insurance companies are now promoting universal life for children. The "kiddie tax" puts children under age 14 in a bad position if they have unearned income of over $1,000. They are taxed at the same rate as their parents. Universal life is pushed as a good way for children to build a tax-deferred college fund while obtaining life insurance protection. As I discussed in Chapter 11, life insurance for children is a bad idea unless someone is dependent on their income. The investment component and tax advantages do not make up for life insurance protection that is not needed.

With universal life, you can decide how much of the premium you want to go towards the cash reserve portion of the policy. The tax laws only let you set aside a certain amount for that cash reserve. The insurance company selling the policy should make it clear to you how much you can put toward the cash reserve. Going beyond these limits can jeopardize the tax-free status of the proceeds. You also get the same tax benefit found in other life insurance policies. Your beneficiary would pay no income tax on the death benefit.

Interest on universal life policies

Great tax advantages don't make up for a low interest rate. A universal life policy pays no dividends. Instead of dividends, you earn interest on your cash value. The traditional whole life policy pays a very low rate of interest. The interest on a universal life policy is based on the short-term rates at that particular time and is usually tied to bond market interest rates.

All universal life policies promise a competitive rate. There is always a guaranteed minimum interest rate which is far below the rate you expect to get when you purchase a policy of this kind. The guaranteed rate of interest on a universal life policy might only be 4 or 5 percent.

Determine how the rate of return is calculated. Make sure that you know the correct rate after the expenses have been deducted. The quoted interest rate might not take all of the policy charges into account. An insurance company can muddy the water with projections of cash value that might not come to pass. These cash values might be bolstered with interest bonuses that the insurer is not obligated to pay.

A problem can arise if a universal life policy is sold at a time when interest rates are extremely high. When rates fall, owners of universal life policies might have to pay higher premiums to keep the same amount of coverage. If they don't, the value might go down. The death benefit could be reduced or the insurance coverage could even be cancelled.

Borrowing against a universal life policy

The cash value you have built up in your universal life policy can be borrowed. Normally, you would not pay income tax on this transaction. You would pay below-market interest rates. The cash value must be high enough, however, to sustain the policy while money is being borrowed. Remember, you still have to pay the cost of insurance built into the universal life policy, along with the charges. Excessive borrowing can cause the policy to lapse. When a policy lapses, there is no longer a death benefit and there could be tax consequences.

When you withdraw from your cash value, you'll pay taxes. There are situations under the Technical and Miscellaneous Revenue Act of 1988, however, where your withdrawals are not taxed.

Group universal life insurance

I have continually pointed out that your employer is a good source for satisfying your insurance needs. At some point, you might even be able to buy universal life through your employer. These group plans will contain many of the advantages associated with universal life.

They will combine inexpensive insurance protection along with a cash accumulation account. The account will earn interest at a market-sensitive rate. This means it will be close to the current rate of interest. There will be a guaranteed minimum interest rate. It will have a flexible death benefit that could be based on the employee's current salary. Money from the cash accumulation account would be added to the death benefit.

Group universal life insurance plans offer conversion privileges. Normally, there is a waiver of the premium if a disability occurs. You also have the option of buying universal life for a spouse or your children.

How to evaluate universal life

One way to evaluate universal life is to look at the policy illustration. Some companies use unrealistic assumptions about interest rates. Their projections might have bonuses built into them. These bonuses are not guaranteed and are only payable when you hold the policy for a particular length of time. These projections might also be based on unrealistic assumptions about the mortality rate of policyholders.

Rather than looking at projections, take a look at the history of the universal life policy that the company offers. Look at the interest rate history and how well its other life insurance products have performed. Make certain that existing customers are given the same interest rate as new customers.

When evaluating a universal life policy, you should be paying close attention to the expenses. Your actual return on investment will depend on how high those expenses are. Don't be confused by the use of the phrase, "no load." You might think there's no sales commission, but that isn't necessarily the case. A so-called no-load life insurance policy might be one where the sales commission is amortized over a number of years and is not deducted from the initial premium.

In fact, there are a few companies that do offer no-load life insurance. USAA is one in particular. Still, USAA deducts 3 percent from each payment for administrative expenses. There will also be other costs, such as a start-up fee. If you withdraw funds from your investment account, you might also be assessed a fee.

In addition to these expenses, you need to look closely at the surrender charges you owe if you cancel the policy. You might decide you want to cash in your investment after a number of profitable years. This is not as easy as it sounds. There are normally surrender charges. Although these surrender charges will decrease each year, it might be as long as 15 years before you can avoid a surrender charge of some kind. USAA has no surrender charges on its universal life policy.

The cost of the life insurance component will reduce the return on your investment. Because you are getting term insurance along with the investment account, the insurance charges increase as you grow older. If your return on investment is low, you might end up having to put more money in just to keep the death benefit intact.

Evaluating a universal life policy can be extremely difficult. As I mentioned in Chapter 11, there are services that can help you shop around for the best life insurance deals. Several of these services will not offer advice on universal life policies. There are too many variables involved with a universal life policy to do simple price comparisons.

VARIABLE LIFE INSURANCE

By now, you have learned about the various names for whole life insurance. It is sometimes called straight life or ordinary life. Variable life is not just another name for whole life. Variable life combines many of the features of traditional whole life with a new element. It's for the life insurance purchaser who can live with the element of risk.

Variable life is similar in many ways to traditional whole life. You pay a fixed annual premium. You can borrow against your cash value at comparable rates of interest. You can even choose to invest in the same portfolio that whole life money managers are using.

While there are a great many similarities, the crucial distinction between variable life and whole life is choice. You select how you want your premium invested. You decide how much of your premium is to be allocated to the various investment vehicles. You are given a choice of mutual funds that are managed by professionals. You can switch the investment portion of your premium among stocks, bonds, gold, or money market funds.

Along with that freedom of choosing your own investments comes the element risk. Variable life insurance can offer higher investment yields than a traditional whole life policy, but you must assume a greater degree of risk. The death benefit and cash values can vary in relation to how well those investment vehicles perform. A minimum death benefit is guaranteed, but the cash value is not. While whole life guarantees those earnings, variable life does not.

Though there are no guarantees, there is the possibility of earning capital gains on your investment. Choosing the right investments can result in a higher death benefit that is well above the guaranteed level. It can also produce a high cash value. The death benefit cannot drop below the amount of insurance initially purchased.

Even when your investments perform well, you run into some of the same problems we saw with traditional whole life. It takes a number of years for your cash value to build, because of administrative costs and the agent's commission. Therefore, this is a long-term investment because of the up-front costs you will be paying.

You must look at your own tolerance for risk if you choose variable life. Maybe you're not a risk-taker by nature. You must also look at whether you're putting a large percentage of your assets into variable life or a small portion. You can afford to take a greater risk if it's only a portion of your assets, or if it only utilizes a small percentage of your investment nest egg.

You might question whether life insurance is an area in which you should be making speculative investments. The purpose of life insurance seems to contradict the basic concept of variable life. You buy life insurance because of needs. If you have a legitimate need to protect your family, why choose a policy that might be depleted if you make a bad investment decision?

Variable life might be justified if the minimum death benefit guaranteed by the policy satisfies your needs, and you can afford to play with the policy in the hope of achieving a better-than-average return for your family. One alternative would be to buy term insurance and invest your savings in the same mutual funds that you get with variable life.

With variable life, you can minimize the risk by using only that investment capital with which you can afford to speculate. It can add to an already diverse portfolio and might make sense if you are in a high tax bracket. It has legitimate tax savings if you don't need to get at your money. When you are looking for a liquid investment, life insurance is not for you.

Clearly, variable life insurance is not for people with little tolerance for risk. Nonetheless, it is not as risky as jumping into the stock market on your own. When you choose a stock fund, you are buying groups of stock, not just one speculative issue. All of the funds are professionally managed. Your risk can be a controlled one if you have investment savvy and are well-read in the financial area. The true risk-taker would be the purchaser of variable life who chooses investment vehicles with little knowledge.

You'd better have a high tolerance for risk if you choose variable life and possess little investment expertise. It's similar to the choice of a full-service stock broker as opposed to a discount broker. You shouldn't be choosing a discount broker unless you research stocks, map your own trends, and make investment decisions on your own.

The risk is that, if your investments don't perform well, you will be paying a great deal of money for the guaranteed amount of life insurance that remains. In contrast, you might increase your life insurance coverage and build cash value during those years where your investments perform well. With variable life, you cannot bank on keeping that increased coverage or high-cash value. Your investments might not perform as well in later years. You should not be lulled into a false sense of security unless you reduce your risk by switching to more conservative investments.

VARIABLE UNIVERSAL LIFE

Just when you think you're understanding the mechanics of a particular policy, the life insurance industry combines the elements from several products to produce a new one. Worse yet, you can't help but become confused when you see the new product under different names. After first talking about universal life in this chapter, we then turned our attention to variable whole life. We are now going to focus on variable universal life.

Variable universal life blends the features we saw in the two previous policies. You get the investment options found in variable life. You also get the flexible premium and death benefit of universal life. Unlike variable life, however, there isn't necessarily a minimum death benefit, because both universal life and variable universal life have nonguaranteed mortality charges. Even though there will be maximum mortality charges, a lower return on your investment can result in your having to pay a higher premium to cover those mortality charges. If you don't, the death benefit can evaporate.

Variable universal life combines elements from other policies we've examined. When you see these features from other policies, it's not surprising that there are so many names for variable universal life. It has been called by such names as Universal Variable Life, Flexible-Premium Variable Life, and Universal Life II.

Variable life and variable universal life are worth considering if you are in a high tax bracket, have reasonable risk tolerance, and have long-term investment goals. These policies usually let you choose from mutual fund families, which you can even switch by phone. You can assume as much or as little risk as you want. You can invest aggressively or defensively according to market conditions. The insurers' portfolios are usually managed by well-known mutual fund companies. Your cash value will depend upon your investment success.

ANNUITIES

Although I discuss annuities in conjunction with life insurance, they are different in many ways. An annuity is an investment contract between you and the insurance company. You receive a return on your investment that supplements your contribution. At some point, you can choose to "annuitize" your investment in order to provide income for a specified period of time or for a person's lifetime.

To understand how an annuity works, it is important to distinguish between the "accumulation phase" and the "payout phase" of a particular investment. When you buy a deferred annuity, your investment, along with your earnings, grow during the accumulation phase. Your funds continue to build until you reach the payout phase which is the point where you begin receiving income from your investment. If you die during the accumulation phase, your beneficiaries will get the investment value of your account. If that value is less than the total premiums paid, they will get the larger amount.

You might even take a large amount of money, buy an annuity, and start payments immediately. This is called an immediate annuity. Unlike the deferred annuity, there is no accumulation phase. You go immediately to the payout phase.

In either case, you must make some important decisions when you reach the payout phase of the annuity. You are given an assortment of choices. The amount of your payout will depend on your selection. An annuity is quite flexible until you decide which payout you want. At that point, both you and the insurance company are locked in to that schedule.

To make these payments to you, the insurance company makes good use of the money you've given it. As a way of better understanding the annuity, it might help to picture yourself winning the lottery. This is probably something you do anyway after a bad day at work. When you win $100 million in the lottery, your state officials don't run over with a check in that amount. Instead, you receive the money in installments over a number of years. The lottery officials invest a much smaller amount in an annuity, which makes the required payments to you. By investing that smaller sum, the insurance company can make money and can still pay you $100 million over a number of years.

Chances are, you'll be investing a smaller amount if you buy one. You can buy the annuity with a lump sum. This would be a single-premium annuity. You might decide to make a series of payments to the insurance company instead, which is a flexible-premium annuity.

TAX ADVANTAGES AND PROBLEMS

Although you can create a stream of income for years to come with an immediate annuity, it is during the deferred annuity's accumulation phase that a small amount can turn into a very large sum of money. The earnings on your annuity grow without being diminished by taxes. These earnings are not taxable until you withdraw them, and they are spread out over a number of years. When you begin receiving income from an annuity, only part of the income is taxable because you are receiving both interest and a partial return of your principal.

Another advantage of an annuity is that you can postpone receipt of income until you are in a lower tax bracket. It can be useful to supplement a pension, Social Security, or the income you expect to receive from an Individual Retirement Account. In fact, some financial experts are recommending annuities for people who can no longer qualify for IRAs because their income is too high. You are not limited to $2,000 per year with an annuity.

While the person selling the annuity will point to the tax advantages of this investment, it can create tax problems. Unless you are over age 59¹/₂ when you withdraw money from the annuity or cash it in, the IRS imposes a penalty. There is a 10 percent penalty on any earnings withdrawn, along with the tax you owe on the withdrawal. These charges would be in addition to any insurance company fees that might be imposed upon the withdrawal. Like an IRA, there are exceptional situations in which you will not be penalized on the withdrawal. If you die or become disabled, the penalty will not be charged. There are other limited exceptions when the penalty will not be charged, but you should check with your accountant to see if you qualify.

You should approach the purchase of an annuity with the expectation that you will not draw upon it until you're older than age 59¹/₂. To fully exploit the tax advantages, you should plan on holding the annuity for many years so that the earnings can grow without current taxation.

THE FINITE-TERM ANNUITY

The finite-term annuity is sometimes called a certificate of annuity because of its resemblance to a certificate of deposit (CD). You can purchase it with a variety of maturity dates. It also lets you choose when to pay taxes. The minimum investment is usually $5,000 or $10,000. The yield is normally a little less than the going rate on bank CDs. When the maturity date arrives, you can take your money and pay taxes on the gain. If you don't need the money and don't want to pay the taxes at that point in time, you can roll the money over into a new finite-term annuity.

This annuity investment is advantageous for someone who is over 59¹/₂. It's not quite ideal for someone younger than that, because there is a 10 percent early-withdrawal penalty imposed by the government, along with the tax on your gain. There is also the question of safety. It's not quite as safe as a bank CD, although choosing an A+ or A rated insurance company can come close.

FIXED ANNUITIES VS. VARIABLE ANNUITIES

No matter what the tax advantages of an annuity are, you must still pay close attention to the rate of return on your investment. You will be choosing between two kinds of annuities—fixed-rate annuities and variable-rate annuities. As the name suggests, the fixed-rate annuity pays a specified rate, but only for the length of time agreed to by the parties. The rate is adjusted at regular intervals after the initial period is over. The variable-rate annuity fluctuates according to the performance of the investments you designate.

Fixed-rate annuities guarantee a particular interest rate for a specified period of time. After that period is over, only a minimum yield is guaranteed. It used to be that an insurance company would only guarantee a certain interest rate for one or three years. Today, guaranteed rates for as long as 10 years are becoming increasingly common. Fixed-rate annuities invest primarily in bonds and Ginnie Maes.

Don't be enticed by an unusually high interest rate. Although there will be a guaranteed minimum, the current interest rate will only last for so long. After that guaranteed period is over, the rates can fall. In its sales pitch, the company selling the annuity will always tell you how the rate can go up after the guaranteed period, not just down. The danger for you is that it will go down.

Look at the interest rate history of the annuity you're considering. Find out what the interest rate has been for the past five years. Ask how the future interest rate will be calculated and make certain you will get the same rate as new customers. Finally, remember that annuities are a very long-term investment.

VARIABLE ANNUITIES

With variable annuities, your rate of return depends on your investment skills. You will be able to choose from a variety of mutual funds. The investment possibilities are similar to those found in variable life and variable universal life policies. All of the funds should be professionally managed. The interest, dividends, and capital gains are reinvested and tax deferred.

Just as with variable life and variable universal life, there is a certain amount of risk with variable annuities. Although these funds are professionally managed, the rate of return can fluctuate according to market conditions. You face the same risks that you would when investing in any mutual fund. Some of the funds are riskier than others. If you are a seasoned investor, you will recognize these risks and can hold them in check with your knowledge of market conditions. Only you can judge your tolerance for risk and how well your portfolio is diversified.

Choosing a variable annuity doesn't mean you have to roll the dice forever. When you're ready to receive payment, you can choose a payout option that suits you and that does not depend on your skill in choosing investments.

PAYOUT OPTIONS

Annuities are quite different from the life insurance products we've looked at previously. To distinguish these policies, one insurance newsletter stated that an annuity stops paying benefits at the insured's death, and that's where life insurance first begins to pay benefits. While that distinction gives you a general idea of the difference between an annuity and life insurance, it's not totally correct.

You can structure an annuity so that the payout will continue for a specified length of time. This period can extend beyond your lifetime if you choose that option. Therefore, payments from an annuity do not necessarily end on your death. Furthermore, there are life insurance policies that pay benefits prior to death if some catastrophic event occurs.

Despite these exceptions, an annuity is commonly regarded as an investment that pays you benefits until your death. The most compelling argument in its favor is that it can guarantee an income for life. It can be structured so that you cannot outlive your income. When you enter the payout phase of the annuity, you will have a number of options to consider.

You could decide to take the annuity in one lump sum. Obviously, that could cause tax problems in the year you decide to take it. You wouldn't buy an annuity just to have it paid out to you in full.

The simplest option is a straight-life or lifetime-only annuity. The terms of this agreement stipulate that you receive a monthly income for life. With this type of payment schedule, the insurance company estimates how long you'll live. The longer you live, the more it pays you. The catch is that no one gets any money when you die. If you're the negative sort, this option might not charm your socks off. You'll worry about dying on the day after choosing this option.

If you're not confident you'll live longer than the insurance company thinks you will, you can choose a joint-and-survivor annuity. This pays a monthly benefit for as long as both you and your dependent live. In effect, if you don't take full advantage of the annuity, your dependent has a chance to outlive the insurance company's projections. This settlement option also lets you take care of a dependent's income needs. Not surprisingly, your investment would bring a lower monthly income with the joint-and-survivor annuity arrangement. This stands to reason, because your investment fund has to last over two lifetimes, not just one.

Another payout option is receiving income for the rest of your life, with a guarantee. This is called an annuity with life-and-period certain. You are guaranteed that payments will continue for at least the designated period, whether that be 10, 15, or 20 years. This way, you are sure that you'll get your money's worth out of the annuity, even though it might not be you who collects. Your beneficiary would collect for the full guaranteed period, even if you don't make it.

You can also choose an income for a fixed period. You select the length of time you'll receive the annuity payments. The length of time you select will determine how much you get per month. Somebody will get that income for a fixed period, though it might not necessarily be you. If you don't collect the full amount, your beneficiary will receive the rest of the payments until the specified period expires. Living longer than expected won't help you with this option. The payments stop after the specified period ends.

You would think those are all of your options, but there are more. You can approach an annuity from a different perspective. You tell the insurance company how much you need and it calculates the payout accordingly. For example, along with your other income, you need $1,000 per month to live comfortably. The insurance company will use your principal and interest to pay out that $1,000 per month for as long as possible. It is different from the typical annuity payout calculation, because life expectancy is not a consideration. With this payout option, you can outlive your annuity. If you die before the annuity's value is depleted, your beneficiaries receive the balance.

Other options are installment-refund annuities and cash-refund annuities. They return your original annuity investment to your beneficiary if you don't outlive the amount you put in.

You needn't choose any of these options during the accumulation phase of the annuity. You would be wise to wait until you're ready for payments to begin. At that time, you will know what your financial needs are. You also can choose a payment schedule that takes full advantage of the tax laws in effect at that time. No matter which annuity you choose, remember that the monthly payment you're choosing now might look anemic in 20 years. As your dollar's buying power erodes over the years because of inflation, you might find yourself short of monthly income if this is the only source of funds you have.

EVALUATING AN ANNUITY

To evaluate an annuity, you should first look at the safety of your investment. In Chapter 4, I discussed the A.M. Best Company rating system. You should not even consider an annuity unless it is rated A+ or A. When you buy an annuity from a company that is not rated A+ or A by *Best's Insurance Reports*, you are taking a conservative investment and adding an element of risk. This advice applies even if your state has a guaranty association to make good on these life insurance contracts. After purchasing an annuity, you should still keep track of its rating. If the company's rating goes down, you should consider a tax-free exchange from that annuity to another one with an A+ or A rating.

You can't talk about the safety of annuities without mentioning the Baldwin-United problems during the early 1980s. Baldwin-United was a company that marketed annuities. It experienced severe financial difficulties, which resulted in many sleepless nights for its customers. These customers eventually received a return on their investment that was less than expected. The purchasers of Baldwin-United annuities recovered their money because of other insurance companies and stock brokers who made good on the contracts.

Although the safety of an annuity should be your primary concern, there are other factors to consider. Your evaluation should take note of the charges imposed by the insurance company selling the annuity. Ask if there are any administrative expenses, sales commissions, management fees, or surrender charges. These charges can reduce the amount of interest you are actually receiving on the annuity. The salesperson's explanation of these charges can be quite confusing, so be careful. Although a company might be "no-load," in the sense that no sales commission is charged, there could still be less obvious charges. A company might charge a management fee in one form or another. Some companies only assess these fees on smaller annuities. You should be able to find a safe annuity that doesn't charge a sales fee or an administrative fee.

You might be wondering how the salesperson makes his money. He will earn a commission of 8 percent or less. The company selling the annuity absorbs the commission. Although you might not pay the commission directly, it can adversely affect the rate of return that you receive. A salesperson might try to steer you toward an annuity that pays him a higher commission. For this reason, you need to be careful.

Find out about any surrender fees if you cash in the annuity prematurely. These charges are a back-end load. Some companies have eliminated or reduced them entirely. Other companies apply this penalty if you cash in the annuity within five to seven years after you purchase it. With other insurance companies, there might be a gradually reduced surrender fee that might continue for as long as 15 years. Naturally, you wouldn't need to worry about surrender fees with the finite-term annuity. When the term is over, there would not be a surrender charge.

Some annuities let you withdraw up to 10 percent of your accumulated interest without a surrender fee. Others charge an early withdrawal fee. Unfortunately, when you cash in an annuity or withdraw part of the interest, you might still have the tax consequences to consider. If you're younger than age 59 1/2, you could face a stiff penalty as well as extra taxes on the money you receive.

Pay particular attention to whether your annuity contains a bailout clause. Some companies charge you to get this clause. It allows you to cash in your annuity without paying a surrender charge if the interest rate falls by a specified percentage. These bailout clauses vary in their wording. Some are worded harshly, so it's unlikely you'll be able to meet the conditions. The bailout clause will be based upon the initial rate you're getting on your annuity and by what percentage it drops from the initial rate. Obviously, the bailout clause is inappropriate for a variable annuity, because you determine how much interest and capital gains you will earn.

As with so many other types of insurance policies, you will have to shop around for the annuity that's right for you. You should be comparing the company's A.M. Best rating, interest rates, and any fees that the company might charge. Some of these expenses will be more important to you than others. If you might need your money in five years and don't have other sources you can tap, the surrender fee will be more important to you. As a general rule, however, you should not be purchasing an annuity unless you plan on keeping it for many years.

Even after you choose an annuity, you might have to shop around again when you go from the accumulation phase to the payout phase. You'll usually do better converting your present annuity than buying a new one, but not always. If another company can do more with your money, you can switch to another annuity without causing yourself a tax problem. Essentially, you are using your funds at the new company to buy an immediate annuity. When you're looking at your options, shop around to make certain that another company can't offer you a better payout with the same amount of money. Keep in mind, however, that one insurance company might not offer the best monthly payout for every option. Each company's financial data and loss experience will be different. If one company does not believe you will live as long as another company thinks you will, it will offer a better monthly payment.

WHAT'S AHEAD FOR LIFE INSURANCE IN THE 1990s?

I've talked a lot about how your needs determine the amount of life insurance you should have. Companies that market life insurance will try to convince you that you need their products, even when you don't. That is why it is so important for *you* to analyze your family's needs and assess what *you really* must have. It's not expected that there will be any revolutionary new insurance products like universal life or variable universal life as there was in the 1980s. Rather, there will be a creative packaging of existing life insurance products.

Life insurance policies with living benefits will be actively marketed. As America continues aging, life insurance will be promoted as a tool to meet the expenses associated with a serious illness or to pay for the cost of long-term health care. Insurance companies might also focus more on the sale of annuities, because they can be an excellent retirement investment.

13

Life insurance and estate planning

THERE'S A GREAT DEAL MORE TO ESTATE PLANNING THAN JUST WRITING A will. Through estate planning, you can distribute your assets as you see fit. You can minimize the delay and expense of probate. An estate plan can help you reduce taxes at the time of death and can even minimize the taxes you owe during your lifetime.

Unfortunately, estate planning is a complicated endeavor. Many attorneys are not qualified to handle a case in this field and will refer you to a specialist who has significant experience and expertise in this branch of the law. You will find that the nationally advertised law firms like Hyatt Legal Services will not handle intricate estate planning. They will, however, prepare wills and advise clients on probate matters.

It is not surprising that some lawyers shy away from estate planning. There have been frequent changes in estate and gift tax laws. At one point, the American Bar Association passed a resolution asking Congress to bring stability to estate planning because estate lawyers have complained that changes in the law couldn't be understood.

Estate planning involves many areas of the law. Preparing an estate plan requires an in-depth knowledge of the law of taxes, wills, property, insurance, and trusts. Because so many attorneys turn down these cases because they lack the expertise to handle them, it should make you think twice when a life insurance agent offers you estate planning advice.

Many life insurance agents will volunteer to help you with your estate planning. Some of them have studied extensively to develop their expertise in this field. Despite their qualifications, there is still a problem in using someone's advice who has a vested interest in selling you insurance. Insurance policies are not the only tools to use in the estate planning process. There are trusts and other arrangements to carry out the estate plan.

USES OF LIFE INSURANCE IN ESTATE PLANNING

Life insurance can serve a very basic purpose in the estate planning process. It can be used to build an estate where none already exists. One life insurance sales brochure carries this concept one step further. The brochure suggests that you buy the coverage to create an "instant estate."

Many people find it difficult to build an estate over a lifetime. Paying for educations, weddings, homes, and other expenses eats away at their savings. It is difficult enough to save for retirement, let alone build an estate. Younger people don't even get the opportunity to attempt to build an estate if they die prematurely. They might own a house but the mortgage offsets the value of that asset. Life insurance is viewed by some as a vehicle to create that estate. Without life insurance, there might not be any unencumbered assets for surviving family members to use.

The fact that life insurance can be used to create an estate does not change our discussion of who needs life insurance. If no one is dependent on the person for support, there would be no need to create an estate with life insurance. Children, for example, do not need life insurance, because the family is not dependent on them for support.

In addition to its role in creating an estate, life insurance can be useful in other ways. For those who have very large estates, life insurance can provide liquidity. There will be estate taxes and settlement costs to pay, and life insurance policies can be used to pay those costs rather than liquidating the assets in the estate to meet those obligations. For estates of any size, life insurance can preserve the assets that comprise them. Life insurance can be used to pay the expenses associated with death, so that a house or some other asset does not need to be sold to provide funds. Life insurance can be a ready source of cash for a family at the time of death. The proceeds of the policy go directly to the beneficiaries the without the delays of the probate process.

LIFE INSURANCE AND ESTATE TAXES

To understand the role of life insurance in the area of estate planning, some background on estate taxes is in order. There is an unlimited marital deduction that lets property pass from one spouse to the other without federal estate taxes. The taxes are deferred until the death of the second spouse. As a general rule, the federal estate tax does not apply to estates valued at less than $600,000. For estates that are larger than that amount, there can be significant taxes and settlement costs. On estates of any size, there are state inheritance taxes to consider.

Although the proceeds of a life insurance policy aren't subject to income tax on the part of the beneficiary, there might be estate taxes. A $100,000 life insurance policy will be included, along with other property left by you, in your estate. If your gross estate totals more than $600,000, there could be estate taxes to pay. To avoid estate taxes, you should consider assigning that life insurance policy to someone else. You can even assign a group life insurance policy. After that assignment, you can't change beneficiaries or surrender or cancel the policy.

After you have assigned a life insurance policy, you can no longer retain any "incident of ownership." The power to change a beneficiary demonstrates that you maintain control over the policy. Therefore, you are still viewed as owning it. Accordingly, the policy proceeds would still be included in your gross estate. As an additional matter, you cannot transfer the policy within three years of your death. A transfer within that time frame is regarded as having been made to avoid the inclusion of the policy in your estate.

This rule discourages people from transferring ownership of a policy in anticipation of death. You must not own the policy for at least three years prior to your death. An owner can borrow against the cash value of the policy, if it is a whole life policy, and choose the beneficiaries. It is the beneficiaries who receive the proceeds of the policy at the death of the person insured.

If your spouse is the sole beneficiary of your life insurance policy, there is no need to transfer ownership of it. Even if it is a large policy, there will be no estate taxes because of the unlimited marital deduction. As a practical matter, however, the proceeds of the policy might eventually be taxed as part of the spouse's assets at death. When you are advised for estate planning purposes to transfer ownership of a life insurance policy to a spouse, you are risking the loss of coverage in the event of a divorce. If that were to happen, your spouse might exploit the cash value of the policy or designate different beneficiaries.

One solution to potential problems of this type is to transfer ownership of the policy to an irrevocable life insurance trust. The trustee will carry out the instructions given at the time the trust is established. Unfortunately, these trusts are expensive to create and maintain. Some experts suggest these trusts are only worthwhile if you have assets that are well in excess of $1 million.

There is another potential problem when transferring ownership of a life insurance policy that you need to be aware of. Transferring ownership of a cash-value policy could cause problems with the gift tax. This tax becomes an issue if the cash value is over $10,000 which is the limit for a single individual. There is no gift tax on transfers between spouses. You should also keep in mind that you can't change beneficiaries or surrender or cancel the policy after you assign it to someone else. While this might make sense from an estate planning standpoint, it could frustrate some action you would like to take during your lifetime.

These same considerations affect any new life insurance policy that you want to buy. If estate taxes are going to be a problem, you should consider having someone else buy the life insurance policy on you. The policy cannot be purchased with your money. If you do not own the policy, it will not be part of your taxable estate. While this might reduce estate taxes, it can also cause some of the problems noted above when you do not own a life insurance policy.

SECOND-TO-DIE LIFE INSURANCE POLICIES

A number of companies are offering second-to-die life insurance policies as an estate planning tool. You might see these policies marketed as Joint and Last Survivor Life. They cover two lives rather than just one. The policy does not pay benefits until the second spouse has died. The policies are designed for couples whose heirs will have to pay estate taxes and settlement costs, even though they have used estate planning techniques. The death benefit from these second-to-die policies is designed to cover those expenses.

A second-to-die policy is radically different than your typical life insurance contract. With second-to-die policies, two lives are insured under the same policy. The policy does not pay its benefit until the death of both parties, not just one. If a husband and wife are insured under a policy of this type, and one of them dies, no money is paid out at that time. There is no benefit paid until the surviving spouse dies, because no estate taxes are likely to be owed until that time.

Naturally, second-to-die policies are less expensive than those that pay out on the death of one person. There is less risk to the insurance company with this arrangement. They can also be less expensive for another reason. One of the two people might be a "rated" risk. The person, because of a health problem or some other factor, is considered to be a greater risk and is charged more for insurance. The insurance company is less concerned with that problem, because there is another person who must also die before payment is due.

Usually only couples with very large estates should consider buying a second-to-die policy. Anyone whose estate is large enough to consider this should consult with an attorney who practices in this area, not a life insurance salesperson. Rather than buying a specialized policy to pay estate taxes, these couples should be considering other ways to more efficiently distribute property to their heirs.

The sales literature for second-to-die policies illustrates one of their drawbacks. The company offers to split the policy into two separate ones if federal estate tax laws change. Therefore, if you bought this policy for the purpose of paying estate taxes, your reason for buying it would disappear if the law changes. Instead of getting your money back, you get two policies that you might not have wanted in the first place. A change in the unlimited marital deduction could eliminate the need for second-to-die policies. Further changes, however, might create the need for additional life insurance products.

SELLING LIFE INSURANCE THROUGH ESTATE PLANNING

In the course of the estate planning process, you might be encouraged to buy additional life insurance. Recent changes in the tax laws have focused attention on the charitable remainder unitrust. With the unitrust, you transfer cash or other property to the trust. At designated intervals, the trust makes payments to you and your spouse during your lifetimes. After your deaths, the cash and property remaining go to a charity of your choice. When you establish the trust, you get a tax deduction.

You're probably wondering what this could possibly have to do with life insurance. Well, the life insurance salesperson has plans for the tax money you saved by setting up the unitrust. The salesperson will suggest that you are short-changing your heirs by setting up this trust with a charity as a beneficiary. Conveniently, you can use the tax savings from the trust to buy life insurance for your heirs. Therefore, an estate planning suggestion can indirectly lead to a life insurance sales pitch.

You will also get more direct insurance sales pitches that play upon your charitable instincts. An insurance agency will work hand-in-hand with a university or charitable institution and suggest that individuals make gifts of life insurance.

14

Disability insurance

MY WIFE'S FORMER DENTIST WAS IN HIS 30s WHEN HE SLIPPED ON A PATCH OF ice. The elbow injury he suffered wouldn't have been too bad for most of us. Most of us though, aren't dentists. Being unable to use our elbow for leverage during dental procedures isn't that important to us.

My brother-in-law's a periodontist. On the day before my wife and I got married, he and I were playing tennis. He turned his ankle and fell on his arm. For a month or two, we all worried that he wouldn't be able to return to his growing dental practice.

Aside from both of these men being dentists, they had one other thing in common. Both were seemingly too young to be in need of disability insurance, yet both jeopardized lucrative, prosperous careers. There's a happy ending for one of the dentists. My brother-in-law has a prosperous periodontal practice in Westchester County, New York. He says he might let me drive his new Porsche one day; the other dentist is selling real estate.

EARNING POTENTIAL

When you get your paycheck, it doesn't seem like much. After they take the taxes out, they're never paying you what you think you're worth. Nevertheless, the ability to earn an income is a valuable resource that must be protected. If you earn $3,000 per month or $36,000 per year, you will make over a million dollars before you retire. If you earn more, the lifetime totals will be amazing. For young people, the ability to earn a living is their greatest financial asset.

How's your cash flow? Are you finding it tough making it from payday to payday? Are you having difficulty putting away money to meet financial obligations such as a child's education? Consider how well you'd do if you became disabled and were unable to collect a paycheck. If you're not ready to "take that job and shove it," you're probably not ready for the devastating impact of a disability.

Maybe you've dreamed of early retirement. Chances are, you'd be reading this book on a beach with a fishing pole in hand if you could afford to retire right now. Most of us will need to work until close to the normal retirement age. A disability can cause a premature retirement without any alternative source of funds and without any paycheck. A disability can put an end to the millions of dollars you can expect to earn over your lifetime. Oh sure, you won't have those commuting expenses and clothes won't be a high priority item, but the prospect of life without an income is a frightening one.

Until you reach that point in life where you're receiving a stream of income from your investments, disability insurance should be a high priority. As you become less dependent on a paycheck, your need for disability insurance should decrease. Your assets can be used to generate income. Your ability to earn a living is no longer your greatest asset, just one way to make money.

THE RISK OF BECOMING DISABLED

It's a morbid thought, but we all risk becoming disabled because of sickness or an accident. Morbidity is your potential for becoming disabled, based on your current health and life expectancy. And the risk is significant. Statistics show that a 35-year-old is 3.7 times more likely to become disabled than die.

Despite those odds, you're much more likely to have bought life insurance than a disability policy. Since the day you were born, or shortly thereafter, it's been drummed into your head about the need for life insurance. Becoming disabled is a less publicized danger, even though it is more likely to occur during most stages of your life. While the statistics quoted above don't necessarily mean you will suffer a long-term disability, that prospect should be guarded against if you're the insurance planner for your family.

INSURANCE THROUGH YOUR EMPLOYER

If you're like most people, the only disability insurance you have is through your employer. Depending on your years with the company, and the type of benefits offered, it's quite likely you only have a short-term disability policy through work. You might only get a certain number of weeks of disability pay for each year of your employment.

New York requires that most employers provide short-term disability insurance. The Disability Benefits Law obligates the employer to provide this disability insurance for injuries, illnesses, and pregnancy. The typical employer-provided disability policy will pay a specified percentage of your weekly salary for a stipulated number of weeks. The number of weeks you are entitled to will depend on the length of your employment with the company.

Even if your employer offers a long-term disability benefit, you still might need an individual disability policy. The benefit amount could be too small and the benefit period might be too short. It's also unlikely that your disability benefits are portable. When they're not, it means you can't take the policy with you when you change jobs or leave your place of employment. As with any policy that requires you to be healthy in order to buy it, the risk is not qualifying to buy another one. Furthermore, if your employer pays the premium, the benefit is taxable.

Don't count on Social Security disability benefits to pick up the slack. More people are turned down than succeed in obtaining Social Security disability benefits. There's even talk of tightening the requirements for obtaining these benefits. On top of that, the benefits are unlikely to replace all of the income you're losing because of the disability.

DISABILITY INSURANCE LIMITATIONS

Once you realize that you should have disability insurance, you must determine how much you need. Surprisingly, insurance carriers will limit the amount of coverage you can buy. That in itself is a real man-bites-dog story. You've spent a lifetime avoiding people who are trying to sell you more insurance. No matter how much life insurance you have, a salesperson will always try to sell you more. Disability insurance is a different ball game.

There are a number of reasons for the limitation. Primarily, the insurance company wants you to have an incentive to go back to work. The logic is that if you let someone have too much disability insurance, you are opening the door to discretionary disabilities. The individual could go back to work but doesn't because there is no financial incentive to do so. In setting a limit on the amount of disability insurance you can buy, the carrier will also look at your net worth and how much unearned income you are receiving. These extra funds from sources other than working could, when combined with a disability income check, discourage someone from going back to work. With too much money coming in, an individual might not be motivated to make a full recovery from the disability.

In addition to placing a limit on the amount of insurance you can buy, there are situations where a company won't even sell you a policy. If the earnings from your job represent less than 50 percent of your annual income, your chances of getting disability insurance are slim. Disability insurance is designed to replace work-related income. You are a better risk, from the carrier's vantage point, if you desperately need to work to maintain your life-style. Having other sources of income means you might someday view a disability check as gravy and will lose the motivation to go back to work.

You might also find companies who are unwilling to sell you disability insurance if you are engaged in a hazardous occupation. Some carriers avoid selling disability insurance to self-employed individuals, because proving income is more difficult. Finally, your medical history could make you a less desirable risk to insure.

HOW MUCH INSURANCE YOU NEED

It is not smart to buy as large a disability policy as the insurance company will allow. You should analyze your finances and needs carefully. It is generally assumed that you will want enough after-tax income to maintain your family's standard of living. The problems arise when you must decide how well you can expect your family to live during a period of disability, whether that be several months or several years.

Naturally, you won't want to give up your house in the event of a disability. Should you, however, buy enough disability insurance so you can still afford the country club, the luxury car or the vacation home? What about your spouse, can he pick up some of the drop-off in income? These are the types of decisions you must make when you're purchasing disability insurance.

To avoid being overinsured, you should be looking to cover your bare bones monthly expenses. Although you should allow some margin for error, you must expect to give up some things if you become disabled. The kids will have to go to a state college or give up summer camp.

A good rule of thumb is that you should try to cover 60 percent of your salary. Because many families need two incomes to make ends meet, a comprehensive disability policy on each working parent is a necessity to replace the income of a wage-earner who becomes disabled. In the ever-growing number of single parent homes, the importance of disability insurance can't be stressed enough.

You might wonder how 60 percent of your income can be sufficient to fully cover your family. You will most likely have less expenses if you are disabled and can't work. In addition to those savings, if you pay the premium yourself, the benefit will be tax free. Since you probably lose a third of your paycheck to taxes anyway, the 60 percent of your regular wages should provide sufficient coverage.

HOW LONG DO I NEED IT?

We've addressed the question of how much disability insurance you need. The next question to answer is how long you need it. I've already discussed how the need for disability insurance diminishes as you grow older and have enough assets to generate income without a paycheck. The catch is that you might never reach that point where you have accumulated assets, especially if you have a mid-career disability that lasts for an extended period.

The typical disability policy pays a full benefit until you reach age 65. There are a variety of life-extension riders that will continue the benefit for your lifetime, however. These riders will pay benefits for life if you are totally and permanently disabled prior to age 60. This extra coverage is quite expensive and would not be necessary if your retirement needs have already been satisfied. If you have a large IRA and your pension is vested, it is not as important to continue disability checks beyond your 65th birthday.

HOW TO EVALUATE A DISABILITY POLICY

You don't want to spend good money on a disability policy that will only pay in very limited situations. A narrow definition of total disability will restrict your ability to collect on the policy. When you are reviewing the definition of total disability, your primary consideration should be the language "own occupation" versus "any occupation."

"Own occupation" definition

You definitely should buy a policy that defines total disability as being unable to work in your own occupation. This type of language entitles you to your full disability payment even if you are still able to do work of some type. A less valuable policy will define total disability as the inability to work in any occupation. With a pure "own-occupation" definition, you can collect no matter how much you are earning in some other line of work.

To understand the importance of the "own-occupation" definition of total disability, let's look again at our two dentists. The less fortunate dentist ended up selling real estate instead of practicing dentistry. If his disability policy did not have an "own-occupation" definition of total disability, his real estate work would prevent him from collecting benefits.

Suppose a surgeon develops arthritis. Because of this condition, he can no longer do surgery but is still able to teach at a medical school. An "own-occupation" clause would let him collect the benefits from his policy. A policy with an "any occupation" definition of total disability would be of no use to the surgeon. As long as the physician can work in any occupation, the definition of total disability is not satisfied. Therefore, no disability benefits would be forthcoming.

It is not enough that the insurance company defines total disability as the inability to work in your own occupation. The carrier can insert another clause that takes away this positive feature. There might be additional language which states that the benefit is offset by income earned while engaged in any occupation. Therefore, although you meet the definition of total disability in the contract, your benefit is reduced by money you make from any work you find. If the policy has an offset provision, the "own occupation" clause will be rendered useless.

Residual disability

You should also be extremely concerned with how the policy handles a residual disability. This aspect of the policy would be especially important if you are only able to return to work on a part-time basis or suffer a reduction in earnings because of a disability. Perhaps, you are a salesperson who lost accounts during the period of disability. The residual disability protection pays a pro rata benefit until you are back on your feet again. Although you are no longer totally disabled, the residual disability provision in the policy recognizes that your income is still damaged by your illness or injury. The residual disability language might read: "Proportionate benefits are payable when you are not totally disabled but still suffer 20 percent or more loss of income because of injury or sickness."

Residual disability protection is also important to self-employed professionals. Suppose you are the sole practitioner in your own law firm and must refer clients to other attorneys while you're out of action. When you do return to work, these clients do not just leave the other attorney and return to you for their legal work. They are likely to continue their relationship with the new attorney. If you've paid attention to the residual disability language in your policy, you will receive a portion of your benefit until you can build up your practice again. The residual disability coverage should not require you to be under continuing medical care, or that you be working less than full time.

Guaranteed renewability

You should also be looking for a policy that's guaranteed renewable. A policy that's conditionally renewable or optionally renewable isn't in your best interest. Even a guaranteed renewable policy has its drawbacks. It does not mean you will pay the same premium forever. A noncancellable policy is guaranteed renewable, and at the same premium. The insurance company can't cancel it for medical reasons or because you submit too many claims. It also can't change the premium before your 65th birthday.

RIDERS

In previous chapters, I've compared riders to bells and whistles. You must separate those riders that are merely decorative from those that offer substantial protection. Riders can help you tailor a policy to meet your family's special needs, but they can also add to an insurance company's profits. While disability insurance is important to have, many riders are not. Some are like buying insurance on your insurance.

Riders can, however, serve a valuable purpose. The "own-occupation" clause and residual disability protection can be added with riders. A rider can even save you money, as you will see with the Social Security rider.

The carrier might try to sell you a rider that provides for a hospital confinement benefit or an outpatient injury benefit. One major disability carrier offers its own version of this type of rider, which is called a Nondisabling Injury Benefit. It pays up to $2,500 for outpatient expenses incurred, even though no monthly disability payment is made. With this rider, you are duplicating other coverage. Your health insurance policy should be your source of protection for this risk.

Another rider to consider is a cost-of-living adjustment (COLA). A COLA rider can be very expensive, and you need to evaluate the COLA rider itself, not just the question of whether to buy one. Some have lifetime caps. Some are calculated using simple interest rather than compound interest. For an older person, the COLA rider is not as important, because inflation will not erode the benefit as much.

A COLA rider provides inflation protection after a disability occurs. An automatic benefit increase rider helps you before a disability occurs. Your coverage is automatically increased each year by a small amount. The extra insurance you are buying should increase your premium, but the rider itself should not.

The guarantee of physical insurability rider is extremely important in any health-related policy. I have mentioned that the amount of disability insurance you can buy is tied to your income. You might be in a profession where your salary increases rapidly. If your health deteriorates as your income skyrockets, you might not be able to cover the new compensation level that you've reached. This rider gives you a guarantee that no matter what your health is at the time, you will be able to purchase additional disability insurance. This rider, if you decide to buy it, should let you buy as much or as little as you want. You should be entitled to this option even if you don't exercise it for an extended period of time.

Because riders can be big money-makers for the insurance company, you will be offered a wide variety of them. One will bolster your retirement savings. Another will supplement your child's college fund. The sales pitch is that a disability will cut deeply into your savings for retirement and education for your children. Riders like these are attractive but can raise the premium significantly.

There are even riders that will let you gamble on your need for disability insurance. Companies offer cash value and return-of-premium riders. The cash value rider entitles you to a refund on your disability insurance premiums after a very long wait. All claim payments are deducted from this cash value. The return-of-premium rider gives you a refund at the end of a specified period of time. One rider of this type refunds a portion of the premium after six years, which is offset by any benefits that are paid.

With these riders, you are betting that you will not need disability insurance. These riders are very expensive. Rather than increasing the amount of money you spend on insurance, you should stick with a comprehensive disability policy without these riders. The tax treatment of these refunds is also an issue.

DIFFERENT FORMS OF DISABILITY INSURANCE

There are other sources of disability coverage apart from Social Security disability benefits. You should get workers' compensation if you're injured in the course of your employment or develop an illness because of a hazard you've been exposed to at work. There might also be income loss protection available under your auto policy if you are injured in an accident while operating a motor vehicle.

There are also a number of mail-order disability policies you might have noticed. Although buying insurance through the mail would seem, at first glance, to be an inexpensive way to buy insurance, most of the policies do not measure up to the standards we have set forth previously. They will offer income replacement rather than protecting your ability to work in your own occupation. In addition, a residual disability is unlikely to be covered.

Read any mail-order policies carefully. I have mentioned that a good disability policy is expensive. When a policy is too cheap, it should cause you to question how much protection you are getting. The price is often no bargain when you examine the potential benefits.

You should do your own cost-benefit analysis. Don't just look at the premium and monthly benefit you will receive. One disability policy costs $484 per year for a 50-year-old. The monthly benefit of $1,000 looks significant, but the policy loses its luster when you realize that the benefit will only be paid for 24 months at most. The $484 per year will bring a maximum of $24,000 if you need to use it for the entire two years.

There are a great many policies that resemble disability insurance. In the brochures for these policies, there will be references, subtle or overt, to their role in offsetting a loss of income. For example, the hospital indemnity plans pay a specified amount for the period of time that you are hospitalized. They talk about how the benefit use is unrestricted. The brochure proudly points out that you can use this insurance to offset any income loss you suffer because of the hospitalization.

While that extra income from a hospital indemnity plan might be nice, it is no substitute for a comprehensive disability policy that pays regardless of whether you are hospitalized or not. There are many situations that can result in a disability. Even if it is a situation where you are hospitalized, the disability period could last long after you are released from the hospital. As I have warned on many occasions, don't substitute a number of ill-suited policies for one that serves the exact purpose you need.

MORTGAGE DISABILITY INSURANCE

I have talked before about policies that are just too specific. While you do need a disability policy to cover your loss of income, you don't need one that is specifically tied to your mortgage. Instead, you should be looking for a solid disability policy that will meet all of your financial needs during the length of time you are disabled.

When you evaluate your life insurance needs, you should be concerned with all of the financial obligations that your family will be saddled with in the event of your death, not just a mortgage. Similarly, when you are looking for a policy to replace your monthly income in case you are disabled, your monthly mortgage payment is just one factor to consider in determining how much insurance to buy.

When you look at your monthly expenditures, you'll see you have many more expenses than just a mortgage even though it might be the most significant. Along with your house payment, you still must pay property taxes, school taxes, upkeep, utilities, and a host of other expenses. Having a disability policy that only takes care of the monthly mortgage payment is a start, but it is certainly not enough to cover all of the expenses you have. A comprehensive disability policy that replaces 60 percent of your monthly income is far superior to mortgage disability insurance.

Mortgage disability insurance isn't like mortgage life insurance. The bank won't force you to buy it if you don't have enough equity in your home. In a worst-case scenario, it's you, not the bank, who loses out. Without the ability to meet your mortgage payment, you could risk losing your home. When the house is sold, the bank's interest in your dwelling will be returned. It's incumbent upon you to buy a comprehensive policy that can help you meet all of your financial obligations.

When you're buying a disability policy to protect the income you need to pay a mortgage or other debts, keep in mind what kind of mortgage you have. With a fixed-rate mortgage, you know precisely what your monthly obligation will be. With an adjustable-rate mortgage, the monthly payment might become considerably higher.

HOW TO SAVE MONEY ON DISABILITY INSURANCE

As with any insurance purchase, there are good and bad ways to save money. Even though the disability insurance carrier will place constraints on the amount you can buy, you can do your part by not being overinsured. If you live on far less than what you earn, there is no need to insure the excess. The purpose of this policy is to guard against catastrophe, not to replace every penny you earn.

Consider a Social Security rider. With it, you can insure for a lesser amount than you might have to without it. The rider lets the insurance carrier take the risk of whether you'll qualify for these benefits. The rider guarantees a specified amount, whether that includes Social Security disability income benefits or not. If you don't qualify, this rider kicks in the difference.

You should be shopping around for every policy, no matter how small or how large, because the prices will vary significantly. Be certain to price the same policy with the same options. Never go with a company rated less than A by A.M. Best Company, even if the policy is less expensive. Always compare the exact coverage and riders from company to company.

Elimination period

When you're choosing a disability insurance policy, you can save money through the process of elimination. Selecting the right elimination period can save you a great deal of money when you buy disability insurance. The elimination period is the amount of time you must wait until benefits begin after you become disabled. If you choose a longer waiting period, you will save money on disability insurance.

The elimination period is a lot like the deductible on your car insurance. Your automobile policy costs less when you choose a high deductible. Similarly, stretching the elimination period reduces the premium you will pay for a disability insurance policy.

Elimination periods commonly run from 30 to 180 days. You can even opt for 365 days. You'll pay less for the policy if you're willing to wait longer for benefits to begin. Your choice of the right elimination period will depend on the amount you have saved in your family's emergency fund. Financial planners recommend that you set aside funds in the event of an emergency. If your emergency fund is in place, you should be able to cope with the waiting period until disability benefits begin. Remember too that you are allowed to tap your IRA before age $59^{1/2}$ without penalty if you become disabled.

Utilizing a longer elimination period is compatible with the true purpose of insurance, which is to protect you against a financial catastrophe. Although you might view 30 days without a paycheck as a disaster, it hardly compares with the financial chaos caused by a lengthy disability. The real financial disaster awaits the individual who picks a short elimination period at the expense of long-term benefits. It is far more important to have a benefit period that runs, at a minimum, to the age of 65. You might not get your benefits as quickly, but you can be certain that your checks will be coming throughout the length of your disability.

The money you save by lengthening the elimination period can be used to increase the benefits that will be far more important to you in the long run. If you are disabled for an extended period, or even for life, you'll wish you had opted for a higher monthly benefit as well as disability benefits that last until your wage-earning days are over.

Shoot for the longest elimination period you can handle. You might have a short-term disability policy through work to help you through this time frame. Even though waiting for benefits to begin can cause apprehension, it is far more frightening to think about being disabled for life without the proper coverage to make up for the loss of income.

Keep in mind that disability insurance is long-term protection. Most of us could overcome a cash flow crunch of several months duration, but being unable to work for life would be a blow that few people could overcome.

Beating the high cost of disability insurance

In the near term, a step-rated policy can be a way to save money. Although you will pay later for these savings in the early years, it can help make a disability policy more affordable. If you expect your income to grow significantly over the years, the step-rated policy can be a useful tool. You will pay one premium initially. The premium then rises to its permanent level at a specified age.

You might think you're saving money by purchasing a group association plan or an income replacement plan. These policies, although less expensive, might have the unfavorable clauses we've discussed previously. You'll lose the benefits as soon as you're capable of working in any occupation, not just your own. They might not be noncancellable or guaranteed renewable.

Another way to beat the high cost of disability insurance is to stop buying coverage on a piecemeal basis. Don't buy the waiver-of-premium rider when you purchase life insurance. It will only be effective in very limited circumstances. If you can't work and don't have a monthly income, paying your life insurance premiums will be the least of your problems.

Instead of buying incidental disability coverage in other policies, you should be applying the extra money toward one solid policy containing the features mentioned previously. If that policy is too expensive, lengthen the elimination period. As you grow older, you might reach a point when you no longer need the policy. When you can live comfortably on the income from other sources, you've reached the point when your disability policy has outlived its usefulness.

15

Health insurance

IF YOU WANT TO KNOW THE RISKS OF NOT HAVING GOOD HEALTH INSURANCE, go for the early bird special at any restaurant in South Florida and listen to the conversation at nearby tables. Better yet, sit at the pool at any condo. You'll invariably be a party to a conversation like this one:

"$18,000? That's peanuts! When I had my bypass operation, the bill was $29,000. Every day, four different doctors came in who I never saw before. Each one charged me $50 a visit, and they never did anything but nod their heads up and down."

The "Can You Top This?" discussion goes back and forth for 20 minutes or so then it finally ends with, "So young man, having good health insurance is the most important thing you can do."

I love South Florida, because even I look young to most of the residents. Although they might not be on target in that assessment, they have correctly identified an extremely important area of concern for the family insurance planner. It is vital to guard against the risk of illness through the right health insurance. A catastrophic illness can wipe out the funds you've saved to retire in South Florida, or to live comfortably anywhere else.

The need for comprehensive health insurance is not restricted to the residents of a retirement community. In any area or at any age, your assets can be devastated by a serious illness. Consider the economic damage you'd suffer if you were hospitalized at over $250 per day. When you consider the cost of drugs, medical testing, and other charges during a typical day in the hospital, you might be paying more than $1,000 per day when you're hospitalized. If you're used to staying at a motel for $30 per night, the cost of a hospital stay is probably too rich for your blood.

It's not just the hospital stay that will deplete your family's savings. Transplant surgery could easily generate a hospital bill of over $100,000. Or suppose you need a defibrillator, a device that is implanted and can correct an irregular heartbeat. Each one of these devices costs in the neighborhood of $15,000, not counting the surgery. Worse yet, the defibrillator must be replaced every two years. Even if you could raise the capital for one surgical implant, try raising the cash on a regular basis. Maybe your medical problems will be less expensive, and you'll only require a clot-dissolving drug which runs over $2,000 on each occasion you need it. When you read in Ann Landers' column about hospital bills with $7 charges for aspirin, you'll recognize that good health care coverage is a priority for the family insurance planner.

HEALTH INSURANCE THROUGH YOUR EMPLOYER

For most people, good health insurance starts with their employer. If you're used to getting health insurance through your employer, you might already be getting memo's altering the terms of this important employee benefit. Chances are, your coverage is becoming more expensive. Employers are making a concerted effort to shift more of the cost to you. Because of skyrocketing medical costs, they hope to curtail expenses through a variety of programs.

You can expect your employer to shift part of the financial burden to you. The days of "first dollar coverage" are coming to an end, unless you enroll in an HMO, which I will discuss later in this chapter. With a conventional group-health insurance plan, you can expect to pay higher deductibles. No matter how benevolent your employer is, you can expect to see higher deductibles as a way to off-set the ever-increasing cost of medical care. Some companies have now implemented deductibles based on a fixed percentage of your salary.

You are also going to see more cost-control measures such as mandatory second opinions. Before you are hospitalized in a nonemergency situation or before you undergo surgery, you will be required to have a second physician certify that the treatment is medically necessary. Your employer's plan might require that you discuss the proposed treatment with a medical representative of the insurance company, who will then decide if a second opinion is needed. Having this safety mechanism can prevent needless surgery. There are those experts, however, who offer the persuasive argument that cost rather than the well-being of the patient becomes the overriding issue.

These preadmission approval programs are an attempt by employers to manage the care of their employees and to control costs. Employers are also narrowing the choice of doctors and hospitals you can use as you will see later in this chapter when we discuss preferred provider organizations (PPOs). They are negotiating agreements with groups of doctors and hospitals to provide medical treatment at a lower cost. With HMOs, the medical provider agrees to accept a prepaid fee for a particular service. With PPOs, the provider offers a discount on the services rendered. An employee not using the preferred provider would have to pay a higher portion of the cost. These attempts to control costs are in everyone's best interest, unless the quality of medical care is sacrificed.

In addition to the changes in employer-sponsored health plans, the benefits packages are changing too. Many companies now allow you to tailor your coverage to the specific needs that you have. Some companies have gone with a cafeterialike plan that allows the employee to customize his own benefit package. With cafeteria plans, which resemble cafeterias because they let you select the benefits you want, just as you would food items in a cafeteria, you are given an allotment of flex dollars. You select the type of medical plan you want, or you might decide to allocate those flex dollars to purchase other types of insurance coverage or benefits. You might even be able to take the cash or apply the funds to your 401(k) retirement account.

In essence, you can choose to not be covered by any type of health insurance coverage. The cafeteria plan permits this option, and might be viewed as enticing an employee to forego health insurance in exchange for some other benefit. Even in a more conventional benefit package, the trend toward a higher contribution by employees toward their health care costs might spell danger for many short-term thinkers. Unlike in the past, where employees received health insurance automatically, they are now given a choice of not having any health insurance and the risks of that decision are enormous. Self-insurance is one thing but gambling on staying healthy is a foolish bet.

To control costs, some companies don't offer coverage to an employee's spouse unless the worker is the principal wage earner in the family. As employers' costs rise for providing health insurance, you will see many new methods for curtailing these expenses. Employers want their employees to become more cost-conscious about their use of medical benefits.

Employers and insurance companies promote books such as *Take Care of Yourself: A Consumer's Guide to Medical Care*. Books like this one encourage personal responsibility for maintaining your health. The thrust of the program is to make you think twice before going to the doctor. Visits to the Emergency Room of a local hospital might be avoided. The book suggests that annual physicals might not be necessary. As a tool to achieve better health, and as a way to control medical expenses, a book such as this one serves an important purpose. Controlling medical costs can help all of us.

Perhaps, you know better than to go without health insurance. Instead, you think you can get a better deal by going elsewhere. Even with the trend for employers to pass on more of their costs to employees, you are still likely to get the best health insurance policy for the money from your employer. There are a number of advantages to these group policies. The premium will be much lower, and your employer usually will pay a sizeable portion of the premium. In addition, an experienced negotiator from your company will work to obtain the most favorable terms available.

These group plans are also a better deal because there is no medical screening. They can offer a wider range of benefits, because they cover a larger group of low-risk individuals. Males are generally considered to be a lower risk, if the employees are young and healthy. A company with a predominantly female work force will not be able to get as good a policy for the money, because they're viewed as a higher risk.

The family's insurance planner should take a close look at the medical benefits available through an employer or employers of family members who work. Take a look at how inpatient services are handled. Is a hospital stay covered for 100 percent or will a smaller percentage be paid for by the carrier? You might notice that it pays a lower percentage if you fail to use any of the cost control mechanisms such as a mandatory second opinion or a preadmission certification process.

Another area to consider is how the plan deals with expensive outpatient services such as preadmission testing and emergency care. Make sure you clearly understand the coverage provided for x-rays, radiation, chemotherapy, anesthesia, and prescriptions. Look too at whether chemical dependency and substance abuse programs are covered. The better plans will cover them with certain limitations.

COBRA

The group health insurance benefits offered by your current employer might be the only thing you like about your job. Group health insurance is what keeps many people tied to their employment. Perhaps you've given some thought to opening your own business or are entertaining the notion of retiring early on some beach. You've got it all planned: early retirement, fishing, writing the great American novel, or blissful days with no pinheads getting on your nerves. It all sounds great except for one thing, health insurance.

You might run into a similar dilemma if you're forced to leave your job. The most traumatic part of getting fired could be the realization that you are going to be without health insurance. Even when you're close to retirement age, getting health insurance at a reasonable price can make a significant dent in your savings. Assuming you aren't entitled to an early retirement package that keeps your health insurance in effect until Medicare covers you, you could be in for a rude awakening when you price the cost of a private policy. The price will be steep and it won't be as comprehensive as the one you had with your former employer. Keep in mind that an early-retirement sweetener can leave a sour taste in your mouth, when there's no provision for health insurance at a reasonable price.

Until a plan is devised to provide health insurance for the unemployed, COBRA might come to your rescue. No, it's not a Sylvester Stallone character, but a federal law that can temporarily solve your health insurance problems.

COBRA stands for the Consolidated Omnibus Budget Reconciliation Act of 1985. With a name like that, you can see why it's called COBRA rather than its proper name. COBRA can help ease your transition into a new business, another job, or early retirement.

COBRA allows you to buy health coverage for up to 18 months from the group insurance carrier of your former employer at the same rates you received as an employee. Naturally, you aren't entitled to your employer's contribution, but the insurance should be a lot cheaper than an individual policy. Your employer can add a 2 percent charge to the rate for its administrative expenses. Federal laws are a lot like insurance policies. You can't write them without putting in a great many exceptions. The company you worked for must have 20 or more employees. You also can't utilize the benefits of COBRA if you are fired for gross misconduct. There are also special provisions for spouses of deceased employees who are entitled to the benefits of COBRA for a longer time period, usually 36 months. As you will see below, children who are no longer dependents can also take advantage of COBRA.

COBRA is a temporary solution. You might need a permanent health care insurance solution after you leave your employer. The employer's health insurance policy should allow you to convert the group policy to an individual one. This would be especially important if you were unable to qualify for another medical policy. This conversion privilege should still be available after your COBRA benefit ends.

If you only have to deal with the health insurance issue on a short-term basis while you are between jobs and are not eligible for COBRA, there are insurers that offer a short-term major medical policy. A permanent major medical policy would be preferable if coverage for a long period is needed. It is far better to have a permanent policy if you are in danger of becoming unable to obtain health insurance because of a medical problem.

HEALTH INSURANCE FOR THE HANDICAPPED CHILD

You won't lose your group health insurance policy if you make too many claims, although your employer might run into problems because of them. The only way to lose it is if you don't pay your share of the premiums or if you leave your job. This can be a difficult issue to deal with if you are the parent of a disabled child. Children born with disabilities are automatically covered by their parent's group health insurance policies. Unfortunately, this coverage might not continue forever. It could end at the age of 19 or 22 for full-time students.

Many group health insurance policies do afford coverage indefinitely for the handicapped child. To find out if yours does, look at your employee benefits book under the definition of "dependent." One book defines "dependent" as an unmarried child who is incapable of self-support, physically or mentally handicapped, and fully dependent on you. In reading any legal document, the language is very important. The use of "and" means the dependent must meet all of the above criteria, not just one particular requirement. The coverage for a handicapped child should be discussed with your benefits administrator and with the insurance company that provides the coverage.

A parent in this situation should resolve the health insurance coverage issue before making any job changes. Before accepting a new position, the parent should be absolutely certain that the new employer's carrier will cover the disabled child. Although the family member might be automatically covered, some policies view this as a preexisting condition.

If that is the case, and you must switch positions, you can look to a special risk insurer. There might be policies offered through your state to cover situations such as this one. Check with the insurance department in your state to find out if there are any such plans.

INSURING YOUR OLDER CHILDREN

As the family insurance planner, you must make certain that your nondisabled children are also covered after they no longer meet the definition of "dependent." Some colleges offer health insurance policies, but they might not contain adequate coverage for serious illnesses and could end at the time of graduation. Even if your own health insurance policy has covered them while they were in school, the coverage will end at that time also. There will be situations where your child doesn't go directly from school to a job and will be without health insurance for a short time period.

In this case, a short-term major medical policy might be a solution. Although you can check first with Blue Cross/Blue Shield, there are other companies that offer these short-term health care policies. No matter how healthy your children appear to be, going without insurance is too big a risk to take.

Your children without health insurance might also take advantage of COBRA. If you do buy health insurance through your employer, COBRA might entitle your child to extend coverage at group insurance rates for up to 36 months. While your employer will not contribute to the cost of the coverage, it should be lower in price and more comprehensive than other policies. These are, however, only short-term solutions.

COORDINATING BENEFITS

If more than one family member is employed, pay particular attention to the coordination of benefits clause. The coordination of benefits feature is designed to prevent duplicate benefit payments when more than one family member has medical coverage. A coordination of benefits clause prevents people from profiting from an illness. It is also designed to discourage overinsurance and to avoid duplicate coverage. Georgia, as of this writing, requires carriers to pay their full benefit regardless of other coverage.

The coordination of benefits clause should be considered when you are choosing whether both the husband and wife should maintain health insurance with dependent coverage. As we indicated previously, employees are assuming a greater share of their health insurance costs. Because of this trend, it is no longer safe to assume that both the husband and wife should simply buy a policy and list the spouse as a dependent. Coverage is becoming more and more expensive and is still no guarantee of full coverage.

The coordination of benefits clause works quite simply. The plan covering the employee is primary and will pay the limit of its benefits. The plan covering the dependent is secondary and pays the remaining eligible cost. The language of the coordination of benefits clause varies from company to company, and is becoming more restrictive. At one time, the odds were good that the secondary carrier would pick up the entire balance but won't necessarily be the case in today's environment where medical costs are rising rapidly.

The coordination of benefits issue becomes more complicated when children are involved. If both parents are employed, the issue arises as to which carrier is responsible for the medical bills of a dependent child. Until recently, insurance companies followed a "gender rule" to guarantee uniformity in the handling of these dependent claims. The bills for the children were submitted first to the carrier of the father. That group health insurance policy was considered primary, meaning the bills would first be paid from that source. The gender rule fell out of favor, however, because of the growing divorce rate. Carriers found it difficult to obtain information about the father's health insurance, because the mother generally had custody. The gender rule, which is sometimes called the "male-female rule," also raises questions of sex discrimination.

To avoid these problems, the "birthday rule" was adopted. Under the birthday rule, the parent whose birthday comes first in the year is the primary plan. The plan covering the other parent is secondary and pays the remaining costs to the extent of the coverage. Because the birthday rule was adopted, the claim must be submitted initially to the group insurance carrier of the parent who celebrates a birthday at the earliest date in the year. Therefore, if Mom and Dad each have a separate health policy and Mom's birthday is in March while Dad's is in June, Mom's carrier must process the bill first.

Implementing a birthday rule prevents disagreements between carriers over who is responsible for paying a particular bill. It also prevents side agreements between parents to select the carrier they want to pay a particular bill. I am familiar with a situation where one parent works for a small company and the other parent works for a large company. The parent who is employed by the small company was afraid to send in medical bills thinking that it would adversely affect his job security. He reasoned that the group insurance costs of the smaller company would be affected by his claims whereas the bills would be of little concern to the large company that employs his wife. The birthday rule eliminates decisions of that nature.

EVALUATING YOUR HEALTH INSURANCE

Whether you have coverage through your employer or an individually purchased medical plan, you still must make certain that it adequately meets your needs. There are several important elements to look for in evaluating your medical benefits. The potential financial burden you face is eased by what is called a "stop-loss" clause in the medical plan. In any benefit year, your out-of-pocket expense ends at some particular amount whether that be $500, $1,000, $2,000, or $5,000. A health plan with a low "stop-loss" clause costs you more.

The "stop-loss" clause in the medical plan includes deductibles and any coinsurance payments you must make toward your medical bills. It might not include any extra money you must pay because a doctor's fees are excessive. Your plan should cover at least 80 percent of your medical expenses. You are responsible for the remainder up to the cap set by the "stop-loss" clause.

You should evaluate whether the medical plan has adequate lifetime benefits. Some plans pay an unlimited amount during an individual's lifetime. Others limit the payout to $250,000 or a $1 million maximum. If your plan sets a low figure for lifetime medical benefits, it is wise to consider a "piggyback" medical policy. The policy should have a very high deductible and large maximum payout for each illness. It's a little like the umbrella policy we looked at in Chapter 10, but as an additional layer of protection for medical bills.

Your medical plan should cover basic hospital benefits and outpatient care as well. Many infections must be treated with intravenous antibiotics. You might have to remain in the hospital for the length of the treatment if your policy won't cover home health care visits.

Evaluating health plans is complicated by the diversity of health insurance options that are now available. Traditionally, the only option was a fee-for-service plan, offered by Blue Cross/Blue Shield. With a fee-for-service plan you pay a fixed amount of your health-care expenses before the coverage becomes applicable. This deductible might typically be $150 to $250 for an individual and $500 to $1,000 per family. There will also be a copayment of 20 to 25 percent on all of your medical bills. Finally, there is the "stop-loss" figure I spoke of which stipulates the maximum amount of money you can be out-of-pocket during a calendar year.

Fee-for-service plans don't usually cover routine check-ups and immunizations. There is also the additional problem that arises when charges exceed the usual and customary fee for that service. If a doctor's charge is $100 and most doctors in the area only charge $80, your reimbursement will be based on the lower amount.

Even the fee-for-service plans are becoming more diverse. One unusual plan gives you both a lower deductible *and* a lower premium, in exchange for a higher "stop-loss" figure. If your family has extensive medical bills during a calendar year, this means you would have a larger out-of-pocket loss. This proposal might sound attractive if you are relatively healthy and are unlikely to incur significant medical expense. Your exposure is greater, however, in the event the tide turns and your health takes a turn for the worse.

HMOs

Instead of a conventional reimbursement plan, you might opt for an HMO. A health maintenance organization is a fixed-fee plan or a prepaid health plan. You receive comprehensive medical care for a premium that is paid in advance. All of your medical needs are met, from surgery to emergency care. You might even be entitled to dental, vision care, or physical therapy.

The big selling point for HMOs is that you normally get total health-care coverage with no deductibles and minimal copayments, although there might be some additional charges for hospitalization and certain procedures. Whereas a fee-for-service plan might pay 80 percent of your surgical expenses, the HMO would cover them in full. While your fee-for-service plan would pay 80 percent of the prescriptions you need after the deductible is satisfied, the HMO might charge $2 to $5 for each drug purchased.

All routine care or preventive treatment is included as part of your premium. The premiums you pay for an HMO should be lower or about the same as the more traditional fee-for-service plan. Because of these benefits, belonging to an HMO can mean lower out-of-pocket medical costs.

You might wonder how an HMO can keep these costs so low. The doctor gets a flat fee for each patient enrolled. If the patient stays healthy and requires little service during the year, the doctor has earned a fee for little work. The doctor becomes extremely underpaid, however, when the patient requires constant medical attention during a given year. HMOs appeal mainly to younger people who are usually healthier than their older counterparts.

HMOs also keep their costs down by paying attention to preventive medicine. It's a major selling point and it's why they're called health maintenance organizations. When routine physicals and checkups are permitted at little or no charge, its subscribers are more inclined to utilize these services, which can prevent many long-term complications. Many HMOs also provide cancer screenings, stress reduction classes, programs to help you stop smoking, and other services aimed at keeping patients healthy, which is good business for them in the long run. One HMO offers $175 for a weight loss of 10 pounds or more, and up to $100 reimbursement per year for participation in a fitness program.

Along with these positive steps to control costs, there is some debate as to whether HMOs employ less honorable methods in this area. Some HMOs put pressure on doctors to hospitalize their patients less frequently. A doctor might receive a bonus, if a patient is hospitalized for fewer days. There could be a financial incentive if the doctor avoids sending a patient for expensive tests. The physician might limit costs by not sending a patient to a specialist. Whereas the

popular perception is that doctors overtreat patients, HMOs are often accu
of undertreating in order to keep a lid on expenses. Congress has passed legislation to keep HMOs from using financial rewards to induce physicians to limit
patient care. It should be noted, however, that giving doctors a free reign on
medical treatment and diagnostic testing does not necessarily result in a higher
quality of medical care.

Some HMO critics make the argument that the costs are low because the
service is not particularly good. The physician makes a healthy profit through a
volume of patients. These critics argue that HMO patients wait longer for service and are not treated with the same respect as the patient who has a fee-for-
service insurance plan.

HMOs and freedom of choice

The biggest drawback to HMOs is the lack of choice. With an HMO, you must
choose a "primary care physician" from the list of doctors provided by your carrier. This physician won't necessarily be convenient for you, or the doctor you
would like to treat you. In the best of all worlds, your own personal physician is
one of the group's participating doctors. Unfortunately, this won't normally be
the case. Sometimes, one of the HMO doctors is someone who you'd like to use
but isn't accepting patients at that time.

There are also selected groups of specialists. With a fee-for-service plan,
you could search out the top person in the field, and the plan would pay the fee
up to its usual parameters. If you belong to an HMO, you would have to pay the
fee out of your own pocket.

This lack of choice probably explains why HMOs usually have younger
patients as members. Younger people are less likely to have a family doctor or a
particular specialist who they prefer using. In addition, an area comprised of
more mobile citizens would be more likely to use the services of an HMO,
because they are less tied to specific physicians. These younger members might
also be attracted to the broader maternity benefits usually found in an HMO.
Enrolling in an HMO could lock you into a particular doctor, however.

HMOs versus PPOs

There are two types of HMOs, a group practice plan and an individual practice
plan. A group practice plan provides medical services at a health center that is
staffed by the HMO physicians. These centers are usually equipped with diagnostic equipment, x-ray machines, and laboratory facilities. Complicated procedures are performed at affiliated hospitals. Individual practice plans use
private-practice physicians who receive a fee per patient rather than for each
service they perform. The HMO you select will have a list of physicians who participate in its plan. Some HMOs offer a combination of these two types. You can

either go to the health center or use one of the physicians who participate in their network.

An HMO is not the only health insurance option that is available. A preferred provider organization, or PPO, is a group of doctors in private practice who have agreed to provide medical service at a discount price. The PPO combines certain aspects of the traditional fee-for-service plan and an HMO. It gives you more freedom of choice. When a doctor or hospital is a PPO member, you will generally pay little or none of the cost. When you go to a physician who is not a member of the PPO, you can expect to pay a greater amount.

Insurance companies and corporations are making agreements with PPOs in order to lower health care costs. Companies are developing PPOs that provide prescriptions, vision care, and dental services. PPOs are often a voluntary supplement to health insurance plans.

Both PPOs and HMOs cover your emergency treatment anywhere. They will send you to an outside specialist only if their own physicians are not qualified to handle the problem. You might be a candidate for an HMO or PPO, if you are the type of individual who is reluctant to check out a medical problem because of the anticipated expense. Knowing a visit will be free or of nominal cost might encourage you to have a medical problem looked at before it becomes worse. These organizations might also be useful for the family that is new in the area and really is unaware of physicians that they can use. The life-long resident is less likely to need any assistance in choosing a primary care physician or specialist.

Evaluating an HMO

When evaluating an HMO, there are a number of factors that you should consider. As I mentioned before, your choice of physicians is limited with an HMO. It would be better for someone who is not already attached to certain doctors.

You must also examine the quality of those physicians. Ask how many of the HMO members are board-certified. Board certification means that a doctor has successfully passed an examination in his or her medical specialty. A doctor who is board-eligible has completed required training but hasn't passed the exam as yet. Naturally, if the HMO has a high percentage of board-certified physicians, the quality of medical care is likely to be good.

You should also ask some frank questions to be sure the quality of those physicians isn't undermined by financial incentives. Ask if the doctors get bonuses for avoiding the use of specialists or if a shorter hospital stay results in a better fee for the primary care physician. Ask if the doctor has a financial motive for seeing a patient less often. The economics of practicing medicine could inhibit the proper treatment of the patient.

You should also ask about the turnover rate of its physicians. Little turnover is a good sign. It also can mean that you will develop a rapport with the physicians. They can become familiar with your medical history. It means you won't be dealing with a new doctor each visit, and you can develop a level of trust in the physician's ability. You might find Dr. Welby, but he could be gone the next year. Worse yet, you might not get to see Dr. Welby when you participate in an HMO. Medical aides might handle routine matters rather than a physician.

Consider the financial stability of the HMO. Look for an HMO with a positive operating margin over a number of years. Request copies of its financial statements. Some HMOs are owned by large corporations, which is a good sign that the HMO is financially stable, but it doesn't guarantee that the parent company won't sell off the HMO after a few years. Your employer should allow you to change your enrollment if the HMO goes out of business.

The member retention rate is also an important factor to consider. There is usually a reason why an HMO loses members. You might have to wait too long for an appointment. The members might not be impressed with the attending physicians or the quality of the care provided. The HMO retention rate should be at least 85 percent unless there are special circumstances, such as a large employer moved its facility, taking many of the HMO members with it.

Before signing up with an HMO, investigate its quality by speaking with members and former members. Their experiences will tell you a great deal about whether you'll be satisfied with it. You must look too at the quality of the hospitals that are associated with the HMO. If you've lived in an area for any length of time, you should be familiar with the reputations of the hospitals in the vicinity.

You should also evaluate an HMO by looking at the treatment it covers. It will probably cover routine doctor visits, prescription drugs, physical examinations, inpatient hospital treatment, obstetrics, home health care, radiation and chemotherapy, gynecological treatment, pediatric care, vaccinations, and a full range of medical treatment. There should be provisions made for eye care, hearing problems, and dental treatment. Find out if any copayments are required.

Make sure that you won't have problems when you need medical treatment outside your target area. If you are traveling in another state, find out how emergency treatment is provided for by an HMO. It should cover that treatment in full, except for a small copayment, as long as the medical care is of an emergency nature. In fact, it should cover medical emergencies anywhere in the world. There will be restrictions on non-life-threatening situations. See how emergencies in your local area are handled. Are there provisions for after-hours care?

Just as with a fee-for-service plan, there is treatment an HMO won't cover. Cosmetic surgery, foot care, and treatment of TMJ Syndrome are a few of the exclusions found in several HMO plans. Mental health care might also be limited depending on which plan you have.

LOSS PREVENTION

As you have just learned, HMOs stress the concept of preventive medicine. As the insurance planner for your family, you are charged with the responsibility for loss prevention and risk avoidance along with your obligation to buy the right health insurance. You should be taking steps to reduce your family's health risks. Your family should be engaged in health and wellness activities. Many employers are initiating similar programs as a way to control employee health costs.

As a starting point, here are some steps your family can take to reduce the risk of health-related problems occurring:

- Exercise-fitness programs
- Avoid overexposure the the sun
- Stress reduction exercises
- Weight control
- Proper nutrition and eating habits
- Periodic physical exams for all family members. Medical testing including blood pressure and Pap smears.
- Limit alcohol consumption
- Adequate sleep
- Avoid drug use
- Make the homeplace safer by taking steps to avoid accidents.

While life-style management can only go so far, and you don't want to become obsessed with loss prevention, you can encourage your family to use more discipline in these areas. Just as HMOs offer incentives for members to stop smoking, you can reward yourself and other family members who break the habit. Set the right example by swearing off some of your particularly dangerous vices. Naturally, you're well-aware that nonsmokers are less likely to experience a medical problem. In addition to the indirect effect this will have on your health insurance costs in the future, it will have a direct impact on the price you'll pay for some insurance policies.

If you don't take steps to minimize health risks, your employer might take them for you as part of the ongoing effort to control costs. A growing number of employers are bringing in a nurse to educate women about the risks of doing harm to an unborn child by improper eating habits, drinking, drug use, or smoking. Prenatal care can help an employer control costs. As part of their effort, many employers have created nonsmoking environments. An on-site fitness center also represents an attempt by an employer to reduce health-related risks and control its medical expenses.

COST CONTAINMENT EFFORTS

While you and your employer are working to control health care costs, others will be taking similar measures. Curtailing these medical costs is in the best interest of all consumers. In some states, insurance companies are required to implement these cost control mechanisms. Florida has enacted legislation that obligates a carrier to try to control medical costs.

The Florida law states that no health insurance policy or health services plan can be issued without at least one cost containment provision. The law mentions coinsurance, deductibles, second opinions, bill audits, scheduled benefits, benefits for preadmission testing, and utilization review as possible cost containment provisions. Utilization review is a process in which a nurse, or some other health professional, evaluates the proposed treatment to determine if the surgery or hospitalization is necessary.

That same law also mandates that every health insurance policy delivered in the state of Florida have a coordination of benefits clause. The statute also requires that every health insurance policy use the birthday rule in determining how the benefits are coordinated. It also spells out how to handle health insurance claims where one of the policies is from a state where the birthday rule isn't followed.

WHEN BENEFITS ARE DENIED

The wrong time to learn you have inadequate health insurance is when you submit a claim. You've spent several hours filling out the claim form, and still you get back a denial of benefits that you can't understand. According to humor writer Dave Barry, medical insurance claim forms are designed by mildly retarded cocker spaniels. After several hours spent in completing one, you might agree with his assessment.

I've already discussed some reasons why medical claims are denied. You might not have satisfied the deductible. Perhaps, you sent the form to the wrong carrier and did not comply with the coordination of benefits clause in the insurance contract. More than likely, your claim will be denied because you didn't complete the form correctly. It might be a situation where your physician didn't provide all of the necessary information. These are legitimate reasons for denying a claim, some of which can be corrected.

Medical necessity of treatment

There are other circumstances that give a carrier a legitimate reason to deny your claim, although you can argue the point with them. Almost all health insurance policies have a clause that lets the insurer deny payment if the treatment was not medically necessary. A health insurance policy does not pay for cosmetic surgery, because it isn't medically necessary. A man who needs plastic surgery on his nose could argue that it is medically necessary to correct a deviated septum. Similarly, a breast reduction operation might be challenged as not being medically necessary. A woman could get around a medical necessity denial by showing medical proof that she is experiencing back problems and needs the surgery.

The second opinion requirement in many health insurance policies should prevent the insurance company from invoking the medical-necessity clause. Usually, insurance companies require the second opinion on any elective procedure. If the surgery doesn't require a second opinion, make certain you have evidence that the treatment is needed.

On more and more occasions, insurers are questioning whether medical tests are necessary. The insurance carriers have developed computer programs that monitor whether a lab test or x-ray is necessary in a particular medical situation. The carrier's position is that the tests might not be necessary to diagnose the medical problem or to improve the ailment. An example is x-rays that are taken as a matter of course and don't help in the patient's recovery.

Unfortunately, an insurer's unwillingness to pay for a test will hurt you, not your doctor. When the insurance company finds it is not medically necessary, the physician or hospital could still come to you for payment. Many lab tests are high-profit items for the doctor and can be a significant source of income. Physicians, on the other hand, would argue these tests are medically necessary and they are in danger of malpractice suits if they fail to order them. Later in this chapter, you'll see how to challenge the insurance company that claims your treatment was not medically necessary.

Reasonable and customary charges

Just as a claim can be denied because the treatment was not necessary, a policy might only pay a portion of the services if the charges are excessive. A health insurance policy will only pay the reasonable and customary charge for service rendered by a doctor or hospital. It might be referred to as the usual and customary fee. Insurance companies determine this dollar amount by comparing the usual fees charged by medical providers in the community for the same services. Using this data, they come up with a fee schedule showing the maximum allowance for a given procedure. A dentist might only be allowed $40 for a cleaning and examination based on the typical charges of other dental practitioners in the area.

The percentage paid by your policy will be based on the reasonable and customary amount, not the total amount charged. If your carrier only pays 80 percent of the usual and customary charge, you would get 80 percent of the $40, not the actual amount your dentist charged. When a fee is said to be unreasonably high, your doctor can present additional documentation to show that the procedure was more complicated than the standard one. The physician could also agree to accept a lower fee, but don't bet on it.

Preexisting conditions

The preexisting condition clause can lead to a rejection of your claim, not just a disallowance of part of your bill. The company can deny payment for a medical condition that predates your policy. We saw this problem earlier in the chapter when we discussed problems you face when you change carriers and are the parent of a handicapped child.

You might run into a problem if you buy a health insurance policy, and soon thereafter are diagnosed with a disease. The insurance company might argue that this was a preexisting condition and should not be covered by the policy. Most plans have a time limit after which preexisting conditions are covered without challenge. It's a little like the incontestability clause in a life insurance policy.

The so-called incontestability clause in a health insurance policy might not keep your claim from being denied. In many of these plans, an illness is not covered if you have received any treatment for it during the preceding 12 months. After the effective date of the coverage, you must go 12 consecutive months without treating the problem. Until that time, the illness is treated as a preexisting condition.

When you change health care policies, preexisting conditions can jeopardize your coverage under the new plan. There will be occasions, however, where you can still file a claim against your old policy. Potentially, you could submit the bills to the prior carrier, even though the charges are incurred after the coverage ends. There has been considerable litigation on the issue of health care coverage after an individual has left the health plan. Suppose a pregnant woman loses her health care coverage after her husband's employment is terminated. When she enters the hospital and incurs thousands of dollars in medical expenses, many jurisdictions would find that she has no health insurance coverage.

In some jurisdictions, however, the pregnant woman could argue successfully that her entitlement to medical benefits is vested. In other words, the event that triggered the medical expenses occurred while the coverage was in effect. It would be similar to a situation where someone is diagnosed with cancer and begins treatment. If the medical coverage ends, these later expenses should also be covered. The entitlement vests prior to the contract's end.

Despite the logic to that argument, the courts have not always been persuaded to extend coverage to those medical conditions that began during the policy term. In those cases where they ruled that coverage should be afforded, it has been on the theory that the contract language was ambiguous and the person needing medical treatment reasonably expected the coverage to continue. Other decisions extending coverage rely on the theory that public policy demands this result.

Any decisions to the contrary reason that it is the medical expenses that trigger coverage, not the injury, illness, or medical condition. If a policy clearly spells out that the coverage ends at a given time, the carrier should not be required to pay for medical expenses incurred after the policy has ended. The public's interest is not harmed by terminating coverage if notice of that benefit modification has clearly been given to the insured.

With COBRA, it would be unusual for these situations to arise. If you are suffering from a medical problem that requires treatment, you would never allow your medical coverage to lapse. When your health insurance is through your employer, you can in many cases continue that coverage by virtue of COBRA. Anyone with a continuing medical problem would obviously pay to remain covered under that policy.

There are unfair situations, however, that can arise under COBRA. You lose the continued coverage under COBRA when you become eligible for a new health plan. The new plan's preexisting conditions limitation, however, might pose a problem. In effect, you would not be covered under either the old plan or the new one. This Catch-22 situation will undoubtedly be corrected.

Any person changing jobs should be aware of these potentially dangerous situations, just as I suggested with the parent of a disabled child who is changing positions. Sometimes it's better to be double covered during this time rather than find yourself with no coverage at all. Make certain you consider these extra costs when deciding whether to accept a new position. You should also consider converting the previous group policy to a private one until you make certain that any preexisting conditions are being covered under the new plan. You can always cancel it later if it's not needed.

Be sure to get something in writing from the new carrier. Deal with the new carrier openly rather than concealing the condition. Don't wait for a denial of the claim before addressing the issue directly. Remember, lying on an application isn't a way around the preexisting condition clause. Instead, it can be used as a basis for denying benefits.

INFERTILITY TREATMENT

Infertility can sometimes lead to two health insurance problems. In Pittsburgh, quintuplets were born to a couple that resorted to fertility drugs after not being able to have children. Sadly, two of the quintuplets died. The babies had been critically ill for a lengthy period after the premature birth, and the medical costs were over $1 million and climbing.

This situation raises two issues. It demonstrates the need for a health insurance policy that pays an unlimited or extraordinarily high amount of lifetime benefits. While this would be a very unusual situation, there are more probable events that can test the adequacy of your medical coverage.

It also raises the issue of whether health insurance pays for infertility treatment. Coverage for infertility treatment is nonexistent in some policies. In others, only limited procedures are covered. Many insurance companies refuse to pay for in vitro fertilization, but for a number of different reasons. The carriers use some of the reasons we have just discussed. Some argue that in vitro fertilization is experimental and is not covered. Others argue that the treatment is elective and not medically necessary. Because of the expense of this treatment, carriers will argue that the fees are well beyond the reasonable and customary charges and should not be paid.

Once again, you can supply medical documentation to show the treatment is medically necessary. Treatment for endometriosis would be covered, even though it might also help in a couple's effort to have children. In the 1990s, your state might require that there be coverage in health insurance policies for infertility treatment. Eight states have already acted in this area and others will surely follow.

DON'T TAKE NO FOR AN ANSWER

As I indicated before, and will discuss at length in the last two chapters, don't take your denial letter at face value. Go up the chain of command. Your insurance company might not understand its own rules. Get a supervisor to review the matter if you have the slightest doubt about whether you were properly denied. Read your employee benefits book and see for yourself if the proper decision was made. Believe me, it's a lot easier to read than most insurance policies. If you have an individual policy, read it carefully and make sure that denial is explained more thoroughly than the typical one-line claim form explanation.

If it's a problem with your employer's group insurance carrier, you have certain rights under ERISA, the Employee Retirement Income Security Act. Because of ERISA, the plan administrator must tell you how to submit an appeal if your claim is denied. Some courts have held that workers who are dissatisfied with decisions made by their group health insurance plan, can only sue under ERISA. Under ERISA, you can only recover the benefits in question and your legal expenses. In some jurisdictions, ERISA preempts any action under state law for a bad faith handling of your claim. You will see in Chapter 22 how a wrongful denial of a claim can result in the award of punitive damages. If the health insurance policy is from someone other than your employer, the bad faith remedy would still be available.

There are companies that will handle your medical insurance claim for you. Mediform of Cleveland, Ohio, offers a number of services for people who are having difficulty with their medical bills. For a fee, they will file the appropriate forms, analyze your coverage, and follow up with the insurance company if a legitimate claim has been denied. Medicoll Inc., of Miami, Florida, handles claims for a set fee and a percentage of the recovery. Services such as these are popping up across the country.

"DREAD DISEASE" HEALTH INSURANCE

When medical shows used to be popular on television, critics would jokingly refer to their plots as the disease of the week. The plot of each new show would revolve around a patient with some exotic disease. Dr. Gannon or Dr. Welby would manage to cure the patient within the hour.

Although those diseases made for a successful television show, it's no way to buy insurance. Nevertheless, some insurance companies make a fortune selling "dread disease" insurance. The policy pays off when you suffer from one of the covered diseases. As is the case with so many insurance sales pitches, they play upon your fear of contracting that disease. If you do, these policies pay a stipulated amount, which normally is only a small percentage of your actual medical costs.

These "dread disease" health insurance policies are a bad deal for several reasons. First of all, they only pay you when you experience the precise medical problem defined by the policy. We have stressed time and time again that narrowly-defined coverage is not the right insurance to buy. Although these policies boast that they only cost pennies per day, it's still too much money for the small amount of protection they provide. You're still paying too much for too little coverage.

It's also a bad idea because there are so many horrible diseases out there that you can get. You're only in luck, so to speak, when you happen to get the particular disease covered by the policy. These "dread disease" policies are no substitute for comprehensive health insurance that pays for every medical problem, not just the one that you bought because you got a brochure in the mail.

"Dread disease" health insurance is of little use, even on those rare occasions when it does pay. Because of inflation, the fixed benefit will pay less and less of your actual medical costs as time goes by. What's more, these limited benefits are far less than the cost of hospitalization. There might also be a restriction on collecting that requires hospitalization, rather than medical treatment alone. Finally, you have a narrow range of coverage to begin with, and the actual definition of the dreaded disease is likely to be narrower yet.

Cancer policies are the worst of the lot. They prey upon your worst fears. After exploiting that fear, the insurance company then attempts to show you how this inexpensive policy can eliminate the financial risks. When you hear these promises, however, your first thought should be that you want comprehensive health care coverage, not a policy that only pays for one particular illness. The low price should also warn you that there are few situations in which benefits will be paid. Remember, "dread disease" policies have strict definitions of what constitutes cancer. Health problems brought on by cancer won't necessarily entitle you to benefits. Some states won't permit the sale of these "dread disease" policies because of their drawbacks. Currently, however, there is no federal law prohibiting their sale.

HOSPITAL INDEMNITY PLANS

Hospital indemnity plans are also inexpensive. For a small amount, you might get specified benefits for each day you are hospitalized. One hospital income plan costs $24.40 per month for a family and pays you $60 per day up to a maximum of $24,000 when you are hospitalized for illness or injury. Your spouse and children get lesser amounts per day. The maximum is higher for cancer confinement, and you get a higher amount per day when you're in intensive care.

There are several things wrong with these plans. First, they are no substitute for a health plan that pays a large portion of your hospital costs. Obviously, based on the figures we discussed earlier in the chapter, $60 won't go very far in paying your daily hospital charges. Second, there are strict rules about preexisting conditions. In this particular plan, you have to wait 12 months to avoid a challenge for preexisting conditions. Finally, someone over age 65 isn't covered until the eighth day of confinement for certain illnesses. Because most hospital confinements are under seven days, no benefits would be payable for that group. Individuals under age 65 aren't faced with the seven-day waiting period. Consider, too, that many surgical procedures are being performed on an outpatient basis. Operations from hernia repair to cataract removal are performed without any hospitalization.

You might want to look at your medical history to decide if a policy like this one is necessary. A serious medical problem might run in your family. Perhaps, you expect back problems at some point in your future that could require surgery. If you are quite active or do manual labor as part of your job, these policies might make more sense. If family members are engaged in more dangerous activities such as skiing or riding motorcycles, you are more likely to use the benefits found in a policy such as this one.

There are some advantages to these plans. The benefits can be used for any purpose whatsoever. In some respects, these policies are similar to a medigap policy. You can use the benefits to plug the gaps in your existing medical coverage. A hospital admission can generate additional expenses. You might have a high deductible on your regular plan. You might be responsible for expenses that exceed the reasonable and customary charges that your primary carrier pays. There could be prescription drugs and private-duty nurses to pay for with little assistance from your health insurance plan. While these policies can be a satisfactory supplement, they are no replacement for a comprehensive medical policy. You might also run into indirect expenses caused by a hospital admission such as child care.

Because of these major expenses, your family might be in dire need of a cash payment for each day of your hospital stay. Because the benefit use is unrestricted, you can decide the manner in which to spend it. There is no coordination of benefits, and it is irrelevant if you are receiving other medical benefits. Because you pay the premium for this policy yourself, the benefits are tax-free under current tax law.

Even though this money might come in handy during a time of need, these policies should be avoided. You would be wiser to put the money toward a better health insurance policy. The incidental expenses you pay when hospitalized are losses to shoulder yourself. These small payments were not meant to be covered by insurance. It is the risk of incurring catastrophic expenses that should motivate you to buy insurance.

GROUP ACCIDENT PLANS

You might be getting solicitations in the mail for group accident insurance plans. Your local motor club, or some other group to which you belong, might be the sponsor of the insurance. For $29 per family member that one plan charges, the insurance company will pay a specified amount for medical treatment needed because of an accident.

As examples, the policy pays 100 percent of emergency room charges, doctors fees, x-rays, casts, and splints. This doesn't sound bad until you hear the maximum payments. The ceiling on emergency room visits is $100. You'll get $20 on doctor's visits, $50 on x-rays and $50 on splints.

At those reimbursement levels, you'd better have another medical plan. I don't know if your doctor still charges $20 per visit, but mine doesn't. Remember the additional stipulation before you'll get paid on this policy. The medical treatment must be the result of an accident, not sickness.

Let's look at the return on your investment of $29 if you happen to need medical treatment because of an accident. You'll get $100 if you go to the emergency room for accident-related treatment. This is hardly a favorable return on your investment, if you've held the policy for longer than three years. If you're like most people, you probably haven't had an accident requiring treatment since you broke your arm in the fifth grade.

MAIL-ORDER HEALTH INSURANCE

The "dread disease" policies, hospital indemnity, and group accident plans are typical of the mail-order health insurance proposals you will receive. While there are reputable companies that market policies through the mail, you really don't need these health insurance plans. You will end up spending more money on insurance for very little extra coverage.

Mail-order policies are no substitute for a comprehensive health plan that pays substantial benefits for treatment caused by any illness or accident. You need a policy that pays on the basis of services, not cash indemnity on a daily basis. The cash indemnity plans give you pin money, but you're far better off with a policy that pays a large percentage of the services rendered.

If you do decide to buy a mail-order policy, make sure the health insurance policy is guaranteed renewable. At the time of renewal, you might not be healthy enough to buy another policy. You also run into the preexisting condition problem when you change policies. In the health insurance context, preexisting conditions will be covered after a certain period of time. A good policy will not challenge these preexisting conditions if six months go by without treating them. It's the health insurance version of the incontestability clause that you saw with the life insurance. Make sure it pays for every hospitaliztion, not just those triggered by an accident. It should pay for illnesses *and* accidents.

Look at the daily rate of reimbursement, not just the grand total you could recover in the worst-case scenario. This grand total will usually be highlighted in bold print on the cover of the brochure. You are likely to collect a much smaller amount. You would have to be hospitalized for years to collect the total amount at the daily rate, which is often very low. Check to see if there is a long waiting period before benefits begin. In mail-order policies, it is usually longer.

Finally, make sure the quoted rate is not just an introductory one. Only deal with companies you trust and with companies licensed in your state to sell that policy.

HEALTH COVERAGES IN OTHER POLICIES

When you suffer health-related problems, don't forget the coverages available in your other policies. If you or a family member is injured in an auto accident, there might be medical benefits available in that policy. Medical payments are also available under the homeowners policy. Although it won't cover your family, you can avail yourself of similar coverages if you are injured on someone else's property. Remember, too, you are entitled to medical coverage through workers' compensation if you are injured in a job-related accident.

SAVING MONEY ON HEALTH INSURANCE

Obviously, our friends at the pool in South Florida are right. Good health insurance is a priority in a society with skyrocketing medical costs. Even if your employer is picking up most of the tab, it will not be inexpensive and the costs can only be expected to rise in the 1990s.

When you have to buy a private health insurance policy, and your employer's not there to help negotiate the price and pay part of the premium, you are going to be shocked by the cost. Depending on the company and the coverage you choose, it's going to cost you anywhere from $3,000 to $10,000 per year. As you might expect from the wide range of prices, it's going to pay for you to shop around.

As I stressed before, start your shopping trip with a list of needs. Know exactly what you want and need. Don't let an insurance salesperson talk you into frills that don't necessarily improve the policy. Make sure you buy a guaranteed renewable policy, an indispensable item on any health insurance policy written on an individual basis. It should be renewable as long as you pay the premium.

As we've seen so often, a deductible can bring down the price significantly. Expect a deductible of $300 to $500, and plan on a higher one if you can afford it. Make certain, however, that you can afford that high deductible on more than one occasion. If more than one family member is hospitalized during a given year, you could find yourself strapped. The solution to this problem would be an out-of-pocket limit for the year. You might be able to take advantage of a carry-over deductible found in some policies. Bills incurred in the last three months of a calendar year can be applied to the next calendar year's deductible.

Don't forget that you might also belong to an organization that offers group health insurance programs to its members. Professional, social, and fraternal organizations that you belong to might offer a health insurance plan. Call or write some of those organizations to see what they have in the way of insurance programs. Compare prices and coverage among the various plans. No one will pay a portion of the premium but the group rate will be less expensive.

A good way to save money is to avoid all of those enticing mail-order policies that come your way. Although they are relatively inexpensive, they offer little protection. In particular, stay away from "dread disease" policies. You can also avoid any expensive riders that the carrier wants to attach to your policy. You need medical coverage, not accidental death riders and other endorsements. These riders do not increase the quality of the health care coverage—only the cost.

If you need an individual health insurance policy, you'll find that saving isn't your only problem. You might have difficulty finding a company to insure your family if one of you suffers from a medical problem. In that situation, you should look to your local Blue Cross/Blue Shield when it has an open enrollment period. You might also check with your state's insurance department to see if there is a risk-sharing pool that offers health insurance policies to people in your predicament.

In the 1990s, there is a danger that health insurance costs will continue to escalate rapidly despite the massive cost-containment efforts that are taking place. Some insurers are no longer offering individual health insurance policies, which will drive up the premiums even further than they are now. There will be many who call for national health insurance as one answer to the dilemma. If affordable health insurance can't be offered in any other way, there is no doubt that a legislative solution will be attempted.

16

Medicare

YOU'VE PROBABLY HEARD MORE THAN YOU CAN STAND ABOUT THE CHANGES in Medicare. Just when you thought you understood some of the changes, Congress turned around and repealed the law that caused all of the confusion in the first place. Hopefully, the information in this chapter won't change by the time you're reading it.

Congress had good intentions when it tinkered with Medicare. It had hoped to protect older Americans from the financial devastation caused by sudden illness or injury. Congress realized that ongoing treatment with prescription drugs can be enormously expensive and our legislators wanted to expand Medicare's coverage in that area.

The Medicare Catastrophic Coverage Act was signed into law by former president Reagan on July 1, 1988. On December 13, 1989, the law was repealed. With the repeal of the law, Medicare coverage returned to the way it was before the act was passed.

To help ease the confusion over Medicare coverage, let's start by looking at some things that haven't changed over the past few years. Medicare is still a federal health insurance program that is primarily for people who are 65 and older. Some disabled individuals under the age of 65 also qualify for Medicare benefits.

In addition, Medicare still consists of two parts. As before, Part A pays for hospital expenses. Part B pays for physician charges and other medical services. Medicare will base its payment on what it views as allowable charges. This is the dollar amount of the bill that Medicare feels is reasonable for a particular medical service. It is similar to the "reasonable and customary" standard used by health insurance carriers.

Though the amounts have changed, the Medicare beneficiary still has to deal with deductibles and coinsurance. Coinsurance or a copayment is the portion of the medical bill that the patient must pay. Though some of the language is still the same, the current Medicare law is far different than the coverage provided by the 1988 Act that was later repealed.

PART A BENEFITS

For the immediate future, Medicare will cover far less than it would have, if the 1988 law had remained on the books. The 1988 law had removed the limit on the number of hospital days that Medicare pays for in a year. For that reason and others, the law was viewed as providing catastrophic coverage to Medicare beneficiaries. The current Medicare law is far more limited.

In 1990, Medicare will pay all allowable charges for the first 60 days of inpatient hospital care after a $592 deductible is met. If you are hospitalized for 61 to 90 days, you must pay $148 per day after the 60th day. If you must be hospitalized for longer than 90 days, there are 60 reserve days that you can draw upon in your lifetime. Unfortunately, you must pay $296 for each reserve day used.

Obviously, a patient who is hospitalized for a lengthy period could incur major expenses. There is no limit on your out-of-pocket expenses as there was with the 1988 law. Furthermore, the $592 deductible can be charged on separate admissions in all four quarters of the year. In theory, a patient hospitalized in each quarter would owe $2,368.

Medicare is also not the answer if you need long-term care in a skilled nursing facility. Part A will only pay for 100 days. After the 20th day, the Medicare beneficiary must pay $74 per day.

Under the current Medicare law, hospice care is covered for 210 days. There is no coverage, however, for custodial care in a nursing home. In Chapter 17, you will see the importance of long-term care insurance to cover problems of this nature.

PART B BENEFITS

The coverage for doctor bills and other medical services is found in Part B. Under Part B, Medicare pays for medical care that is both "covered" and "approved." The covered services include physician charges, ambulance fees, diagnostic tests, outpatient treatment, and home health care. Certain medical care is not covered, such as routine medical exams, eyeglasses, hearing aids, and most dental work.

After a $75 deductible is satisfied, Medicare will pay 80 percent of the approved charges. In other words, if your physician charges $125 for a medical service and Medicare only feels that $100 is reasonable, it will only pay $80 or 80 percent of the allowable charge.

The Medicare beneficiary must pay the remaining 20 percent of the allowable charges, along with any charges in excess of the amount approved by Medicare. A physician, however, might agree to accept the amount paid by Medicare as full payment. With Part B benefits, there is also a premium that must be paid which is usually deducted from the person's Social Security check.

MEDICARE INCOME TAX SURCHARGE

The controversy over the Medicare Catastrophic Coverage Act of 1988 wasn't sparked by the expanded benefits provided by that bill. Many citizens were outraged by the income tax surcharge contained in the law to pay for the additional benefits. Had the law not been overturned, Medicare beneficiaries would have paid as much as $1,700 per couple in 1990. The maximum surcharge for an individual would have been $850 in 1990.

When this chapter was drafted for the first time, I was doubtful that the surcharge would remain intact throughout the 1990s. While I expected the tax to be reduced or eliminated, I never thought the catastrophic benefits would be thrown out too. Because the Act has been repealed, Medicare supplemental coverage is worth considering.

MEDIGAP POLICIES

Because Medicare will now provide less benefits, medigap policies take on greater importance. Medigap is the nickname for health insurance supplements designed to plug the gaps in Medicare. Many experts had felt these policies would be superfluous under the Medicare Catastrophic Coverage Act of 1988 but with the more limited Medicare law that is now in effect, medigap policies take on greater importance.

In theory, a family can self-insure against the costs not covered by Medicare. Unfortunately, an illness or accident can generate considerable out-of-pocket expenses. For the Medicare beneficiary who is on a fixed income, these expenses could be devastating. The price of protection, however, is not cheap. It is expected that medigap policies will range in price from $700 to $1,500 so a healthy Medicare recipient should at least consider the self-insurance option.

In deciding whether self-insurance is a viable option, look at the collection policies of the doctors you use on a regular basis. Many physicians agree to accept assignment of Medicare benefits. This means the doctor or medical provider will accept the payment from Medicare and not bill you for the remainder. If the physicians you use accept Medicare assignment, a medigap policy is not as crucial and self-insurance is an option to consider.

Some people won't need a Medicare supplement. If you are eligible for Medicaid, a medigap policy is unnecessary. Medicaid is an assistance program for low-income people. Even if you are ineligible for Medicaid, your former employer might provide additional medical coverage to supplement Medicare. Check to see whether that former employer subsidizes your health care costs in any way.

To decide if you need a medigap policy, it helps to look at the additional coverage you'll get when you purchase one. The insurance regulators in your state will establish the minimum standards for the medigap policies that are offered. In its interim Medicare supplemental insurance guide, the medigap requirements for New York State are outlined. By looking at some of the benefits required in that state, you can determine whether a medigap policy is right for the members of your family on Medicare.

A medigap policy can't just cover a portion of the Part A deductible of $592. It must cover all or none of the deductible. If an insurer offers a policy that covers none of that Part A deductible, it must also offer one that covers the entire deductible.

At a minimum, the medigap policy in New York must cover the copayments required for hospital care on days 61 through 90. It must cover the copayment owed when a Medicare beneficiary uses the lifetime reserve days. After the reserve days are exhausted, the medigap policy must cover 100 percent of the eligible Part A expenses. The lifetime maximum, however, is 365 days.

Because a Medicare beneficiary can be on the hook for 20 percent or more on Part B expenses, New York requires that the medigap policy cover the allowable amount that remains. When you are shopping for medigap policies, you will find coverage that goes beyond that minimum standard. Some medigap policies pay doctor bills in full, even when they're higher than the fees allowed by Medicare. Most Medicare supplements, nonetheless, only pay the difference between what Medicare permits and the approved charge. The amount approved by Medicare is based on the type of illness and the treatment rendered.

In addition to these limitations, Medicare won't cover medical treatment in many foreign countries. A Medicare supplement will sometimes pay for these expenses. If you don't buy one that does, you will need to purchase a travel insurance policy that pays for medical treatment needed while on your trip. The medigap policy would cover those expenses and others. It is a far more valuable policy to have than travel insurance, since it lasts all year long and not just for the duration of your trip.

If you opt for a medigap policy, don't get carried away and buy more than one. Even if the price were not so steep, you would be duplicating coverage. Medigap policies are designed to cover those areas that Medicare doesn't. When you buy more than one, you're buying several policies that were drafted to afford the same coverage and they will invariably overlap.

It is against the law to sell a medigap policy to someone who already has a medicare supplement in force. The policy can only be sold to that individual if the Medicare supplement will replace one that the person already owns. Despite this restriction, there will always be unscrupulous agents who won't abide by the law. Their goal is to sell you the medigap policy that pays them the best commission, not the one that's right for you.

Hospital indemnity policies are sometimes touted as a way to supplement Medicare. Unlike a true medigap policy, this coverage will only become useful when you are hospitalized for an extended period. Because it is not specifically written to plug the coverage gaps in Medicare, the hospital indemnity policy is not nearly as useful. You would be better off with one comprehensive medigap policy.

The same advice applies to "dread disease" policies. Instead of wasting money on them, you should be sticking with one Medicare supplement that pays for medical treatment of any kind and not just one disease.

Because the cost of medigap policies is expected to increase, you should give some thought to joining an HMO instead of buying a Medicare supplemental policy. You would pay an additional fee to the HMO, along with the payment it gets from Medicare. Your hospital and medical costs would be covered, subject to the same limitations that you saw in Chapter 15. Belonging to an HMO might also reduce your prescription drug costs. The current Medicare law will only pay for prescription drugs when they are administered in a hospital or in limited situations following an organ transplant.

HOW TO FIND THE RIGHT MEDIGAP POLICY

In order to find the right medigap policy, you have to follow the advice given for virtually every other insurance product—you have to shop around to find out which company offers the coverage you need for the right price.

As you shop around for the best medigap policy, ask for an outline of the coverage provided by the policy. It should be in language that is easy to understand. The seller of the a medigap policy should also supply you with a guide that explains Medicare benefits.

It is helpful to find out the loss ratio of the medigap policy you're considering. A loss ratio compares the amount a company pays out in claims to the premium collected. A low loss ratio means the company is not paying out much in claims compared to the premium it is charging customers. The medigap carrier should be spending at least sixty cents in benefits for each dollar in premium it receives. Spending seventy cents in benefits out of each dollar taken in is a 70 percent loss ratio. Prudential, for example, had an 83 percent loss ratio on its medigap policies in 1987, which is exceptionally good.

Your state insurance department can make certain that a Medicare supplement meets the 60 percent target. It can adjust the rate filings of medigap insurers to make sure that the carriers hit the 60 percent loss ratio. Medigap policies have also drawn the attention of Congress. Legislation has been introduced that would require a minimum loss ratio of 70 percent on individual medigap policies. If passed, the legislation would require state insurance commissioners to follow a specified procedure before approving rate increases.

When you review a medigap policy, determine if it has been approved by the insurance regulators in your state. When it has been approved, you can be sure that it meets certain minimum standards. Just as we saw with the New York State standard, only certain types of medigap policies will be approved. Finding an approved policy, however, is not the end of your search for the right Medicare supplement.

The medigap policy should be guaranteed renewable for life. Otherwise, you risk cancellation of the policy. At some point, your health might not enable you to qualify for another policy. A conditionally renewable policy is not nearly as good. With that type of policy, the insurance company can stop insuring you for specific reasons set forth in the contract.

Beware of preexisting condition language or time limits until coverage begins. Medicare won't deny your claim, because it involves a preexisting condition, but a medigap policy will. When the Medicare Catastrophic Coverage Act of 1988 was repealed, insurers were ordered to reinstate coverage to anyone who cancelled a medigap policy after January 1, 1989. The insurers were not allowed to deny coverage because of a preexisting condition. Many people had cancelled medigap policies, because they did not appear necessary under the 1988 law.

Check to see if there is any coverage for prescription drugs under the medigap policy. The catastrophic law was to gradually provide increased prescription drug coverage. Obviously, the price of these drugs can be astounding.

As we saw when we looked at the standards for medigap policies in New York State, the insurance department can help you make your choice. In many states, you will be able to obtain literature that lists the insurers who offer these policies. These publications from your state's insurance department will also outline the benefits that must be provided. The insurance department can also direct you to service organizations in your state that provide counseling on these issues. You can also look to consumer publications for advice on making this decision. *Consumer Reports*, for example, has provided a detailed analysis of medigap policies that are on the market.

The federal government is in no way affiliated with the companies that offer health insurance to supplement Medicare. If a salesperson implies that a company is affiliated with the government or Medicare, you should stop dealing with that person immediately. Private insurers sell medigap policies and they are not connected to the government in any way. Watch out for unethical companies and agents that use official-looking cards and letters to generate leads.

Keep in mind when you shop around for a medigap policy that it is not the answer to long-term health care because it will not pay for custodial nursing home care. Medigap policies should only be used to plug the gaps in Medicare.

OUTLOOK FOR MEDICARE IN THE 1990s

You would think that after passing a revamped Medicare law in 1988 and repealing it in 1989, Congress would decide to leave Medicare alone for a few years. Already, there is talk of changing Medicare again. If coverage is expanded, Congress will have to think long and hard about how to fund those benefits. It is doubtful that Congress will risk the outcry it heard when it levied the income tax surcharge in 1988.

In the 1990s, Congress might push to cover nursing home care under Medicare. To pay for federal coverage of long-term care under Medicare, taxpayers might see a surcharge that dwarfs the recently repealed one.

There is only one thing you can be sure of with Medicare. It will not be any easier to understand. There will still be hundreds of regulations that even Medicare processors don't completely understand. The government uses private carriers like Blue Cross/Blue Shield to process and pay many of these Medicare claims. You should not hesitate to go back to the carrier for an explanation of its decision. Follow up on the claim until you fully understand the explanation.

We are already seeing businesses pop up in many states that cater to Medicare beneficiaries who don't understand their coverage. For a fee, these businesses will help file your Medicare claim and follow it through to a conclusion.

Unless Medicare is expanded again in the 1990s, medigap policies will be big business. You can expect to see dozens of advertisements for them. In the near term, they will be very expensive.

As you grow older in the 1990s and become more concerned about your health, you should not be frightened into buying a medigap or any insurance policy. The decision to buy insurance coverage should be an informed one. You should understand your own financial situation and how the policy will protect you in case you encounter health problems.

17

Long-term health care

IN SOME RESPECTS, THE PROSPECT OF GOING TO A NURSING HOME IS MORE difficult to deal with than the inevitability of death. For that reason, there is a tendency to shy away from nursing home coverage. People know they are going to die. When confronted with the issue of needing long-term health care, many people say they would rather die than go into a nursing home.

Later in life, some of these people do end up in a nursing home. Perhaps, you have watched a friend or relative of yours enter a nursing home. As a condition of their admission, they might have been required to turn over their assets, such as a house, to the nursing home. As America grays, you would certainly think there is a better way to pay for nursing home care than to simply turn over assets to the facility. In this chapter, we'll explore the options you have for financing nursing home care.

THE RISK OF NEEDING LONG-TERM HEALTH CARE

For people in need of long-term care, turning over assets to the nursing home is only a partial solution. It might only cover a portion of the expenses generated by the nursing home admission. It has been estimated that 70 percent of all single people admitted to a nursing home are wiped out financially in three months. The admission of a spouse to a nursing home for an extended period can destroy a couple's financial stability, no matter how well off they are.

Today, a 12-month stay in a nursing home might cost $25,000. If costs continue rising as they have, the charges in 30 years might approach $55,000. Without a long-term care policy, the assets someone has worked a lifetime for can be drained by nursing home expenses. The math isn't too difficult. Years of nursing home care at $25,000 per year will exhaust all but the largest estates.

A great many people mistakenly believe that a government program will pick up the tab for nursing home costs. I've already pointed out that Medicare does not pick up nursing home expenses in most instances. The Health Insurance Association of America estimates that less than 2 percent of the country's nursing home costs are covered by Medicare. The other possibility is Medicaid, the medical assistance program that is supervised by the states.

If the person facing long-term care has assets, Medicaid might not be a palatable option. The eligibility requirements for Medicaid are strict. In some states, the person facing nursing home care might only be allowed to keep a few thousand dollars in assets. There are exceptions made for couples, so that the spouse cannot be forced to sell the family's home. A lien, however, might be placed against the home so that payments can be recouped after the spouse's death. A couple's assets, in addition to the house, can be tapped to some extent to pay for the long-term care. Even if you qualify, some long-term care facilities won't accept Medicaid patients.

Long-term care insurance is to protect you in case you have a chronic illness or disability that renders you unable to care for yourself. It's not just for the distasteful possibility that you will need to be in a nursing home. You might be unable to handle your day-to-day activities such as bathing, cooking, or household chores.

I've stated repeatedly that insurance is needed to cover catastrophic financial losses. Long-term care, whether in a nursing home or not, will generate expenses of that magnitude. Your family has a significant exposure, even if no member is in a high-risk group. As the insurance planner for your family, you need to be concerned with the insurance coverage of other relatives, such as parents. They should be advised to purchase a long-term care policy especially when they are in good health. If they can't afford long-term care insurance, you and your siblings should be buying a policy for them. Otherwise, you could be footing a very large bill to see that they are taken care of if they should find themselves needing long-term care.

LONG-TERM CARE POLICIES THROUGH YOUR EMPLOYER

Because of the financial and personal hardship brought on by the need for long-term care, some employers have started offering long-term care policies as an employee benefit. Unfortunately, few employers offer long-term care policies as of this moment. These will, however, become an important employee benefit in the 1990s. Employers are reluctant to make contributions to that long-term care coverage, but the group rate would be considerably cheaper than an individual policy. The group long-term care plans are likely to have less restrictions than an individual policy.

In a group plan, the underwriting base is better, which can result in lower premiums and more comprehensive benefits than an individual policy. A more favorable underwriting base means the plan attracts a wide variety of members, not just individuals who feel they'll need long-term care in the very near future. Having younger employees in the plan helps spread the risk and keeps costs lower. In addition, group rates are negotiated by someone at your company who is trained to get the most favorable deal available. This skill, along with the leverage a large company has, can result in a favorable price. Furthermore, if your employer contributes a portion of the premium on your behalf, you will save significantly on an individual policy.

Employer-sponsored insurance plans usually have a maximum payout over the insured's lifetime. The maximum applies to both nursing-home care and care that takes place in the patient's home. There is a waiting period before benefits begin. The long-term care need not be preceded by a hospital admission.

The premium depends on the age when you enroll for benefits. Therefore, the earlier you enroll, the less your premium will be. Furthermore, these premiums remain the same for your lifetime. Many of these plans allow the employee's parents and in-laws to enroll. You can also continue the coverage after you leave that employer. The coverage is portable.

WHAT KIND OF LONG-TERM CARE DO YOU NEED?

There's more to long-term care than just nursing home coverage. Some care can be administered in the patient's home and can help the individual avoid a nursing home indefinitely. There are four kinds of care you should get in a long-term care policy.

1. Skilled nursing care
2. Intermediate care
3. Custodial care
4. Home health care

Skilled nursing care should be covered. This is the care that is offered by licensed medical professionals. It is performed pursuant to a physicians orders and can include nursing and rehabilitative care. Medicare pays for 100 days of skilled nursing care each year. After the 20th day, the Medicare patient must pay $74 per day.

Intermediate care is done under medical supervision, but is not necessarily conducted by licensed medical professionals. The service must be rendered pursuant to a doctor's orders.

Custodial care is especially important for individuals who have no close relatives to help care for them or who don't wish to saddle someone with tending to their needs. The custodial care coverage pays for someone to help with dressing, bathing, eating, and other functions that can no longer be performed alone.

It is nonmedical care to help with daily hygiene and does not need to be performed by someone with medical skills or training.

Home health care is usually performed at home on a part-time basis by home health aids. It's usually speech therapy, physical therapy, or occupational therapy.

A typical long-term care policy pays a fixed daily amount and a maximum lifetime benefit. You will have a choice of benefits. You might choose $80 per day reimbursement for a maximum of five years. A less expensive policy would pay $60 per day for the same number of years. You can also reduce the daily amount that a policy will pay and decrease the number of years of protection. Some companies will let you buy lifetime coverage. While these fixed-dollar plans are the most common, a few plans pay a percentage of the actual long-term care costs, usually 80 percent.

HOW TO EVALUATE A LONG-TERM CARE POLICY

The first step in evaluating a long-term care policy is to check with the department in your state that handles insurance matters. This branch of state government can be an excellent source of information as you research long-term care insurance. In Chapter 9, you learned how your state's insurance department might provide pamphlets that can help you find the best price on automobile insurance. In the long-term care area, a few state insurance departments are providing an even greater service. They will provide booklets that analyze each long-term care policy offered in your state.

For example, Michigan provides an excellent guide for consumers. It compares the benefits offered in various long-term care policies available in that state. This booklet, and similar guides, can help you keep track of the essential features in the long-term policies you are evaluating. You should call or write your state insurance department to see if this type of guide is available. At the end of this chapter, you will find a long-term care policy checklist from the Health Insurance Association of America that can also help you evaluate a long-term care policy.

As you evaluate the various long-term care policies, price should not be your only consideration. The policy should also cover:

- Chronic ailments. This includes acute conditions.
- Alzheimer's disease. This can be a significant risk to older family members and is responsible for a great many nursing home admissions. Even policies that say they cover organic mental conditions could have restrictive language. It should clearly state that this disease is covered.
- Senility.

- Nervous and muscular disorders. This includes Parkinson's disease and muscular dystrophy. There will be preexisting condition exclusions, however.
- Day care and respite care. Respite care lets the family of a long-term care patient take a well-needed vacation by admitting the patient to a nursing home for a short period.

Avoid a policy that requires a hospital admission before long-term benefits can begin. A policy might have a three-day prior hospitalization requirement, although there are efforts in progress to abolish this prerequisite because there are occasions when an individual won't need to be hospitalized before requiring long-term care. Alzheimer's disease, or some other condition, can force someone directly into a nursing home without being hospitalized first. You should be eligible for benefits when a doctor certifies your need for care.

Earlier in this chapter, I discussed the four levels of care that a long-term care policy should provide. A policy should not require that one level of care be used before allowing a different level of care. A policyholder shouldn't have to use skilled nursing care first to qualify for custodial care. You should be able to use any level of care without having used a different level of care first.

Skilled nursing care, intermediate care, and custodial care should not be treated differently under a long-term care policy. The benefit rate you choose should apply equally to these levels of care. There are some policies that pay less for custodial care. The long-term care policy should also not have a separate maximum for each level of care. Home health care, however, will normally be reimbursed at a lower rate or will pay a specified amount for each service. It might also have a separate and distinct ceiling that is lower than the maximum payout in the policy.

You should consider an inflation rider because long-term care costs are escalating rapidly, and the payment that now appears adequate could offer little protection as costs escalate. A rider of this type would not be as important to an older person who is evaluating a long-term care policy.

There should be no coordination of benefits. Cash benefits should be paid directly to the insured, no matter how many other policies you have purchased. You would be better off, however, with one, solid long-term care policy.

As with any insurance policy, you have to evaluate the carrier offering the insurance. Again, go with a company that is rated A+ or A by *Best's Insurance Reports*. Ask about the insurance company's loss ratio, the amount it pays out in benefits for each premium dollar it collects. Paying out 60 cents or more on each dollar is considered to be a fair loss ratio.

The policy should be guaranteed renewable. As long as you pay the premiums, the company must renew the policy. There should be no age limit on renewability. A conditionally renewable policy means it can be canceled if the company cancels all policies within the state. An insurance carrier might not know for years if it's priced the policy correctly. Having a policy of this type can be dangerous if the carrier later discovers that the policies are not profitable. At that time, you might not be able to get another long-term care policy because of your health.

HOW TO SAVE MONEY ON LONG-TERM CARE

As we saw with disability coverage, there is something akin to a deductible that can save you money. It's called the elimination period. A long-term care policy can be purchased with a longer waiting period until benefits begin, resulting in significant savings. One policy on the market offers a choice between a 20-day waiting period and a 100-day waiting period. Some policies even let you choose a 365-day elimination period. The longer you wait, the greater the savings. The longer waiting period is compatible with the true purpose of insurance, which is to guard against catastrophe. Paying for nursing home care for several months is expensive, but it won't wipe out your family's assets as would a lengthy nursing home stay.

The self-insurance concept that I have stressed repeatedly will only work partially for this risk. One actuary forecasted that one in four people will need long-term care of some type. If you plan on saving for this contingency, you should be putting away $50,000 to $200,000 to cover the cost of long-term care. Your savings program should begin before you reach age 50.

Not surprisingly, the younger you are, the lower your premium will be. The premium will remain at that level for the lifetime of the policy. You're not really saving money by buying a policy at a younger age, because, in all likelihood, you'll spend more money over a lifetime. You do, however, get the benefit of having coverage and a lower premium by buying at a younger age.

Even if your employer is not offering a group plan, an organization that you belong to might offer long-term health care coverage. While there will be no employer contribution, the rates might be lower.

LONG-TERM CARE IN THE 1990s

Long-term care policies are a relatively new concept in insurance. But as the population ages during the 1990s, we will see many more of them being offered. As the baby boomers grow older and recognize the risk of needing long-term care, new products will be offered to tap that market. Along with traditional policies that only pay for long-term care, there will be new forms of insurance that address several needs. There could also be legislative remedies.

In Chapter 11, we looked at life insurance policies with long-term care riders. If long-term care is needed, these riders permit a portion of the death benefit to be applied toward those expenses. There is even talk of a life insurance policy that will pay long-term care expenses without cutting into the death benefit. There are more of these hybrid policies each day. Life insurance policies with long-term care riders are not the answer to your nursing home expenses. If you have purchased the right amount of life insurance to meet your needs, taking part of the death benefit to pay nursing home expenses is robbing Peter to pay Paul.

There's really no substitute for a long-term care policy, even though you might be tempted by insurance plans that sound as if they will serve a similar purpose. At first glance, the hospital indemnity plans might appear to be a useful alternative if you need long-term care. Unfortunately, these plans do not pay benefits if the confinement is in a nursing home, extended care facility, convalescent home, rest home, or a home for the aged. Therefore, even if a family member is receiving medical treatment at one of those facilities, the confinement would not qualify for the indemnity payments.

As you reach the later stages of your life, the risk of needing long-term care becomes more significant. If you need long-term care for an extended period, it can wipe out a lifetime of savings. You also might be forced to rely on your children or other relatives for care. That option is often as unpalatable as entering a nursing home. The following checklist will help you compare policies you might be considering.

Long-term Care Policy Checklist

Policy

1. What services are covered?
   - ☐ Skilled care   A___   B___
   - ☐ Intermediate care   A___   B___
   - ☐ Custodial   A___   B___
   - ☐ Home health care   A___   B___
   - ☐ Other care   A___   B___

2. How much does the policy pay per day for:
   - ☐ Skilled care   A___   B___
   - ☐ Intermediate care   A___   B___
   - ☐ Custodial   A___   B___
   - ☐ Home health care   A___   B___
   - ☐ Other care   A___   B___

3. Does the policy offer a means for increasing benefits to account for expected future costs? If so, how?   A___   B___

   Is there an additional premium?   A___   B___

4. Does the policy have a maximum lifetime benefit? If so, what is it?
   - ☐ Nursing home   A___   B___
   - ☐ Home health   A___   B___

5. Does the policy have a maximum length of coverage per "spell of ill-

Policy

ness" of maximum benefit period? If so, what is it?
   - ☐ Nursing home   A___   B___
   - ☐ Home health   A___   B___

6. How long do I have to wait before preexisting conditions are covered?   A___   B___

7. Is Alzheimer's disease covered?   A___   B___

8. How many days is the elimination or deductible period before benefits begin?   A___   B___

9. Does this policy require: A___   B___
   - ☐ Physician certification of need   A___   B___
   - ☐ A functional assessment   A___   B___
   - ☐ A prior hospital stay for:
     - ☐ Nursing home care   A___   B___
     - ☐ Home health care   A___   B___
   - ☐ A prior nursing home stay for home health care   A___   B___

10. Can the policy be cancelled?   A___   B___

11. Will the policy cover you if you move to another area?   A___   B___

12. What is the age range for enrollment?   A___   B___

13. What does the policy cost?
   - ☐ per month   A___   B___
   - ☐ per year   A___   B___

18

Health insurance for pets

THE VETERINARIAN GIVES YOU THE BAD NEWS. YOUR DOG, SPARKY, NEEDS AN operation. The vet tells you that the surgery will cost $500. Without the surgery, Sparky will die. Now you have to make a choice. Should you put your family in a financial bind by having the surgery done or should you let the family pet die?

To many people, their pet is an important member of the family, and there would be no question that the surgery should be done. Others would question whether they can afford the expense, knowing that the dog might die anyway. Sparky's plight might spark a family to look into pet insurance to ease the financial burden in this situation. A sick pet can hurt the family budget in the same way medical expenses generated by any family member do.

Just when you thought you had dealt with all of the insurance issues you could handle, new policies come along to make your job even more difficult. At least two companies are offering health insurance policies for pets. As of this writing, they are being offered in every state except Tennessee.

The Animal Health Insurance Agency (AHIA) of Danbury, Connecticut, introduced its pet insurance program in 1986. According to its promotional literature, AHIA's first policyholder was Benji. Let's face it. If you owned Benji, you could afford to buy all of the insurance policies your heart desires. Assuming you don't own a canine or feline movie star, you might want to think twice before buying a health insurance policy for your pet. Before buying one, you should be weighing the cost of the policy against the benefit you might receive.

There are two options in the plan offered by AHIA. The first is $1,000 in coverage for each covered injury or illness. The price is $97.50 per year per pet with a $50 deductible. The second option guards against catastrophic illnesses.

It provides $2,500 in coverage with a $250 deductible for a price of $40 per year for each pet.

Only dogs and cats are covered. Coverage can't be transferred to a new owner, but a pro rata refund will be given if ownership of the pet changes hands. There is also a coinsurance clause. After paying the deductible, you are responsible for 30 percent of the bill.

Naturally, there are limitations on what the policy covers. As you might expect, it excludes preexisting conditions. This is no surprise, because virtually every health insurance policy contains this exclusion. There is also a 60-day waiting period for coverage to begin.

AHIA's policy does not provide coverage for preventable diseases. There would be a number of diseases in this category such as distemper, rabies, hepatitis, and leptospirosis. Elective neutering and cosmetic surgery are also not covered. Therefore, you're on your own when your dachshund needs a nose job or your beagle needs a tummy tuck or liposuction.

Older pets will have trouble getting full coverage, just as humans do when they get older and need health insurance. The coverage for older pets is more limited. A pet that is age 10 or older is covered for injury only. Pets will not be covered until they reach the age of three months.

Although health insurance for pets can eliminate difficult decisions on whether you can afford costly medical care for your pet, this is another area where you should bear the risk yourself. You should self-insure for any potential treatment that is needed. From the time you purchase your pet, you have to be prepared for the day when your dog or cat needs treatment. You should be putting funds away, even if your pet is as healthy as an ox now. If you aren't prepared for expenses of that sort, buy a fish, and the worst expense you'll have is buying medicine to cure ich.

You might find yourself buying pet health insurance for the same bad reason that you purchase other policies. Once again, you buy it because you're afraid of running into expensive veterinarian bills at a time when you're short of cash. The purpose of insurance is not to remedy your cash flow problems. These budgeting problems shouldn't motivate you to buy a policy you don't need. You have to take responsibility for these small expeditures that are a natural consequence of your decisions. If you decide to buy a dog or cat, you must be prepared for veterinarian bills.

GETTING YOUR PAWS ON THE RIGHT HEALTH INSURANCE POLICY

Even if you like the idea of pet health insurance, you definitely should skip the coverage for pets that are 10 years old or older. The coverage only covers the dog or cat for medical treatment resulting from an accident. I have repeatedly warned against policies that only pay under limited circumstances. Limiting payment to an injury-related situation narrows the coverage significantly and reduces whatever value it has. Moreover, at that age, it is questionable whether the animal's life span will be extended by the surgery or medical treatment.

Coverage for pets under age 10 is better, but it is still not a good investment. It will cover both illness and injury. The $97.50 price is steep, however, compared to the $1,000 you might recover after paying your $50 deductible. You still must pay $30 out of every $100 that is charged. You're still going to be out-of-pocket on each occasion that your pet is treated. Consequently, you still could face uncomfortable choices on whether your family can afford to give a pet the treatment it needs.

If you go with any option, stick with the catastrophic plan. It lets you self-insure for smaller medical problems. The price is $40 per year not $97.50. It also has a higher limit of $2,500 to cover truly catastrophic medical problems that your dog or cat might suffer. The copayment is also $30 for each $100.

Health insurance for pets is sold the same way other policies are sold. There is the famous pennies-per-day sales pitch. Although this is not a lot of money each day, it adds up to too many dollars each year.

Guilt is also part of the sales pitch. You are reminded that your pet is a member of the family too. While most pet owners feel that way, it does not logically follow that health insurance is a wise purchase. You should take care of your pet, but you shouldn't need pet insurance to do it.

19

Travel insurance

ONE COUPLE I KNOW VERY WELL HAD PLANNED A CRUISE WITH A GROUP OF friends. The four couples were to sail through the Caribbean for 10 days. Even with the group rate that the trip's organizer had arranged, the cruise cost almost $5,000 per couple. The organizer of the trip, who happens to be an insurance salesman, decided that travel insurance was not a good investment.

Because this is a book about insurance, and it wouldn't be much of a story otherwise, you've probably guessed that the couple I know missed out on the cruise with their friends. I felt especially bad, because the people in the story were my in-laws. My father-in-law was admitted to the hospital with bacterial endocarditis six days before the trip and didn't get out for three weeks. It doesn't take much of a mathematician to realize that the ship sailed without them.

You might be thinking of the old saying about the shoemaker's children going barefoot. While I wasn't involved in the decision to go without travel insurance, I was able to persuade the cruise line to give my in-laws a significant credit toward a new cruise. They eventually took the trip after my father-in-law recovered. To arrange this however, I went through the hassle of my life with the cruise line. The brochure made it quite clear that they were not entitled to a penny. The incident caused me to believe that at least one coverage within the travel insurance policy can be a good investment.

TRAVEL RISKS

There's something about travel that worries people. Maybe you're the type who leaves your will on the kitchen table when you leave for vacation. For some, it's just the thought of flying that makes them think about death and insurance. For others thoughts of terrorism or driving on the opposite side of the road in a foreign country frighten them.

There might be legitimate reasons to think about death. You might plan on renting a moped in Bermuda. Your vacation plans might include rock climbing or parasailing in Acapulco. As the parachute rises and lifts you high over the beach, it's too late to ask whether there is any governmental body regulating the safety of this activity or if any two guys with a motorboat can earn a few extra bucks this way.

It's not just the life-and-death problems that cause concern. There are the more routine medical problems that crop up while you're on vacation. Maybe you're eating strange food or just eating too much food. You're overdoing it in the sun with no sun screen or the wrong sun screen. You're playing too much tennis or just trying to cram in too many activities in one vacation week.

The risks associated with traveling can be significant. When my in-laws returned from their replacement cruise, they reported that at least one person died on the cruise and there were two other heart attack victims. One of the heart attacks occurred while snorkeling. Cruises, which would seem to be one of the more relaxing ways to travel, have their share of mishaps. There is even a morgue on the ship, because bodies can't be sent through Customs at some ports.

INSURING AGAINST TRAVEL RISKS

With all the things that can go wrong, there is a need for travel insurance, but only to a limited extent. Although travel insurance can be a way to protect your vacation investment, you will often end up buying duplicate coverage. In addition, you should be able to self-insure against some of the risks covered by the policy.

Initially, it's important to clarify what we mean by travel insurance. There are a number of travel insurance policies on the market today, a far cry from the days where there was only the over-the-counter life insurance policy sold at every airport. For a few dollars, you could buy an immense amount of flight insurance. Despite the seemingly high amount of coverage, flight insurance was and still is a bad deal. In that era, you could end the travel insurance chapter right here. It was enough to say you were wasting your money by guarding against a remote risk. You would be better off putting your money toward a life insurance policy that protects you all year long.

Today's travel insurance policy offers many more benefits. Primarily, policies cover trip interruption and cancellation, baggage loss or damage, and medical coverage. You don't have to buy all the coverage. You can pick and choose the coverage you need and skip the coverage you don't need. Cruise lines often have their own version of travel insurance, which includes cancellation charge waivers and baggage protection.

It costs a great deal of money to go on vacation these days. Because of the expense involved, no one really wants to add to the price by buying travel insurance. Unlike some forms of insurance, there is no law requiring you to have it. It's very easy to ignore the insurance, because you're looking forward to the vacation and can't imagine anything spoiling it.

As easy as travel insurance is to overlook, the risk you take by going without it is significant. With many airfares, there is a significant penalty for cancelling. Many tour operators and hotels will not refund your deposit and other prepaid charges, no matter how good your excuse is for not taking the vacation you've booked.

Cruise lines also penalize would-be vacationers who aren't able to take their trip. A cancellation within 14 days of departure can result in the loss of 100 percent of your fare on some cruise lines. With virtually every cruise ship, you will lose your entire payment if you fail to show up at the dock for departure.

Before you assail the airlines, tour operators, and the cruise lines for being cold hearted, you have to concede that there are a number of good reasons for their position on cancellations. Assuming you were advised of these penalties, you have assumed the risk of a problem by agreeing to the stipulated terms. As far as the airline is concerned, you were given the option to select a fare that permitted cancellation, but instead, you went with the lower fare, which included a harsh cancellation penalty. In the case of the cruise ship, it will be too late to sell your cabin to someone else if you are forced to cancel at the last minute. Again, your cruise brochure should make it clear that you are risking the loss of your money.

The risk of loss falls squarely on your shoulders, even if you have a legitimate excuse for not being able to take your vacation. You might argue that you can ill-afford to take the loss. The airline, tour operator, or cruise line, on the other hand, can afford these losses and should expect a certain number of no-shows on each and every trip. The flip side of the coin is that you can purchase travel insurance to protect yourself. Letting you off the hook is unfair to those individuals who have purchased travel insurance. It also would lead to higher prices for all travelers.

If you have the financial means to do it, you can self-insure against this risk. Many people unknowingly self-insure against the risks associated with travel. They don't realize that the airline, tour operator, or cruise ship won't refund their money if they are unable to take the trip. The penalties can be in black-and-white, but they feel an exception will be made if they have a valid reason for not going. As long as you are making a decision to self-insure based on all of the facts and can afford the loss of thousands of dollars, this is a viable option. You cannot count on an exception being made, however.

TRIP CANCELLATION/INTERRUPTION COVERAGE

While travel insurance is normally sold in a package, you can usually buy the specific coverage you need. If you need anything in the way of travel insurance, it will most likely be the trip cancellation/interruption coverage. This coverage will reimburse you for the non-refundable portion of your trip if you must cancel for one of the covered reasons. It will also reimburse you for non-refundable payments you've made when your trip is interrupted for one of the covered reasons. It will normally pay your airfare to rejoin the trip or to return home, depending on the nature of the emergency.

The usual price for trip interruption/cancellation coverage is $5.50 per $100. Assuming your trip costs $2,000, and you need to cover the entire amount, you would pay $110. ($2,000 divided by 100 = 20 × $5.50.) If all of the trip's price is non-refundable, you would need to pay the $110 to cover it in full. When you know that certain payments will be refunded in the event of cancellation, you would not need to cover the entire amount.

At first glance, this coverage might to seem to be a bad deal. It is a policy of limited duration, which I have discouraged you from buying. The difference, however, is that you don't go on vacation every day of the year. You might only be able to afford one week per year. You save all year for that trip. For a relatively small amount of money, you can protect your vacation investment. The risk is just too significant to deal with when you can couch your bets with trip interruption/cancellation coverage.

It's not like flight insurance where you're buying life insurance to cover your several hours in the air. You are covering more than just the seven days of your trip, or longer. You're buying peace of mind for the weeks and months preceding the trip.

Even after you arrive at your destination, you're not out of the woods yet. There are still things that can go wrong, and these possibilities might justify the purchase of trip cancellation/interruption insurance. While you're away, you might get a call telling you that a family member is ill. You yourself might become ill or have an accident, which could put an end to your vacation. The trip interruption coverage reimburses the non-refundable and unused portion of your trip. It also pays any additional air costs necessitated by these unplanned events. If you've ever priced a one-way fare where you don't give advance notice or stay over the required length of time, you'll realize how expensive a change of plans can be.

To evaluate the value of the trip cancellation/interruption coverage, you should be looking at what type of protection you'll get for your money. This coverage will pay, up to the limit you've selected, if an immediate family member dies. The policies will differ, however, on what relatives are covered.

This coverage will also pay benefits if you or a family member becomes ill and must cancel your trip. You should examine the policy closely before buying it to determine which family members are included. You might not have coverage if your favorite aunt becomes ill and her life is in jeopardy. Before buying the insurance, make certain it is clear which family members are covered. Relationship requirements vary from company to company. The policy using the language "immediate family member," would not cover an uncle or aunt.

The policy might cover your close relatives, but this still would be of little value in certain situations. Your best friend might become ill, but it's unlikely that any policy will pay for your cancellation expenses under those circumstances. Some policies do pay, however, when a traveling companion or business partner becomes ill.

MEDICAL DOCUMENTATION OF CLAIMS

The trip cancellation/interruption coverage pays for lost deposits and additional expenses that result from an unforseeable illness, injury, or death of a family member. Naturally, you will need to present medical proof before you can collect on the policy. All medical claims require a doctor's certificate. As we saw in our discussion of health-related policies, there is always a preexisting condition exclusion and it will be strictly enforced.

The insurance company can refuse to pay your claim if you cancel or interrupt your trip because of a preexisting medical condition. The medical condition, whether it's your own or a family member's, must not predate your purchase of the policy. The doctor's report will be crucial in determining whether or not the medical problem is a preexisting condition.

Some companies are quite strict in their interpretation of the preexisting condition exclusion. If the illness was treated within a year prior to the trip, they will deny the claim. A prescription to treat that illness will be viewed as evidence of the preexisting condition. On the other hand, you can argue that it was not. If a doctor releases a patient and gives him a clean bill of health, it should not be a preexisting condition if the problem flares up at a later date.

Some travel insurance policies have their own version of the incontestability clause that we saw in life insurance contracts. These clauses state that if you buy the policy more than 60 days prior to the trip, the company will not assert the preexisting condition exclusion as a defense.

Death is never a preexisting condition. If a sick family member dies, which causes you to cancel the trip, the policy will pay the agreed benefit. The insurance company cannot argue that the death resulted from an illness that was a preexisting condition.

In addition to these medical requirements, and the documentation required to support your claim, some policies have an additional provision. The relative who dies or whose illness forces this cancellation must reside in either the United States or Canada. The rationale is that the insurance company wants to corroborate your story. Using a relative outside the country as an excuse could open the door for fraud.

CANCELLATION DUE TO SPECIFIC EMERGENCIES

There are other occurrences that qualify for the trip cancellation/interruption coverage depending on the particular policy you purchased. If your car breaks down on the way to the airport or you have a flat tire, one travel insurance policy compensates you for any money you can't get back or for additional costs you incur. Naturally, you would have to prove that this event occurred.

In some policies, broken pipes on the day of a trip will be a valid reason to activate the coverage. If an incident like this happened a few days before the trip, however, you would have time to call a plumber and take care of the repairs beforehand. There are even policies that allow you to cancel and be reimbursed if jury duty stands in the way of your trip.

Although trip cancellation/interruption coverage can be a wise purchase, there is no need to overinsure. You only need to insure against the non-refundable portion of the trip. Some argue that it is not needed at all, because many airlines will not penalize you for cancelling a flight because of an extreme emergency. Airlines with this generous policy will require unequivocal proof of that emergency. If airfare was the only expense associated with a trip, this might be a compelling argument. Unfortunately, the airline you're using might not be so benevolent. In addition, a charter flight or tour operator might not accept any excuse for cancelling the trip.

Remember, it's not just your own health you're insuring. A vacation will be of no value if you spend the time worrying about the folks back home. You're insuring their health too. Trip cancellation/interruption coverage lets you avoid making some very difficult decisions. Suppose you must decide whether to go on your trip even though a family member is very ill. The thought of losing thousands of dollars could convince you to leave even though you will not enjoy your vacation.

On the other hand, trip cancellation/interruption coverage is of no value if it does not give you peace of mind. After examining the policy, you might find that it actually covers very little risk. The few family members it covers might not be prone to illness or accident. You might fear that a preexisting condition will invalidate the policy. If that is the case, you should not buy the coverage. This is an appropriate decision as long as you recognize the potential consequences.

Again, be aware of the risk you are facing. If you're driving to the beach and you'll lose a night's deposit at the hotel if you cancel, you obviously don't need travel insurance. Only buy enough insurance to cover what you can't afford to lose.

CRUISES: CANCELLATION FEE WAIVERS

The cancellation fee waiver is a variation of trip cancellation insurance. This quasi-insurance policy is offered by many of the major cruise lines. I mentioned earlier that there are severe penalties for cancelling a cruise. The cancellation fee waiver allows you to cancel until 24 hours prior to sailing. A typical seven-day cruise might offer a $50 per person cancellation fee waiver. If the price of that cruise is $1,500, you might assume you're paying less than the $5.50 per $100 figure that a trip cancellation policy usually costs. Despite the fact that it's less expensive, it's not necessarily a better bargain.

You are only buying protection until 24 hours prior to the ship's sailing. There are still a number of problems that can occur until the ship leaves the dock. On top of that, you are getting little in the way of trip interruption coverage. With rare exceptions, the coverage offered by the cruise lines is of little use if you must disembark because of problems at home or even your own illness at sea.

On the positive side, these waivers are normally much broader than trip cancellation coverage. A passenger usually can cancel for any reason prior to the 24 hour deadline. Therefore, the preexisting condition question is not raised. These waivers usually include baggage protection. Although this coverage is unnecessary in most instances, it can't normally be separated from the waiver. Considering the low price of the waiver, and the expense of a cruise, these cancellation fee waivers are a good deal.

BAGGAGE PROTECTION

Baggage protection in a travel insurance policy is advisable in very few cases. The baggage protection is of little use. Unless you're carrying a purchase of special value, your homeowners policy should cover you. You will also have an action against the common carrier that provided the transportation if it is responsible for your loss. The only advantage is that the baggage policy has no deductible, but that's hardly a reason to buy it.

On a smaller scale, you might have a problem getting fragile gifts back home in one piece. Some of the better stores offer replacement goods if a gift does not make it home in its original condition. A few credit card companies are now offering coverage for theft, damage, or fire on items bought with their card.

MEDICAL COVERAGE

In addition to the risk of a medical problem that forces you to cancel, you should also consider the medical problems that might require treatment while you are away. Most travel insurance policies include medical coverage that you either purchase separately or as part of a package. There are also health insurance plans you can purchase separately for travel that cover a wide range of medical services. For most people, their regular health insurance policy is sufficient to meet their travel-related medical problems.

There is one important reason why your regular health insurance plan is better-suited for your needs. A travel insurance medical plan might be subject to the preexisting medical condition exclusion. When you purchase a new health insurance policy, this exclusion will be a potential obstacle to your recovery. Your existing medical insurance, assuming you have carried it for awhile, will not have this barrier to recovery.

Make certain your regular health insurance coverage applies while you are out of the country. If you belong to an HMO, find out the procedure for receiving medical treatment outside its territory. Find out too if your health insurance policy will pay for an emergency evacuation for medical reasons, a coverage offered by most travel insurance policies. Even if your insurance does cover medical treatment in a foreign country, the health care providers might be unwilling to bill your insurance company directly. You'll have to be reimbursed later by your health insurer.

If you have Medicare, you might have a problem because it does not cover medical treatment in many countries. It does cover treatment in Mexico and Canada, but only in emergency situations. If you have a medigap policy, however, the treatment might be covered and you can skip the medical coverage available in travel insurance policies. Not all medigap policies do cover medical treatment in another country, however.

This is another area where credit card companies are offering protection as an incidental benefit of membership. Your premium credit card might entitle you to limited emergency medical services and evacuation privileges. Some credit card companies will also help you locate a physician in a foreign country.

The life and accident insurance offered in travel policies is not a good buy. Although the amount charged is small, you are actually paying an exorbitant amount. If you need more coverage in these areas, buy a policy that covers you all year long, not just for the time you're on vacation. You can also get this life insurance coverage for free by charging your tickets on many credit cards.

BANKRUPTCY PROTECTION

When my wife and I were married, we planned a honeymoon to Curacao, which is off the coast of Venezuela. We ended up having our honeymoon in Ft. Lauderdale. Somewhere in between, the tour operator for the Curacao trip filed for bankruptcy.

The good news is that because my wife's employer sponsored the Curacao trip, they reimbursed the money we lost because of the bankruptcy. Although this worked out to our advantage, there are other risks that must be guarded against when you travel other than lost baggage, illness, or accidents. The risk that a cruise line, airline, or tour operator will default is now a fact of life when you take a trip.

A travel insurance policy might be the answer to protecting against this type of risk. A few travel insurance policies offer limited protection if your tour operator, cruise ship, or airline defaults for whatever reason. These policies won't help if your travel agency files for bankruptcy while it is still holding your deposit or payment for the trip. Once the funds are forwarded to the appropriate party, the travel insurance policy would provide some measure of protection.

When you are dealing with reputable companies that have solid financial histories, you shouldn't need protection of this type. This is a risk that you deal with every day without buying insurance. You put money down on furniture or some other product and risk the party going out of business. When you travel, you should be following the same rules of common sense that you use in any business transaction. You shouldn't be dealing with companies that you don't trust and know little about.

20

Insurance and the tax laws

IF YOU'RE THE TYPE OF PERSON WHO WON'T MAKE A MOVE WITHOUT STUDY-ing the tax implications, the purchase of insurance can leave you standing in your tracks. There are many tax regulations affecting the insurance policies you purchase. I've touched upon a number of them in our discussion of the various policies on the market, but it might help to take a broader look at how insurance and the tax laws are interconnected.

CASUALTY AND THEFT LOSS DEDUCTIONS

Throughout this book, you've been encouraged to raise deductibles and handle more risk yourself. I have suggested many situations where self-insurance is better than paying someone to take the risk for you. In some situations, this will mean taking a loss that is not covered by insurance. Worse yet, the tax laws will not reduce the financial impact caused by that loss. Because of this, you might be unwilling to implement a self-insurance program in your own household.

There is a dichotomy here. As your income increases, it gets easier to let losses fall on your own shoulders. You can afford to pay for certain losses out of your own pocket. Unfortunately, as your income gets larger, it becomes harder to take a tax deduction for casualty and theft losses. It is unlikely that you will qualify for a tax write-off in the event that you do suffer a loss.

The IRS defines "casualty" as the damage, destruction, or loss of property resulting from an identifiable event that is sudden, unexpected, or unusual. The key words are sudden, unexpected, and unusual. It can't be a gradual or progressive deterioration. When your gutters rot away after 20 years, this would not be a casualty loss.

You can have an event that qualifies as a casualty, but won't necessarily qualify as a covered loss under your policy. We discussed how earthquake damage requires special coverage and isn't covered by the standard homeowners policy. Therefore, it would qualify as a casualty, yet it would not necessarily be a covered loss if you did not purchase the appropriate endorsement.

Suppose you drop the collision coverage on your old car, which I have recommended. You have an auto accident and the $2,000 car is totally destroyed. This would be a casualty loss that would not be covered by your auto insurance. The damage done by a fire or storm would also fall within the definition of casualty. Although these are all examples of a casualty, you cannot necessarily deduct them on your tax return. The rules pertaining to deductions of this type have been tightened considerably. If your income is significant, the odds are good that you won't be able to take the deduction. You can only deduct a casualty or theft loss if it exceeds 10 percent of your adjusted gross income.

To understand the rule, it might help to look at a hypothetical situation. Let's suppose you have an adjusted gross income of $50,000 per year. To even think about deducting a casualty or theft loss, it would have to be more than 10 percent of that adjusted gross income, or $5,000.

Let's carry our hypothetical situation further. You suffer a casualty loss of $10,000. The tax laws state that the first $100 of a casualty or theft loss is not deductible, unless business property is involved. Because of that rule, you must reduce your $10,000 loss by $100, leaving you $9,900.

You're not ready to fill in your tax return yet. You must reduce the $9,900 again. You need to subtract any insurance recovery or reimbursement you get from some other source. To make the hypothetical easier for an author who isn't very good in math, we'll assume that you receive $900 from your insurance carrier. You now are $9,000 in the hole.

Before taking a $9,000 deduction on your tax return, you have to do one more thing. You must reduce your loss by 10 percent of your adjusted gross income, which worked out to be $5,000 in our example. Your deduction would be $4,000, a far cry from the $9,100 loss that you suffered after your insurance reimbursement.

Because of this limitation on deductions, your small losses will not help you on your taxes. It might make you less willing to self-insure and more willing to pay insurance premiums to guard against these losses. On the other hand, remember that insurance premiums can rarely be used as a deduction unless they are business-related.

MEDICAL EXPENSE DEDUCTIONS

Fewer people would object to paying insurance premiums if they were deductible. In a nonbusiness situation, you can rarely take your insurance payments as a deduction. A limited exception is health insurance premiums that you pay.

They count toward the medical expense deduction that you might be entitled to take on your income tax return.

Unfortunately, your expenses must exceed a percentage of your adjusted gross income, just as we saw with the deduction for casualty and theft losses. Your unreimbursed medical expenses must exceed 7.5 percent of your adjusted gross income to qualify as a deduction. Unless your adjusted gross income is small, you would need to incur significant medical expenses in order to qualify for this deduction.

LIFE INSURANCE

Throughout our discussion of life insurance, you heard about its tax advantages. It might help to look at them more closely. One of the advantages of permanent life insurance is the so-called "inside buildup" of the cash value. From time to time, there have been proposals to tax this increased cash value on permanent life insurance policies and annuities. The life insurance industry argues that taxing increases in cash value is like taxing people on the increased value of their home before it is sold. They argue it is unrealized income and should not be taxed. The insurance industry argues that this inside buildup should not be taxed because permanent life insurance is not an investment vehicle and is simply a purchase of protection.

The insurance industry also contends that because you do not have access to that inside buildup, it should not be taxed. It might be argued, however, that you do have access. A policy loan lets you take that money without paying it back, even though it is deducted from the death benefit. It also seems inconsistent for the insurance industry to contend that whole life is not an investment vehicle when many salespeople use that argument in their sales pitch.

SINGLE-PREMIUM WHOLE LIFE

In any life insurance sales pitch, the tax advantages of whole life policies are stressed. You need only look at single-premium whole life for an illustration of an investment that lost favor because of changes in the tax laws. Policies issued after June 20, 1988 no longer have the tax break that was a selling feature for single-premium whole life. For policies issued after that date, any money you borrow from the policy is considered to be taxable income.

Single-premium whole life lost its tax break when Congress cracked down on tax shelters. Whereas the typical whole life policy is paid for over the years in a series of payments, the single-premium variety ran into trouble because one large payment was used to buy it. The purchaser was permitted to begin borrowing immediately against the cash value. While this was going on, the cash value was still growing tax-free. The purchaser of the single-premium whole life policy was able to collect tax-free income on the investment.

The single-premium whole life policy's fall from favor demonstrates that people were not buying it as protection against death, but were buying it as a tax-saving vehicle. The changes in the tax treatment of single-premium whole life do not affect other whole life policies. You can still borrow against your cash value without tax consequences.

TAXES IN THE 1990s

You can count on one thing in the 1990s . . . change. Undoubtably, the tax laws will keep changing. While many of the tax-related topics we've discussed have remained the same for many years, some of these regulations have changed in the past few years and undoubtably will change again.

Although the Medicare surcharge has been eliminated, a different tax might replace it in the 1990s to fund medical benefits for the elderly. Despite powerful lobbying, some of the tax breaks associated with life insurance might be restricted. There will be changes in the estate tax laws, which will affect the growth of certain life insurance products. Whenever these changes occur, new insurance products will be created to conform with the new tax regulations.

No matter what changes occur, you should not let the lack of a tax deduction dissuade you from higher deductibles. You should not buy more insurance simply because you won't be able to take a loss as a deduction. Conversely, you should not let the tax advantages be the basis for your decision to buy certain insurance products. A tax break will not make up for an otherwise mediocre investment. Similarly, a tax benefit shouldn't encourage you to buy more insurance than you need.

21

Claim tips

YOU SEE THE COMMERCIALS ALL THE TIME. THEY PROMISE FAST AND FAIR claim handling. The commercials show an adjuster driving 60 miles to inspect a fire loss. Despite their promises of claim service, you can't get them to even return a phone call, let alone come out to look at your damages. Whether you have a claim against your own carrier or against someone else's, most people seem to feel that the service isn't nearly as fair or as fast as the insurance companies promise.

When it's your car that's damaged, the insurance company can never fix it fast enough. You look out the window and see the crushed door panel. It reminds you that the insurance company still hasn't set up an appointment to write an appraisal. While it's unlikely that the service will ever be as good as it's advertised, you can speed the process along. You can also make certain that you are treated fairly.

HOW TO DEAL EFFECTIVELY WITH INSURANCE COMPANIES

Most people don't enjoy dealing with insurance companies. Generally, a problem has occurred when you turn to them for help and you're not in the best of moods. It's not a good time to learn what your policy doesn't cover. At stressful times like that, it's not unusual that you'll feel mistreated by the insurance company.

There are many people who believe insurance companies originated the saying, "The check's in the mail." If they didn't, they should at least be paying royalties to the originator, because the words are constantly on their lips.

Seriously, an insurance company is like every other company. It has good employees and bad employees. Most of them would prefer settling the claim for the amount you've asked. It would make their job a lot easier. More often than not, insurance company employees are busy. Most problems are caused by their inability to deal with their workload, rather than some malicious desire to cheat you on your claim.

Unfortunately, there are no hard-and-fast rules on which companies will give you better claim service. Companies go through cycles. During some years, service is a priority and they are well staffed. At other times, they're trying to cut expenses by keeping staff at a minimum.

The principles of dealing with an insurance company are applicable, no matter what type of claim you are pursuing. You might have a health insurance claim that has been denied or a homeowners insurance problem. When it comes to claims, the following advice should be true regardless of the policy that is involved.

BEATING THE BUREAUCRACY

To get your claim processed quickly and easily, you first must understand that insurance companies are usually bureaucracies. Recently, pharmacy bills were sent in for payment to the workers' compensation department of a major insurance carrier. They were returned to the employee with a form, asking him what type of claim he had. This continued to happen on every occasion when the bills were submitted. Finally, he hired an attorney to deal with this insurance company.

As it turned out, the pharmacy bills were computerized. The pharmacy refused to put a file number or department name on the bills, saying that there were not enough lines on the computer screen to input this information. On each occasion, these bills came to the mailroom of the large insurance company. Without the department name or file number on the bills, they were invariably returned with the same form letter asking for identifying information.

Unless you identify your claim sufficiently, there are a dozen places your claim form or bills might go. Unidentified medical bills might pertain to an automobile accident, a workers' compensation claim, a health insurance matter, a bodily injury lawsuit, or several other departments that might be found in a large insurance company. Usually, there is no central computer that can pick out your name and what department is handling your claim. Each department has its own computer, but your correspondence might never get there for a name search to be of any value.

Because insurance companies are bureaucracies, you can't just call on the switchboard and say you want to be connected to the guy you were talking to about your car. You should write down the name of everyone with whom you speak. The insurance company might have hundreds of employees who work both inside and outside the office. There might be more than one employee who is working on your claim. An appraiser will call to set up an appointment to look at your car. A claim representative or supervisor from the Auto Damage Unit might call you to find out the facts of your accident. Another claim department employee might be responsible for paying your medical bills if you are injured in the accident.

DOCUMENTING YOUR CLAIM

Keeping track of names isn't just so you can reach them easily when you need information. It's an integral part of the most important aspect in resolving your claim. Above all, you have to document your claim. While this process won't guarantee that your claim will be accepted, it will guarantee that all promises are lived up to and that you are treated fairly by the insurance company. You should keep a paper trail in case you need it later.

You can bet that the insurance carrier is keeping track of every call made to you and of every conversation you have. Each company has quality assurance guidelines that require that employees record the names, dates, and substance of every conversation during the claim process. You should also keep your own log, in case there are disputes over what transpired, and it will expedite matters if you need to follow up for additional information.

Whenever possible, send letters confirming conversations you've had with the insurance carrier. This will help you verify any agreements or representations that were made. It will allow you to put your position in writing. The receipt of your letter might also trigger additional work on your claim and will help bring it to a conclusion more quickly.

As part of your documentation effort, you can prove your own case if necessary. If your health insurance claim is denied because the carrier feels it was not medically necessary, you can call upon your own doctor to refute that decision. A little medical research of your own might uncover facts to dispute the carrier's position. The person handling your claim might not possess any knowledge of medicine that is superior to your own. The claim handler is relying upon rigid guidelines and doesn't necessarily understand the medical reasons for the denial. No medical situation is exactly alike and you can demonstrate why your claim is different.

If you have a claim against someone's liability policy, you can also develop your own evidence. There might be other witnesses that the insurance company hasn't contacted. Perhaps there have been other accidents in the same area that can be pointed to in support of your position. You should know your claim better than the insurance company employee, who is handling hundreds of them.

Nothing is more convincing to insurance companies than paper. They thrive on it. For you to deal effectively with them, you have to operate on their level. The better you document your claim, the better chance you have of getting a fair shake. You can tell the insurance company personnel how badly you were injured in an accident, but it means more to them if a doctor verifies those injuries in a report. Make sure all lost wages are verified, as well as any incidental expenses.

With certain types of claims, you must think about documentation before the loss occurs. It's like taking a tax deduction without keeping the necessary back-up documentation. You should keep all receipts, invoices, appraisals, and other records in case you have a loss involving your property. Consider making video-tapes of your most priceless possessions. At a minimum, keep a household inventory and photographs of your belongings in a safety deposit box.

It is also important to document the coverage you have. While you might know what drawer a particular policy is in, someone might have to be the insur-ance planner in your absence someday. All of your insurance papers should be in one place. If they aren't, your beneficiaries might be unaware of a valuable pol-icy. Otherwise, they might be writing to insurance companies to see if there is a policy in your name.

Keeping all of your insurance policies in one place can also make matters easier for you. If you've made the mistake of buying mail-order policies over the years, they're as hard to keep track of as savings bonds. A periodic review of your insurance-related documentation will guarantee that you are not paying for policies you don't need. In addition, this review will make you aware of any essential policies that might lapse.

When you start keeping your insurance papers in one place, don't forget about the free coverage you get through a credit card or auto club. When you get a brochure describing this incidental coverage, make sure it stays in the desig-nated area. Keep all correspondence with your agent and insurance company there also, along with the notes from your conversations with them.

EXPEDITING YOUR CLAIM

While documentation is the most important part of the claim process, there are other steps you can take to ease the frustration that is almost inevitable. Be organized. Don't send in a stack of bills and hope the insurance company employees will make sense of it. You should be more familiar than they are with when and where you got the bills. Make it easier for them to process your claim. You might be able to get your money sooner if you help them with their job. Remember, people avoid more difficult tasks.

Being polite is another way to facilitate the resolution of your claim. This means you will often have to show patience with people who test the limits of your patience. Don't be nasty until you have to be. Be rational and logical. It's a tough combination to beat.

Send a letter of explanation along with the claim form, if you feel it is not self-explanatory. If it's already been sent to the primary insurance carrier, make certain that the secondary insurer knows that. Anticipate the problems before they occur.

Whenever you mail anything to the insurance carrier, make certain you've identified it with a file number and the name of the person handling the claim. It's often not enough to put that identifying information on the envelope. Put it on everything in case the material is separated from the envelope. A small item like this can keep your correspondence from sitting in a pile of unidentified mail for days or weeks.

CLAIM HANDLING: THE MYTHS AND THE REALITIES

When you feel an insurance company is giving you a hard time, many terrible thoughts will run through your head. You probably aren't too fond of insurance companies, and a bad experience with a claim will only make matters worse. As angry as you might become, there are some misconceptions that should be cleared up before you go on the rampage.

First, the adjusters for the company do not make money on your claim. They aren't getting a percentage of whatever they can save on your claim. Their performance, however, might be evaluated based on those savings. Their supervisor might be looking at the fair value of your claim and how much was paid in relation to that value.

People who work for an insurance company are motivated to resolve your claim in a timely manner. As the claim lingers, its value tends to increase. There is a greater chance of litigation, which the insurance company would like to avoid. Claim department personnel are under pressure to resolve your claim promptly and to close your file as quickly as possible. Their supervisors will keep records on the number of claims they close, and this will be factored into their performance evaluation.

A common misconception is that the people in the claim department love to argue. In reality, they usually are people who would rather not argue with you over the value of your stolen stereo. Many are burned out from too many years of arguing. If they can justify a settlement, they will try to do so within the parameters established by their superiors.

Claim department employees would prefer to avoid an argument with you. With so many insurance companies emphasizing the importance of customer relations, these arguments are frowned on by management. The employee knows you will complain to his boss if he is anything less than polite or courteous. He could be disciplined for a severe infraction of company procedures.

This doesn't mean you won't run into an insurance company employee who is hostile and disinterested in resolving your claim. You usually can hear it in the employee's voice when he answers the phone. You should not tolerate this treatment. In the next chapter, we will look at ways to go around a roadblock at your insurance company, which also apply to dealing with a surly claim handler.

Even if you do believe that claim employees are argumentative, recognize that most of them don't have time to debate the merits of your claim for hours. Going round and round with you does not help them get their other work done. Most problems are caused by an overworked or inefficient claim staff, rather than by adjusters with evil motives. The busier they are, the better chance you have of making your point.

Another myth is that every claim is only worth a specific amount. The amount an insurance company can pay you for your auto damage, fire loss, stolen property, or health insurance claim is negotiable in almost every situation. The insurance company can bend its depreciation schedule. It can reevaluate its allowance on a health insurance claim if the treatment was more involved than it realized initially. The policy limit is the only figure that is carved in stone.

The insurance company has even greater flexibility in the settlement of your bodily injury claim against its policyholder. While an insurance company has guidelines to estimate how much your pain and suffering is worth, it can raise its offer depending on the facts in your case.

The value of your claim can be affected by how badly the company wants to settle. During certain periods, companies take a tougher stand on liability claims. At other times, settling claims is a higher priority and the carrier wants to avoid litigation at all cost. The settlement value of your claim depends on the attitude of the company at that particular point in time. Furthermore, each adjuster will evaluate your claim differently.

You might be dealing with a company that wants to resolve your bodily injury claim with a structured settlement. Instead of paying you all of your money in a lump sum, the carrier sets up an annuity to pay all or part of your settlement on a monthly basis. This can be an economical arrangement for the insurance carrier. Some companies are pushing to resolve as many claims as possible this way. In a questionable liability situation, your willingness to accept a settlement of this kind might motivate the carrier to settle.

GOOD FAITH GOES BOTH WAYS

We talked in Chapter 7 about the obligation to act in good faith. This is also your responsibility, not just the insurance company's. When you present a claim, remember that obligation. It's easy to rationalize unethical behavior when you're dealing with an insurance company. You might feel justified in padding your claim, because you've paid high premiums for so many years. Insurance fraud can't be rationalized under any circumstances, however. Submitting an inflated or fraudulent claim is every bit as reprehensible as is unethical behavior by an insurance company.

22
Where to turn to for help

THERE WILL ALWAYS BE TIMES WHEN YOU REACH AN IMPASSE IN THE CLAIM process. Your claim is denied or you feel you are not getting the fair value that is owed to you. You've stated your case to the person handling your claim and it's getting you nowhere. At that point, if you still feel you're right and believe you are not being treated fairly, it's time to take further action.

While you might eventually have to hire an attorney, there are still avenues you can pursue before taking that step. You can start by going up the chain of command. Office managers are usually very responsive to phone calls in which a complaint is registered. Surprisingly, these calls often generate more of a response than a lawsuit. In a typical insurance company, there are dozens of lawsuits each day. The employees simply turn them over to a member of their legal staff.

On the other hand, a supervisor or manager is forced to deal with an irate phone call. The manager will usually try to resolve the complaint amicably. One manager of a large claim department always insisted that these problems be resolved so that he did not have to hear from the complaining party again. When you go up the chain of command, you will make certain that there is another review of the facts surrounding your claim.

If you still do not receive a satisfactory explanation, it might be time for a letter. The letter should be sent to the insurance company's home office. Many insurance companies have a procedure established to review these complaints. They will either conduct an independent review of the facts or will follow up with the local office to hear its side. It's unlikely that the company's home office will simply file the letter away or allow the allegations to remain unanswered.

When you complain to the company's home office, there will be paperwork for the local staff to complete. In that paperwork, they will have to justify their treatment of you. In the course of reviewing the actions taken, the carrier might realize it has not acted exactly as it should have. If the local staff hasn't, the home office might question their handling of your claim.

BAD FAITH

The most serious allegation you can make is that the company's employees are acting in bad faith. Whenever two parties sign a contract, there is an implied duty of good faith. The contract between you and the insurance company is no different. When insurance companies accept your premium and agree to insure you, they promise to act in good faith when dealing with you. It need not be explicitly stated in the insurance contract. They are obligated to act accordingly, whether it is written in the contract or not.

Bad faith is something more than just neglect. It's a failure to fulfill a contractual obligation because of a sinister motive. It's conscious wrongdoing, not a legitimate dispute over one's obligations under the contract. If appropriate, your letter to the home office should raise that issue and should state why you believe this to be the case.

Before raising this issue, take a moment to separate your emotions from your perception of the problem. Make absolutely certain you are dealing with a genuine case where the insurance company did not live up to its obligation, and it's not just an honest difference of opinion. It's a serious charge and not just an argument to make so that you can gain leverage.

It would be similar to suing a doctor for malpractice when the results aren't as favorable as you hoped. It would be the equivalent of reporting a lawyer to the disciplinary board just because he lost your case. Only if the lawyer didn't use his best efforts would you have a basis for your action. This is not a step to take when you feel the need to retaliate or because of sour grapes.

The bad faith doctrine should not be used as leverage to get your own way on a claim. The insurance company will not fold its tents and surrender when you mention the words ''bad faith.'' If you are looking at your situation objectively and are still having problems, you might be encountering someone who is either incompetent or overworked. In most cases, you will be dealing with bad service rather than bad faith.

Despite my opinion, you should be on the lookout for situations where you are not being treated fairly and the conduct is purposeful. An act of bad faith can occur in a number of ways. If you are presenting a claim, the insurance company employee might misinform you about the applicable statute of limitations, the time limit you have to initiate a lawsuit. Some policies have an internal limit on presenting claims, as health insurance contracts often do. When you are given advice by an insurance company representative, you should confirm it in writing, because you must be able to document your allegations.

The insurance company must investigate the loss promptly. If there are coverage questions, you should be notified of the problems in a timely manner. The insurance company must tell you why your claim is being denied. Its staff should not deal directly with you when you are represented by an attorney. Some obvious examples of bad faith would be failing to settle a legitimate claim in the hope it will go away or forcing someone to engage counsel to resolve a matter that clearly has merit. Acting in bad faith can result in sanctions against the insurance company and can lead to litigation.

TURNING TO YOUR AGENT FOR HELP

In Chapter 1, I mentioned a survey conducted for *Best's Review* dealing with the readability of insurance policies. In that same survey, the Gallup Organization asked consumers what they do if they find a portion of the policy to be confusing. Sixty-four percent of the participants said they would call the agent who sold them the policy for an explanation. Based on that finding, it's clear that an agent, if you have one, can assist you in dealing with the insurance company.

Your agent should be able to explain the portion of the policy that affects your problems with the insurance company. He can also direct you to the right person to resolve your claim. Your agent probably deals with the insurance company on a daily basis. He knows who to call if you're not getting satisfaction. In an ideal world where service is important to companies and carriers are responsive to customers, an agent would be superfluous. Unfortunately, you might need an agent to flex his muscles to get a response. If you've chosen a company that values its reputation for customer service, you shouldn't need an agent to get the service you've paid a great deal for but aren't getting.

Insurance agents should go to bat for their customers if they have a legitimate claim. Most have clout with the companies they represent. The agent also owes you the duty of good faith. When the agent assumes an active role in handling your claim, he must disclose all information to you. If you are entitled to additional benefits that you're not aware of, the agent is obligated to advise you of them.

TURNING TO OTHER SOURCES FOR HELP

No matter where you live, there will be a state official who is in charge of insurance matters. In most states, that person will be the insurance commissioner, superintendent of insurance, or director of insurance. In Minnesota, the department of commerce has responsibility for insurance problems. The responsible department in your state has employees who are assigned to investigate and follow up on consumer complaints. The carrier will be forced to explain its position to the investigator from that department.

Assuming the insurance department in your state is unable to help, you can try some of the other informal procedures that claimants have used in order to resolve their claims. Some claimants have called on congressmen or state legislators. Others have contacted television consumer reporters who investigate complaints. There might be a column in your local newspaper that helps resolve consumer complaints. Use your imagination.

TURNING TO AN ATTORNEY FOR HELP

At some point when you're dealing with an insurance company, you might question whether you should hire an attorney. While an attorney won't be needed on every claim, there will be occasions where it can help to hire one. There are no clear-cut answers to this question. To help find an answer, it is useful to look at why people hire a lawyer on an insurance claim.

One study investigated why auto accident victims hire attorneys. Some of the results are applicable to all types of insurance claims, whether you are negotiating with a liability insurance carrier or are simply dealing with your own insurance company. Many of the respondents hired an attorney because they wanted to be sure they were adequately protected. Another large group hired a lawyer because someone suggested it was a good idea. A delay in the settlement process prompted many to engage counsel. Others hired a lawyer because they were dissatisfied with the amount of money offered by the insurance company.

Obviously, some of these reasons to get a lawyer are better than others. After you have tried all of the informal means of leverage, hiring an attorney is the next logical step. A lawyer can often break the stalemate that exists between you and the insurance company. An attorney should also be a better negotiator than you are, because that is how he makes his living. An experienced lawyer should be able to document your damages more thoroughly than you can. In addition, the lawyer can make certain that the insurance company is correctly applying the applicable law to your specific situation.

Although there are advantages to hiring an attorney, many people can handle a claim themselves. Having a lawyer will not always expedite the process. Many people believe that their problems are over when they hire a lawyer or threaten to hire an attorney. Surprisingly, the threat that you will hire a lawyer does not frighten insurance companies. In many cases, claim department employees would rather deal with an attorney than with a hostile claimant.

Having an attorney will not necessarily speed up the resolution of your claim. Attorneys are often in no hurry to resolve your claim. With a bodily injury claim, they feel it is in yours and their best interest to wait to settle. In many instances, this can be a good strategy. You might not realize the full extent of your injuries and could settle prematurely. Waiting to settle lets the attorney argue that your period of disability was longer and that you suffered for a longer time.

Choosing the right attorney

Sometimes an attorney will have too many cases to handle and cannot pay as much attention to your claim as it deserves. There are many instances where the insurance company will write to the claimant's lawyer for months in the hope of settling the claim. The insurance carrier asks for documentation of the medical bills and lost wages that are of the utmost importance in determining the value of the claim. Whether it is because of the attorney's high volume of cases or because of a particular strategy, the attorney won't respond to these requests for proof of the damages sustained. Therefore, the case remains unsettled.

Your choice of attorneys might cause the insurance company to be more optimistic about its chances of resisting your claim. In a case of questionable liability, the insurance company could reevaluate its willingness to settle after you are represented. You might choose someone who is inexperienced in trial work. The insurance company might then decide to take its chances in court. When the insurance company believes its policyholder is clearly responsible for the loss, this would not happen.

On the other hand, your choice of the right attorney might add significantly to your settlement. Many insurance companies will allocate more money to the settlement pot when evaluating a claim if they are faced with a well-known trial lawyer who has won big verdicts against them in the past. They are less willing to face that attorney in court and will be more inclined to settle.

The impact of a lawyer on your settlement

In many situations retaining counsel won't speed up your settlement or even guarantee that you will get more money. According to one survey, having a lawyer won't always put more money in your pocket. Although the settlements are larger, the amount you actually receive after the lawyer's fee is less.

Depending on the type of insurance claim you have, you might be able to find a lawyer who will only charge a fee if you win. If you have a serious bodily injury case and a relatively good chance of winning, an attorney will handle this case on a contingency basis. Except for costs, you will pay this attorney 25 to 40 percent of your recovery and only if you win.

Although a contingency fee arrangement is often beneficial to the client, you might be unwilling to pay this large a fee when the insurance company seems willing to settle. One Saturday morning, a radio talk show host offered advice for settling a claim without paying a contingency fee. He suggested that you consult with an attorney to review your case and tell you what the claim is worth. The attorney's hourly charge would be small in comparison to the extra money you might obtain on your claim.

The advice is good but has its limitations. An attorney with an active civil litigation practice would only have his appetite whetted by the general details of your case. There are a few attorneys who engage in a practice that resembles "low-balling." An unethical car dealer, who knows you're just starting to price around for a car, will give you a quote that is quite low. As you price the same car at various dealerships, you find you can't match the price. You go back to the dealer who "low-balled" you, only to find that the price you are going to pay isn't as good as the one quoted originally. By then, you are so sick of car shopping, you buy the car anyway.

Similarly, an attorney who you consult with for an hour might tell you your case is worth an amount well in excess of the figure you can actually get. When you go back to the insurance company and try to get that amount, you invariably fail. As a result, you retain the attorney to handle your case. Eventually, you get paid far less on the claim than the attorney promised. After the attorney's fee, you might even get less than you would have on your own.

Once you agree to the contingency fee arrangement, and the attorney takes over the handling of your case, the estimated settlement value of your claim is gradually reduced. During the settlement process, the attorney will diminish your expectations. He will talk about other factors and circumstances that have decreased the value of your claim. You might end up with a great deal less cash than you were led to believe you would receive.

It's similar to an unethical technique that a few real estate agents use. They tell you your house is worth an extremely high amount in order to get the listing. When you're fortunate enough to get an offer that is far less than that amount, the agent will then encourage you to take it.

When an attorney is handling your claim on a contingency basis, remember that the percentages favor the lawyer. He has a number of cases on his desk. If he sells you short, he can make it up on the next one. If he's getting one-third of your recovery, he gets $20,000 of your $60,000. If you get $75,000, he gets $25,000 of it. That $5,000 difference might not mean a whole lot to him, but the extra money means a great deal to you.

If you don't like the idea of paying a large fee to an attorney, you can handle your own claim. In many cases, the insurance company is more than willing to resolve the claim quickly and fairly. Claim department employees are constantly advised to resolve claims before an individual hires a lawyer. Insurance carriers don't encourage this practice so they can cheat you out of money. The philosophy is that both you and the insurance company benefit from the arrangement.

There is no middleman extracting a fee. Insurance companies feel that the involvement of an attorney inflates the value of the claim and also prolongs the amount of time it takes to bring the matter to a conclusion.

In deciding whether you need an attorney, be cautious and trust your instincts. If you are at all skeptical about whether you are getting a fair shake from the insurance company, engage an attorney. You should treat your dealings with an insurance company as you would any consumer situation. If you don't trust the insurance company representative, and don't feel you're being treated fairly, you should be looking for a lawyer.

It is wrong, however, to assume that you will need an attorney in every situation. Many people are quite capable of dealing with the insurance company without representation. They do just as well on their own as any attorney would. Hiring an attorney on small claims can be cost prohibitive. You probably will have to hire the lawyer on an hourly basis, rather than having a contingency fee arrangement.

This is an area where any advice I give will be questioned by some group with a vested interest. If I say you always need an attorney, I'll be accused of drumming up business for the legal community. If I say you don't need an attorney, I'll be criticized for sticking up for insurance companies. As a lawyer, and as someone who has worked for an insurance company, I believe you don't need an attorney in every situation.

It's a lot like the problem you run into when you're buying a home. Attorneys will argue that you must see a lawyer before you sign any agreement of this kind. For the thousands of home sales that go right even though an attorney has not reviewed the agreement, the few cases where things go wrong are pointed to as justification for always having a lawyer. The situation involving an insurance claim is comparable. There will be occasions where the failure to obtain legal advice results in problems.

At some point, you might have no choice but to turn to an attorney for help. You should hire a lawyer if the insurance company has improperly denied your claim and isn't budging from its position. You should also seek representation if the carrier is stalling or is giving you the runaround. It is also quite clear that if you are already represented, the insurance company should not contact you directly. If an insurance carrier attempts to work around your lawyer, you are dealing with an unethical company and you should advise your attorney immediately.

Before you are represented, it is improper for the insurance company to advise you against seeking legal advice. Although an insurance company would prefer to negotiate with you directly, it should never try to keep you from seeing a lawyer. When an insurance company pressures you on this issue, or on any issue, you should question its motives and should seek legal advice.

UNFAIR CLAIMS PRACTICES ACT

You might need an attorney to advise you of any laws in your state pertaining to the handling of insurance claims. Most states have statutes that prohibit unfair and deceptive claims practices. The legislation establishes certain standards that an insurance company must adhere to in processing your claim. The regulations apply to both first-party claims and third-party claims.

Your state should also have a variation of an unfair claims practices act. In this law, your state will have adopted a set of rules governing the conduct of insurance companies. This legislation is very similar from state to state, because the laws will be based on the model act developed by the National Association of Insurance Commissioners.

The purpose of these statutes is to stop arbitrary decisions on the part of an insurance company. These laws impose a penalty on an insurance company that refuses to pay a claim or delays making payment without a valid reason. Were there no checks and balances, an insurance company could view claims with disdain. In most instances, it could turn down small claims without justification and be confident that no legal action would result from the denial. Without additional penalties, these claims would simply be denied, and the insurance company would know that the amounts in dispute are too small to be pursued. Certainly, this policy would not be a public relations bonanza, but it would save money. Some of these statutes allow the recovery of attorneys' fees.

You can use an unfair claims practices act as a basis for a bad faith action against an insurance company. Many knowledgeable attorneys expect there to be an explosion of bad faith lawsuits against insurance companies in the 1990s. These cases can result in an award of punitive damages. In the course of these lawsuits, the conduct of the insurance company is closely examined to see if all legal and ethical standards have been met.

The underlying claims might be quite small, but if the pattern of behavior exhibited by the insurance company is heinous, a large award for bad faith is possible. These bad faith actions can arise out of the mishandling of a property, theft, uninsured motorist, collision, or some other claim.

OTHER REMEDIES

Using state laws and common law principles, a number of legal actions have been brought against insurance companies by dissatisfied claimants. You will probably need an attorney to advise you, because these remedies aren't available in every jurisdiction. There also might be limitations on your right to sue. In Chapter 15, we looked at health insurance claims. On those claims, you might be forced to use the exclusive remedies under ERISA rather than any statutory action you might have by virtue of an unfair claims practices act.

Your lawyer can advise you of any particular remedies that are available in your state. There have been suits where claimants have attempted to show that the insurance company has intentionally or negligently inflicted emotional distress.

Hopefully, your problem will not reach the point where litigation is necessary. Virtually all insurance companies would prefer to avoid lawsuits wherever possible. The policy itself might provide an alternative to litigation. There might be a provision in it that provides for an arbitrator to settle disputes.

FINDING HELP IN THE 1990s

The 1990s should be the decade of the consumer so far as insurance is concerned. There will be many more attempts to regulate the conduct of insurance companies on a state and national level. Consequently, you might find additional places to turn to when you're having an insurance problem. Some states will establish a consumer advocate or insurance counsel position. This person will be empowered to act on behalf of consumers in the area of insurance.

There might also be increased competition for your business in the 1990s. This will have a favorable impact on price. It should also result in an increased emphasis on customer service by insurance companies. Carriers will be more responsive to your needs and problems.

No matter what direction the 1990s take, you must learn to help yourself when you're having problems with an insurance company. If you feel you are not receiving a fair deal, don't take it lying down. You hold a great deal of power when dealing with an insurance company. A better understanding of insurance only adds to that power, and guarantees that you will get the protection you've paid for in the policy.

Index

money saving tips for, 96-100
multicar discounts, 99
new car selection vs. rates, 99
no-fault laws, 40, 85
old cars and depreciation, 98
personal accident insurance, 102
personal injury protection (PIP), 85, 88, 98
personal liability umbrella and, 88, 103-106
physical damage coverage, 85, 91-92
premiums, determination of, 84-85, 96
property damage liability coverage, 86-87
rates vs. service, 97
rental cars, 91-92
repairs after accident, 93-94, 98
risk analysis, 7-8
shopping around for, 97
split-limit coverage, 86, 104
theft, 98
towing, labor, 91
underinsured motorist coverage, 90
uninsured motorist coverage, 89-90

B

bad faith doctrine, 224-225
baggage protection, travel insurance, 210
bankruptcy protection, travel insurance, 211-212
benefits, 2, 15
Best's Insurance Reports, 1, 28, 198
Blue Cross/Blue Shield, 169, 171, 186
breach of contract, 36, 54, 55
breach of duty, 37, 55
broad form policy, homeowners insurance, 63
budgeting, 11
burial insurance, 120-121
business use of home, homeowners insurance, 77

C

cafeteria plans, 21, 166
cancellation fee waivers, cruises, 210
cancer insurance policies, 15, 121, 132, 182-183, 191
cash value, life insurance, 112-113, 112

catastrophic medical expense coverage, auto insurance, 89
causation, 37
chartered life underwriter (CLU), 24
civil action (see lawsuits)
claims, 53-56, 92, 217-222
co-op homeowners insurance, 81
coinsurance clause, homeowners insurance, 67
collateral source rule, lawsuits, 38-39
collectibles insurance, 10, 72
collision coverage, auto insurance, 90, 97, 98, 100
collision damage waivers, 100-102
Communicable Diseases Exclusion, 75, 76
comparative negligence, 37-38, 95
comparison shopping, 12-13
compensatory damages, lawsuits, 39-40
complaints, 30-31, 223-231
comprehensive coverage, auto insurance, 90-91, 97, 98, 100
condominium homeowners insurance, 81
consolidated omnibus budget reconciliation act (COBRA), 21, 167-168
consumer advocacy groups, complaints and, 231
Consumer Reports, 30, 97, 192
contents insurance, homeowners insurance, 64, 68-73, 81
contracts, breach of, 36, 54, 55
contracts, policy, 50-53
  age, misrepresentation of, 52
  agent's liability for problems with, 55-56
  breach of contract, 54, 55
  carrier, cooperating with, 54-55
  concealing information on, 52
  estoppel, doctrine of, 55
  fraud, 52, 53
  good faith clause for, 52
  incontestability clause in, 52, 55
  misrepresentation of facts in, 52
  waiver, doctrine of, 55
convertible term life insurance, 109
cost, 10, 11
cost-of-living adjustment (COLA) rider, disability insurance, 159
coverage, 2, 15-18, 51-55
credit card theft, 57, 74, 211
credit life insurance, 22-23, 120

I